WITH ALL YOUR MIND

WITH ALL YOUR MIND
A Christian Philosophy

by

Yandall Woodfin

SCRIPTA PUBLISHING, INC.
P.O. Box 6180
Fort Worth, Texas 76115

Reproduced by special permission
of Abingdon Press

WITH ALL YOUR MIND: A CHRISTIAN PHILOSOPHY

Library of Congress Cataloging in Publication Data

Woodfin, Yandall, 1929-
With all your mind.
Includes bibliographical references and index.
1. Philosophy and religion. 2. Philosophical theology. I. Title.
BT40.W66 230 80-24453

ISBN 0-687-45839-0

Acknowledgment is made to the following journals in which some of this material appeared in a different form:

"Ontological Thresholds and Christological Method," *Religious Studies*, 8:2 (June, 1972), 137-46. Used by permission of Cambridge University Press.

"The Futurity of Beauty: Aesthetic Intimation and Eschatological Design," *Theologische Zeitschrift*, 29:4 (Juli/August, 1973), 265-79.

"The Theology of Preaching: A Search for the Authentic," *Scottish Journal of Theology*, 23:4 (November, 1970), 408-19. Used by permission of Scottish Academic Press.

"*Knowing* That You Know God: A Christian Approach to Knowledge," *Southwestern Journal of Theology*, 21:2 (Spring, 1979), 71-90.

"An Axiology of Revelation: Divine Self-validation Vis-à-vis Categorical Verification," *Southwestern Journal of Theology*, 26:2 (Spring, 1974), 47-67.

"The Sound of Meaning: A Christian Approach to Language," *Southwestern Journal of Theology*, 19:2 (Spring, 1977), 100-109.

"A Meditation on the Depth of *Personal* Faith," adapted from *Collage*, April 1978. © Copyright 1978 The Sunday School Board of the Southern Baptist Convention. All rights reserved. Used by permission.

"The Beauty of the Lord," adapted from *Proclaim*, July-Sept. 1979. © Copyright 1979 The Sunday School Board of the Southern Baptist Convention. All rights reserved. Used by permission.

MANUFACTURED BY THE PARTHENON PRESS AT NASHVILLE, TENNESSEE, UNITED STATES OF AMERICA

To Leta,
  my wife,
    whose love and spirit of venture
      brighten the valleys
        and make the mountains worth climbing.
And to Carol, Linda, Rosemary, and Yandall,
  my children,
    whose joy and promise
      echo the grace of the Lord of the Hill.

ACKNOWLEDGMENTS

Although I have no desire to claim, as in the legend of the dwarf who stands on the shoulders of the giant, that I see farther than those on whose shoulders I stand, I do wish to express profound gratitude for those giants in literature, philosophy, and theology who were my teachers and who remain my models and inspiration: C. S. Lewis and H. H. Farmer of Cambridge University; Emile Cailliet of Princeton Theological Seminary; T. F. Torrance and John McIntyre of the University of Edinburgh; Charles Duthie of London University; Stewart Newman and Charles Trentham, who taught me at Southwestern Baptist Theological Seminary; and my professors and present colleagues, James Leo Garrett and John Newport, also of Southwestern.

Many of the themes of this book have appeared in previous articles in *Religious Studies*, *Theologische Zeitschrift*, *Scottish Journal of Theology*, *Southwestern Journal of Theology*, *Collage*, and *Proclaim*. I am grateful to the editors and boards of these journals for allowing me to share some of this material in the wider context of this book.

Among a host of friends who have in their own special way contributed to this project, I wish to thank Boyd and Connie Hunt, Thorwald Lorenzen, William Hendricks, Bert Dominy, Trent Butler, Lacoste Munn, Günter Wagner, and Bruce Corley. Along with these, Harold Freeman, Justice Anderson, William Estep, C. W. Brister, Jimmie Nelson, Fisher Humphreys, J. D. Hughey, and John D. W. Watts have given their encouragement along the way. To Glenda Fontenot, William and Floye Tolar, Keith and Jonlyn Parker, Oz and Jean Osborne, Miller and Annette Brister, Jack and Charlotte Robinson, I would like also to express appreciation for their friendship and support in this endeavor.

Finally, let me thank my associates and students at Baylor University, Southwestern Seminary, and the Baptist Theological Seminary in Rüschlikon, Zürich, Switzerland, who shaped the contours of this study in many unseen ways. Its limitations are, of course, my own; yet I am happy, in the words of an old Gaelic saying, that "I, too, can turn my face to the wind, and cast my handful of seed on high."

Yandall Woodfin

CONTENTS

PART II: EXPLORING THE FRONTIERS

INTRODUCTION

RELIGION SEEKING A WORLD-VIEW

Some people think of philosophy like the two little ladies who once heard a lecture by Paul Tillich. One said to her friend, "Isn't he confusing?" whereupon she replied wistfully, "Yes, but isn't he confusing on a *high level*?" While philosophy is a challenging venture it cannot be blamed for the complexities and depth of the reality it seeks to understand. Very early in western thought Pythagoras described philosophy as the "love of wisdom." He meant not only that one should seek an appropriate intellectual response to reality but that one should find joy in the pursuit of truth and live wisely according to its precepts and values. Since philosophy understood in its broadest sense is man's effort to respond rationally and reflectively to the reality which surrounds him, it actually has no special sphere of its own and must choose and defend its own particular method of interpreting that reality. Philosophy must therefore ask such questions as: How can one *know*? (epistemology); How should one use *reason*? (logic); Is life really *going* anywhere? (history); What *is* reality? (ontology); What is the *value* of reality and its various manifestations? (axiology); What is the significance of *beauty*? (aesthetics); and How can one *speak* meaningfully? (language). The wise philosopher will endeavor to approach these questions in a spirit of openness and free inquiry following the truth wherever it leads. When one becomes convinced that the ground of all that exists is the God who makes himself known in the person of Jesus Christ and the accompanying presence of the Holy Spirit—and this is accepted in the *same* spirit of openness which characterizes genuine philosophy—then the basic concerns of philosophy can be approached from a Christian perspective, and the result is a *Christian philosophy*. One can then apply one's convictions in these areas to such specific problems as the relation of the Christian faith to world religions, the tensions between science and religion, and the perennial problem of evil and suffering.

Socrates maintained at his trial that "the unexamined life is not worth living" and soon sealed this conviction with his death. Surely the Christian, in the light of Christ's conquest of death, should be prepared to demonstrate with intellectual discipline and integrity that the unexamined faith is not worth believing. Alfred North Whitehead once declared quite simply but profoundly that the Christian faith has always been a religion seeking a world-view. The work which follows is one effort to meet this need for today and is offered in obedience to Christ's command to love God, "with all your mind" (Mark 12:30).

PART I

MAPPING THE LANDSCAPE

CHAPTER I

Knowing That You Know God

Finding a place to begin a theory of knowledge or epistemology[1] resembles a certain adventure which befell two lovable characters in *Winnie the Pooh:*

> One fine winter's day when Piglet was brushing away the snow in front of his house, he happened to look up, and there was Winnie-the-Pooh. Pooh was walking round and round in a circle, thinking of something else, and when Piglet called to him, he just went on walking.
>
> "Hallo!" said Piglet, "what are *you* doing?"
>
> "Hunting," said Pooh.
>
> "Hunting what?"
>
> "Tracking something," said Winnie-the-Pooh very mysteriously.
>
> "Tracking what?" said Piglet, coming closer.
>
> "That's just what I ask myself. I ask myself, What?"
>
> "What do you think you'll answer?"
>
> "I shall have to wait until I catch up with it," said Winnie-the-Pooh.

Now Pooh and Piglet continue their search together by walking around in a circle until they become enamored with their own tracks and are convinced that the creatures they are tracking are becoming even more numerous and perhaps dangerous. Finally Christopher Robin, sitting in the tree above them, sees their folly and scolds gently: " 'Silly old Bear,' he said, 'what *were* you doing? First you went round the spinney twice by yourself, and then Piglet ran after you and you went round again together, and then you were just going round a fourth time.' "[2] There is really no single place to begin formulating a theory of knowledge for, as Pooh illustrates, one must know what it is one is tracking before one can be sure one has found it and knows it. And there is always the danger that one will become so involved in the process of knowing that one will distort what is being known.

It is thus very difficult to avoid begging the question in any search for a theory of knowledge because one usually assumes, consciously or unconsciously, that the reality under investigation should determine the method used in the inquiry. Although this is a valid presupposition, it is for epistemology the basic issue—"How does one know the reality in question?" By its very nature, therefore, any epistemology will appear circular or tautological in its manner of pursuit and subsequent confirmation. For example, consider the process involved in determining how one can know friendship. There are admittedly certain recognizable channels of response through which people become involved with one another and begin to form patterns of association which provide the structure of their friendship: a certain intuitive affinity of interests, practical support during a crisis, memory of some shared moment, a common goal and hope for its fulfillment, etc. All these comprise essential elements for any enduring personal relationship. However, knowledge of the way the experience is known can never be attained apart from actually living within the reality of the friendship itself. In other words, there appears to be no ultimate distinction possible between an epistemological method and one's theory of reality, or ontology, for as Paul Tillich perceives: "Epistemology, the 'knowledge' of knowing, is a part of ontology, the knowledge of being, for knowing is an event within the totality of events."[3] Every epistemological assertion is inherently ontological and must reflect some understanding of and participation in the reality which is being known. On the other hand, it should be recognized that epistemology is in the final analysis a schematic explanation of the knowing process and remains one or more steps removed from the initial experience which lies at the base of every knowledge claim.

The Problem of Religious Knowledge

Perhaps the most crucial issue confronting a Christian theory of knowledge is the apparent unwillingness on the part of the believer to allow anything, however painfully tragic, to stand as valid evidence against his belief and trust in God. For example, the apostle Paul proclaims: "I am sure that neither death, nor life, nor angels, nor principalities, nor things present, nor things to come, nor powers, nor height, nor depth, nor anything else in all creation, will be able to separate us from the love of God in Christ Jesus our Lord" (Rom. 8:38-39). There is no mistaking his language! There is nothing conceivable in the light of his faith which could persuade him that God does not exist or that he could ever be left alone without the love of Christ. Now the epistemological counterpart to this religious conviction that nothing should be allowed to count against the existence of God is the logical possibility that this might also mean there is no evidence *for* belief in God. This two-edged sword of the verification issue is nowhere more graphically portrayed than in John Wisdom's now classic parable of the garden:

> Two people return to their long-neglected garden and find among the weeds a few of the old plants surprisingly vigorous. One says to the other "It must be that a gardener has been coming and doing something about these plants." Upon inquiry they find that no neighbor has ever seen anyone at work in their garden. The first man says to the other "He must have worked while people slept." The other says "No, someone would have heard him and besides, anybody who cared about the plants would have kept down these weeds." The first man says "Look at the way these are arranged. There is purpose and a feeling for beauty here. I believe that someone comes, someone invisible to mortal eyes. I believe that the more carefully we look the more we shall find confirmation of this." They examine the garden ever so

> carefully and sometimes they come on new things suggesting that a gardener comes and sometimes they come on new things suggesting the contrary and even that a malicious person has been at work. Besides examining the garden carefully they also study what happens to gardens left without attention. Each learns all the other learns about this and about the garden. Consequently, when after all this, one says "I still believe a gardener comes" while the other says "I don't," their different words now reflect no difference as to what they have found in the garden, no difference as to what they would find in the garden if they looked further and no difference about how fast untended gardens fall into disorder.

There can be little denial that the parable up to this stage vividly and poignantly captures many of the ambiguities and uncertainties of human existence wherever issues of purpose and value are concerned. Wisdom pauses, however, to point out that at this juncture in the parable:

> the gardener hypothesis has ceased to be experimental, the difference between one who accepts and one who rejects it is not now a matter of the one expecting something the other does not expect. What is the difference between them? The one says "A gardener comes unseen and unheard. He is manifested only in his works with which we are all familiar," the other says "there is no gardener," and with this difference in what they say about the gardener goes a difference in how they feel towards the garden, in spite of the fact that neither expects anything of it which the other does not expect.[4]

There are many preliminary questions one feels compelled to ask Wisdom about this parable, or more significantly perhaps, about the world picture reflected in this drama, such as: "Where did you originally get your garden?" "Is there any way to avoid the question concerning the existence of a gardener?" "How does the concept of design in the garden take shape in your thinking?" "Why do you value the flowers?" "Do you really feel there ought to be a gardener somewhere?" These questions, as will be shown later, correspond to those proposed in the classical arguments for the existence of God. The crucial issue at this juncture is, however, whether one should be allowed to decide the matter of God's existence and our knowledge of him on empirical grounds alone.

Any attempt to examine the method by which God may be known must not be allowed to isolate the inquiry from the rich fullness of that environment in which a true knowledge of an infinite, loving personal being, could take place. To do this would be somewhat like testing the potential of human affection by limiting the criteria to quantitatively measurable expressions of love. While granting that tangible manifestations are relevant and indispensable within a loving relationship, what kind of love could be proved or disproved by confining the examination to certain demanded responses within a given space and time? What love could stand the empirical test that the very next word or act which comes from a companion should determine once and for all whether love exists. And even if the possibilities for certain observable indicators should be extended indefinitely, would they ever add up to love? It is, therefore, only in the context of an ontological breadth where one at least has the spiritual space to believe—"Behold, he will slay me; I have no hope; yet I will defend my ways to his face" (Job 13:15); "If I make my bed in Sheol, thou art there!" (Ps. 139:8); "In all these things we are more than conquerors through him who loved us" (Rom. 8:37)—that a meaningful investigation of a Christian epistemology can take place. It is, furthermore, by no means self-evident that the believer is predetermined to believe in God regardless of any evidence to the contrary. Did not the apostle Paul concede, "If Christ has not been raised, then our preaching is in vain and your faith is in vain"? (I Cor. 15:14). The sequence in which Christian knowledge is related to assurance seems to be that we first become convinced of the validity of divine revelation, which generates a qualitative personal commitment within us, which then and only then enables us to confess that nothing could ever transpire to destroy our faith.

An Approach to General Knowledge

Before attempting the actual construction of a Christian theory of knowledge, one should recognize that all knowing, regardless of its sphere or point of reference, comes as one in simple faith organizes his sense impressions (or the perceptions which have been formed from an earlier association with sense data) into patterns of meaning and understanding. Immanuel Kant strives for a proper balance between these two faculties when he explains:

> If the *receptivity* of our mind, its power of receiving representations in so far as it is in any wise affected, is to be entitled sensibility, then the mind's power of producing representations from itself, the *spontaneity* of knowledge, should be called the understanding. . . . Without sensibility no object would be given to us, without understanding no object would be thought. Thoughts without content are empty, intuitions without concepts are blind. It is, therefore, just as necessary to make our concepts sensible, that is, to add the object to them in intuition, as to make our intuitions intelligible, that is, to bring them under concepts. These two powers or capacities cannot exchange their functions. The understanding can intuit nothing, the senses can think nothing. Only through their union can knowledge arise.[8]

Most people involved in this knowing process are naive realists who assume the objectivity, unity, and stability of the external world; the reality of their own personal center of awareness and of other selves; the trustworthiness with which physical stimuli pass over into conscious experience; and the possibility of communication between persons. While it is impossible to isolate reality into tight compartments and delineate the specific areas in consciousness where sensibility and understanding meet in the process of knowing, there do appear to be some broad channels of awareness through which knowledge comes. These channels are, according to their most distinguishable characteristics, the *intuitive, pragmatic,* and *rational/reflective* avenues of response.

The *intuitive* channel is characterized by an inner,

immediate, experiential convincingness or compellingness accompanying a knowledge claim. The *pragmatic* response is distinguished by its concern for the functional effectiveness of truth in some clearly demarcated realm of activity. *Rational/reflective* comprehension is recognized by the presence of conceptual coherence and consistency within a given rational context, or "logical set," and also by the degree to which a claim corresponds compatibly with truth in other areas of experience or fields of knowledge. There is no necessary chronological priority among these channels because a claim may enter experience in any sequence or combination; furthermore, there should be no final assessment regarding their relative value since all are essential. Responsible interpreters will no doubt continue to swing from one emphasis to another from age to age in order to maintain a proper epistemological balance. Moreover, the three channels are unavoidably involved in every legitimate investigation of knowledge. Various aspects of response may receive more conscious attention than others at times, but the whole person is nonetheless engaged. We may not wholly commit ourselves to what we know, and we surely may not know all there is to know about the object of consideration; but the active respondent to any valid knowledge must be the indivisible self.

1. Some knowledge claims are perceived *intuitively* as they present themselves to us with an intrinsic compellingness which inwardly and immediately convinces us of their validity. Long ago Aristotle admonished his followers to realize that some truths really need no formal demonstration when he warned that "it is lack of education not to know that it is necessary to seek demonstration of some propositions and not of others."[6] It was also the intuitive avenue of response to which Blaise Pascal later gave classical expression in his famous declaration that "the heart has its reasons, which reason does not know. We feel it in a thousand things."[7] Even science must depend on this tacit dimension as the physicist Michael Polanyi admits when he says of knowledge in this realm:

> [it] is not made but discovered, and as such it claims to establish contact with reality beyond the clues on which it relies. It commits us, passionately and far beyond our comprehension, to a vision of reality. Of this responsibility we cannot divest ourselves by setting up objective criteria of verifiability—or falsifiability, or testability, or what you will. For we live in it as in the garment of our own skin. Like love, to which it is akin, this commitment is a "shirt of flame," blazing with passion and, also like love, consumed by devotion to a universal demand.*

And who has not experienced that spontaneous intensity of feeling which seems to illuminate the whole of life and the world around? Eunice Tietjens describes this awareness in "The Most-Sacred Mountain":

> The stone grows old.
> Eternity
> Is not for stones.
> But I shall go down from this airy space, this swift white peace, this stinging exultation;
> And time will close about me, and my soul stir to the rhythm of the daily round.
> Yet, having known, life will not press so close, and always I shall feel time ravel thin about me;
> For once I stood
> In the white windy presence of eternity.*

Observe how this way of knowing is virtually contentless, is in itself nonverifiable or falsifiable and is primarily individualistically oriented and emotionally perceived. It will become, however, increasingly clear that knowledge is not possible unless this intuitive channel, within its proper limits, can be trusted.

2. Fortunately, one is not left with intuitive impressions alone for one may also take *pragmatic* verification into account. Here one asks, "Do my intuitive impressions conform to the practical experiences of everyday life? Do these insights issue in workable discourse and useful, constructive activity or progress toward a chosen goal?" In other words, truth claims are expected to meet the *needs* of life. While the concept of need might have a biological, social, or even transcendent personal reference, it means in

this connection that inescapable relationship to the world around one upon which full personal existence depends. The pragmatic approach to truth seeks, therefore, to respond intuitively to some consciousness of need or dependence and then proceeds to draw a rational or conceptual circle around that area. Whatever enables one to perform effectively within that context shall be considered "truth." John Dewey summarizes the distinctive thrust of pragmatic verification clearly when he declares:

> Now an idea or conception is a claim or injunction or plan to *act* in a certain way as the way to arrive at the clearing up of a specific situation. When the claim or pretension or plan is acted upon it guides us truly or falsely; it leads us to our end or away from it. Its active, dynamic function is the all-important thing about it, and in the quality of activity induced by it lies all its truth and falsity. The hypothesis that works is the *true* one; and *truth* is an abstract noun applied to the collection of cases, actual, foreseen and desired, that receive confirmation in their works and consequences.[10]

Just as the intuitive dimension cannot bear the total weight of the knowing process, so the pragmatic method would remain lifeless and beneath consciousness apart from an intuitive awakening, and beyond comprehension without some rational boundaries and conceptual objectives.

3. The intuitive and pragmatic avenues of knowledge can and must be supplemented by *rational/reflective* experience.[11] Though reason is as elusive as the structure of personality itself, it may be described as that mental faculty (which is distinguished from sensibility, psychological states, and the capacity to choose) which possesses a degree of spontaneous, self-evident power of comprehension. It is capable of receiving and projecting various relationships between ideas and thus extending knowledge beyond the conditions of possible experience. John B. Cobb, Jr., struggles to define reason with these subtle distinctions:

> By "reason" I mean a kind of activity that presupposes an openness to the forms given in the objective pole of experience in some independence of their primary emotional impact. Once these forms are distanced in this sense, their mutual relations can be examined. This makes possible contemplation, analysis, classification, generalization, and speculation.[12]

The path toward reason therefore appears to follow this pattern: *Sense impressions* provide the initial spatial and temporal occasions or points of contact through which the mystery of thought begins to become tangible and take shape in one's awareness, or *apprehension*. When this consciousness of some confrontation emerges in greater intensity and becomes increasingly distinguishable from other shades of apprehension, it may be designated as a recognizable *perception*. Once a perception is clear enough to be imaged or verbalized it can be considered a *concept*, or *idea*. The process of consciously *relating* ideas coherently and consistently is called *reasoning*. Rational thinking therefore consists in drawing inferences that correspond appropriately to given data, or premises, and developing purposeful, legitimate conclusions. This reasoning process cannot take place without an intuitive risk, and it has no validity, or at least no relevance, apart from pragmatic concerns. Yet the rational component is indispensable for conceptualizing an insight and setting reasonable guidelines for pragmatic functioning. And perhaps above all it is necessary for correlating the evidence provided by both the intuitive and pragmatic channels.

A Christian Theory of Knowledge

The way is now open to construct a positive Christian theory of knowledge. If the approach toward general knowledge has been trustworthy, it appears congruous to propose that the Christian claim to know God must be received through these same *intuitive, pragmatic*, and *rational/reflective* channels. Even though knowledge of God, according to Christian belief, is possible only by a gracious quickening and illumination of the human spirit through the immediate personal presence of God, this knowledge, as long as man remains a creature in time and space, will be *mediated through* experience. And since the object, or better still, the subject of Christian knowledge is the *person* of God himself and not just something about him, one might expect that God may be known in a manner analogous to friendship or trust among persons. God is indeed suprapersonal but never subpersonal, and however infinite his qualities may be they must still be appropriated by finite men through an experience which is distinctly personal.

1. The New Testament abounds with instances where God speaks through the intuitive channel to evoke that inner, tacit response called faith:

> Blessed are you, Simon Bar-Jona! For flesh and blood has not revealed this to you, but my Father who is in heaven. (Matt. 16:17)

> The doors were shut, but Jesus came and stood among them, and said, "Peace be with you." Then he said to Thomas, "Put your finger here, and see my hands; and put out your hand, and place it in my side; do not be faithless, but believing." Thomas answered him, "My Lord and my God!" Jesus said to him, "Have you believed because you have seen me? Blessed are those who have not seen and yet believe." (John 20:26-29)

> When we cry, "Abba! Father!" it is the Spirit himself bearing witness with our spirit that we are children of God. (Rom. 8:15-16)

> Now we have received not the spirit of the world, but the Spirit which is from God, that we might understand. (I Cor. 2:12)

> Now faith is the assurance of things hoped for, the conviction of things not seen. For by it the men of old received divine approval. By faith we understand that the world was created by the word of God, so that what is seen was made out of things which do not appear. (Heb. 11:1-3)

Through an intuitive awareness one may discover an intrinsic convincingness or trustworthiness about the person of Christ which evokes an immediate inner conviction concerning his inherent truth and value. There is an awesome yet magnetic transcendence in Christ's life and work which simply becomes apparent to the reasons of the heart. John Oman captures the essence of this encounter between Christ and his followers in these sensitive lines:

> The great demonstration of the Christ is just that He never sets Himself, as the absolute external authority of the perfect truth, in opposition to the imperfect authority of the finite and sinful spirit within, but that He has only one appeal, which is to the likeness of God and the teaching of God within. . . . His "I say unto you" did not end inquiry, but began it. Hear something, it said, which the humble heart will recognize as true, and which the experience of obedience will confirm. And surely herein is the weightiest proof of the perfect truth. It does not dominate and silence the inward voices but awakes them and makes them its chief witness.[13]

Now man's capacity to respond intuitively is surely not to be identified as the Holy Spirit but rather that faculty of immediate perception to which the objective reality of God as personal Spirit makes his appeal through Christ. Christian faith, therefore, is not to be understood as mere subjective credulity but rather, in the words of H. H. Farmer, as that intuitive

> awareness of an overshadowing reality which is not perceptible to the senses, nor demonstrable by logical inference from the perception of the senses, nor as yet expressible in precise terms; but which is known with certitude to be somehow the source of all that has been experienced, and the promise of all that will assuredly be even yet more fully experienced, of good in man's life.[14]

Only where Christian belief corresponds appropriately to such a comprehensive, objective reality may it truly claim *knowledge of God*. It remains the task of the pragmatic and rational/reflective approaches, therefore, to explore more carefully the epistemological validity and ontological content of that which is received through intuitive perception.

2. It will be remembered from the earlier discussion of the

pragmatic avenue that any claim based on this evidence must function within a designated sphere. We follow this procedure in Christian philosophy by describing conceptually what we believe to be the character of God, and then in turn giving witness that Christian experience produces godlike people. This is in fact the kind of pragmatic demonstration found in the opening lines of the Gospel of John: "In the beginning was the Word, and the Word was with God, and the Word was God. . . . The true light that enlightens every man was coming into the world. . . . But to all who received him, who believed in his name, he gave power to become children of God" (John 1:1, 9, 12). The pragmatic approach is found frequently in the New Testament and appears very early in Christ's mission: Nathaniel asks Philip, "Can anything good come out of Nazareth?" and the answer is a straightforward, "Come and see" (John 1:46). Paul Tillich employs John 3:21, "But he who does what is true comes to the light, that it may be clearly seen that his deeds have been wrought in God," to emphasize the pragmatic theme that "only in the active realization of the true does truth become manifest."[15] Christ himself appears to be willing to risk his whole ministry upon a pragmatic confirmation when he declares, "If any man's will is to do his will, he shall know whether the teaching is from God or whether I am speaking on my own authority" (John 7:17). And the apostle Paul does not hesitate to call on the practical power of his gospel to defend his apostolic authority and the Lord whom he proclaims: "Since you desire proof that Christ is speaking in me, He is not weak in dealing with you, but is powerful in you" (II Cor. 13:3). And what could be more daringly pragmatic than the invitation to prove through experience that "whoever would draw near to God must believe that he exists and that he rewards those who see him" (Heb. 11:6)? Dr. Daniel Fuller in his *Easter Faith and History* reveals the hidden pragmatic structure of New Testament apologetics when he analyzes the passage in Acts which says that Barnabas "was a good man, full of the Holy Spirit and of faith. And (as a result), a large company was added to the Lord" (Acts 11:24). Professor Fuller proceeds to demonstrate quite pragmatically that the spirit and character of Barnabas could not possibly have been created by a world which is characterized by selfishness and death. So we begin to perceive that his strength comes from outside this world—indeed from the risen Christ whom he proclaims. In a word, "the hearers, sensing the supernaturalness of Barnabas, are confronted with sufficient evidence to credit his message regarding the risen Christ."[16] While the various components of this chain of practical consequences are not without their own particular need for justification, the pragmatic pattern of evidence used here is convincing within the realm of its given context and stated goals.

In one of the earliest postbiblical defenses of the Christian faith, Justin Martyr employs the pragmatic thesis in this glowing testimony to the transforming power of the gospel:

> After our conversion by the Word . . . we who devoted ourselves to the arts of magic now consecrate ourselves to the good and unbegotten God; we who loved above all else the ways of acquiring riches and possessions now hand over to a community fund what we possess, and share it with every needy person; we who hated and killed one another and would not share our hearth with those of another tribe because of their [different] customs, now, after the coming of Christ, live together with them, and pray for our enemies, and try to convince those who hate us unjustly, so that they who live according to the good commands of Christ may have a firm hope of receiving the same reward as ourselves from God who governs all.[17]

This kind of bold confidence in the effectiveness of Christian faith to enable one to meet the basic needs and stern realities of life is representative of the church's pragmatic defense throughout its history. Centuries later John Wesley boasts concerning his evangelical followers, "My people die well." And although each of us is aware that there are regrettable limitations in his own personal life, he need have no apology for maintaining that Christians by and large *live well*. However that may be, one can hold the Christian faith to be *true* only to the degree that it is capable of demonstrating its claim in the arena of pragmatic confirmation.

Just as the intuitive response cannot stand alone, so the pragmatic avenue when isolated from the other channels proves ineffectual in demonstrating the validity of Christian truth. Some have objected, for example, that the Christian faith is not really true but that it produces effective practical results simply because men *believe* it is true. This objection, nevertheless, does not explain adequately the cumulative historical evidence that reality is not merely at the disposal of what one believes to be true, but has its own way of sustaining or rejecting various models or systems of belief. On the other hand, the faith of a Christian is creative primarily because he believes that it is an adequate portrayal of reality. When men are no longer convinced of the ontological support for their motivation and practical actions, the pragmatic results invariably diminish or disappear altogether. Moreover, the intuitive and the pragmatic taken together cannot account for the validity of Christian knowledge, for both of these responses raise questions regarding the *intelligibility* of the Christian revelation and its relationship to reality as a whole. These are issues which can only be resolved by reason.

3. There are, however, confirming elements from the rational/reflective channel which provide necessary conceptual integration for the conviction that one can know God in Christ. In a strict sense there is no such activity as "pure reason" or "mere reason," for one cannot even think about reasoning itself in a nonrelational sense, but must always think about something which is polarized or dependent upon a particular point of reference. That is why this mode of receiving is deliberately called rational *and* reflective. Reason may, therefore, be a legitimate means of obtaining knowledge of God when it is a coherent and consistent conceptual *reflection* upon that which has been given through divine revelation. To be sure, the very fact that man needs revelation is an affront to his rational autonomy. Yet at the same time, the need which revelation has to be

received intelligently is evidence not only for the value of the rational/reflective human capacity but also for the rational quality of God's revelation.

Allow Paul's sermon at Mars Hill to provide the principle illustration for the way reason is used constructively within a Christian frame of reference (Acts 17:16-34). There can be little doubt that knowledge of God according to Paul's witness on this occasion is derived from its christological source for, according to Luke, he "preached Jesus and the resurrection" (Acts 17:18). Paul's purpose is unapologetically evangelistic, εὐαγγελίζετο; however, his method of persuasion is very clearly rationalistic in the best sense of the word. He is not just quoting from the Old Testament and demonstrating how Christ corresponds fittingly to its message and promise, but is seeking also to reason earnestly with his hearers. He is not afraid to point out the inconsistencies in their position and commend the logical coherence of his own personal faith. His pattern of argument runs logically though not necessarily formally or chronologically along these lines: "You are very religious," yet in self-contradiction you boldly confess you do not know whom or what you worship because within your own cultural milieu you recognize that God is one in whom "we live and move and have our being," and "even some of your poets have said, 'For we are indeed his offspring.' " You ought not, therefore, "to think that the deity is like gold, or silver, or stone, a representation by the art and imagination of man." If God is indeed your Creator, it is ridiculous for you to seek to serve him "by human hands, as though he needed anything," or to think that you can establish his presence through your idolatrous symbols (Acts 17:22, 23, 28, 29, and 25). The rational inconsistencies of Athenian religion can be seen at a glance when this collage of concepts and their relationships are projected graphically (see page 33).

On the other hand, Paul commends the Christian message, not only because it is founded on the resurrection of Christ, but because its conceptual relationships are free from this kind of contradiction. The basic Christian theses interlock with one another in an

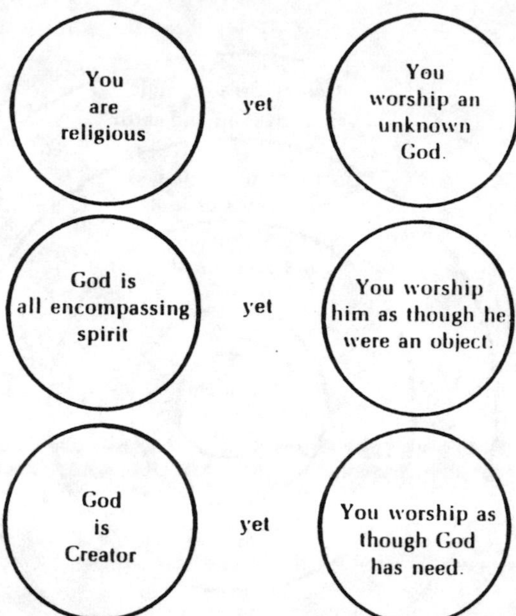

ever-enlarging network of congruence. According to the Christian proclamation, God is the one "who made the world and everything in it, being Lord of heaven and earth." The logical corollary is, therefore, that God "does not live in shrines made by man" (Acts 17:24). God has, moreover, made everyone in the human race, "having determined . . . that they should seek God, in the hope that they might feel after him and find him" (vv. 26-27). All men are, consequently, ultimately responsible to God for the knowledge of him which they possess, however fragmentary or inconclusive this knowledge may be. God has even fixed a day on which he will judge the world by one whom he has appointed—and this one he has confirmed "by raising him from the dead" (v. 31). The rational coherence and consistency of these themes may also be seen more clearly in diagram form (see page 34).

Quite naturally the question as to the factual or historical validity of these propositions as they are presented by Paul remains open for consideration and especially for empirical examination. This would be the case, however, for any set of logical theses, since logic as

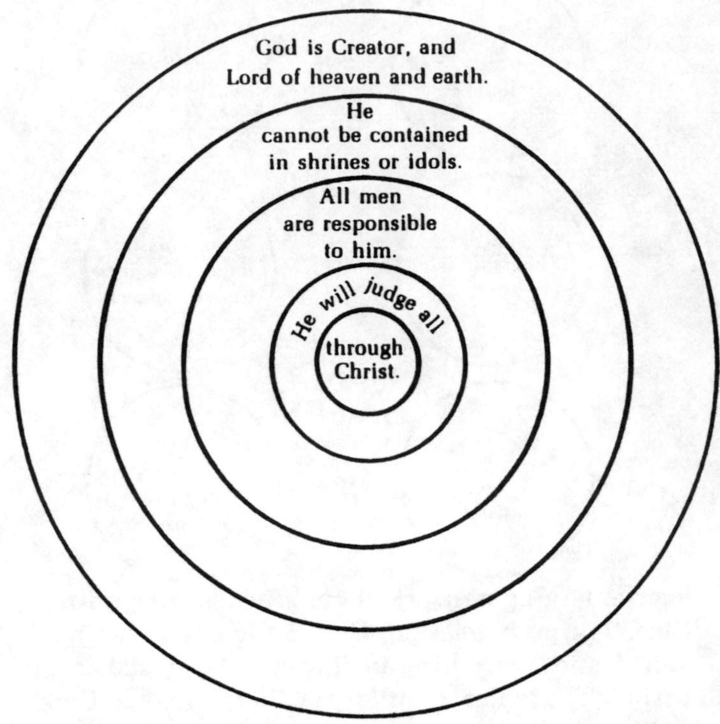

such makes no claim for the actuality or facticity of the things or events to which its propositions refer. It does insist that, provided the factual evidence is trustworthy, we can only think rationally when our thoughts can be related to one another in a coherent and consistent manner. Paul is, therefore, not only confident of the historicity of Christ's resurrection, but is also convinced that the gospel possesses its own inherent rationale.

Eschatological Verification

If the Christian faith is not only a historical and existential affirmation concerning God's appearance in his Son but in addition an eschatological hope which will eventually be confirmed or invalidated, there is a need to defend this faith against the charge that such a futuristic claim for knowledge is *irrational*. It is at just this point that the parable of the garden by John Wisdom, presented earlier, reveals its most profound limitation as a paradigm for Christian knowledge. While the story may be devastating to faith if viewed merely on the empirical plane, it fails to take into account the futuristic dimension of Christian hope. The parable concludes, it will be remembered, that the two spectators feel differently about the garden, "in spite of the fact that neither expects anything of it which the other does not expect." It is here, however, that the parable deliberately excludes the possibility of a drastically different eschatological *expectation*. For it is the essence of hope—and this is supremely true of Christian hope—that it believes the universe is not closed to the possibility of a redemptive breakthrough that can transform the past and renew the future. The early Christian believers, for example, are confident of the knowledge they possess yet at the same time look forward to a fuller revelation which would only come in God's good time. How often they confess, "For now we see in a mirror dimly, but then face to face. Now I know in part; then I shall understand fully, even as I have been fully understood" (I Cor. 13:12); or, "Beloved, we are God's children now; it does not yet appear what we shall be, but we know that when he appears we shall be like him, for we shall see him as he is" (I John 3:2). Such "evidence in waiting" is surely no perfect knowledge but there is, nonetheless, enough present assurance in Christ for one to exclaim: "I know whom I have believed, and I am sure that he is able to guard until that Day what has been entrusted to me" (II Tim. 1:12). The Christian, moreover, shows he or she *does expect* something different from the gardener by believing that death and destruction in this present world can be met creatively through inner

Christian strength and also by awaiting confidently the final victory of God's kingdom. Far from being a weakness of Christian belief, this kind of realistic openness to the cosmos as it is now experienced in process could well be a crucial witness of the truthfulness of the gospel in that it corresponds to the dynamic quality of the ultimate reality it seeks to interpret. Indeed, it may be the high priority given to a futuristic consummation of the Kingdom of God which can only finally be confirmed in the eschaton that provides the most distinctive characteristic for a Christian epistemology.

The basic problem in epistemology, it may be concluded, is perhaps not so much how one knows as it is the ontological question concerning the nature of the reality which is being known. This way of confronting the issue is significant for a Christian theory of knowledge because there is in God's giving himself in Christ an epistemological paradox or inversion. Here the determining factor is not *how* one may know God but that God really wants to make himself known through Christ. On one occasion, as T. F. Torrance observes, Jesus asks his hearers, "Why do you not understand what I say (λαλιὰν, my speech)?" and proceeds then to answer, "It is because you cannot bear to hear my word (λόγον, meaning)" (John 8:43). Notice that the usual order of approaching the problem of knowledge with questions concerned mainly with the intelligibility of language or concepts is reversed when Christ implies one cannot really understand his words unless one is first willing to perceive the far-reaching consequences of his meaning and acknowledge the reasonableness of his message.[18] The decisive question for a Christian epistemology, therefore, eventually becomes quite simply—Do you really *want* to know God? Carl Jung, the Swiss psychiatrist, tells about the man who once came to a rabbi and asked, "In the olden days there were men who saw the face of God. Why don't they anymore?" whereupon the rabbi replied, "because nowadays no one can stoop so low."[19] But according to the Christian faith, it is God himself who stoops toward man in Christ Jesus

> who, though he was in the form of God, did not count equality with God a thing to be grasped, but emptied himself, taking the form of a servant, being born in the likeness of men. And being found in human form he humbled himself and became obedient unto death, even death on a cross. Therefore God has highly exalted him and bestowed on him the name which is above every name, that at the name of Jesus every knee should bow, in heaven and on earth and under the earth, and every tongue confess that Jesus Christ is Lord, to the glory of God the Father. (Phil. 2:6-11)

To know God, therefore, through this humble servant and Lord of Glory one must be prepared, and moreover continually, to become as a little child. Professor James Stewart of the University of Edinburgh enjoys sharing the story of one of his former colleagues, who, though a minister of the Church of Scotland, was affectionately called "Rabbi Duncan" because of his knowledge of Semitic languages. One day some students began joking among themselves wondering what language the renowned scholar used in his prayers. Knowing his meticulous daily schedule, they made their way to his rooms in the college nearby and knelt quietly outside his door—where to their sobering surprise they could barely hear him whisper the words of Charles Wesley's beloved hymn:

> Gentle Jesus, meek and mild,
> Look upon a little child,
> Pity my simplicity,
> Suffer me to come to thee.

When one is willing to receive Christ in such profound simplicity, then, as Paul writes to the Galatians, one may "come to know God" or what is infinitely more important, "rather to be known" by him (Gal. 4:9).

CHAPTER II

Come Let Us Reason

Ever since Martin Luther spoke of reason as a "whore" and "the bride of the Devil," there has been tension among many believers concerning the relationship between reason and revelation or, more precisely, the role of logic in Christian thought. This issue is best illustrated historically and systematically by an examination of the classical arguments for the existence of God. These arguments are significant not only because they embody man's intellectual striving with the basic religious questions of the centuries and appear to have a perennial capacity for survival, but also because they seem to retain their relevance and appeal for the contemporary mind. While the traditional arguments are all rational efforts to demonstrate the existence of a supreme being, there are ontological and moral arguments which presume to defend the existence of God on purely formal deductive grounds, and cosmological and teleological approaches which are more inductive reflections upon the empirical world. They are all, however, excellent examples of man's aspiration to discover a rationale for his own existence and the transcendent quality of his environment. The noble grandeur of these Promethean attempts to prove God is comparable only to their tragic limitations. A knowledge of them is, nevertheless, invaluable for understanding the rational norms which are actually employed in responding appropriately to the Christian revelation.[1]

The Classical Arguments

The *ontological* argument strives to comprehend and express the philosophical-theological ramifications of the concept of *perfection*. We all appear to know, as Walt Whitman envisions, that

> In this broad earth of ours,
> Amid the measureless grossness and the slag,
> Enclosed and safe within its central heart,
> Nestles the seed perfection.[2]

In spite of this argument's rarified logical form, there is no doubt that Anselm, its foremost interpreter, intends his reasoning to give conceptual shape to the knowledge of God which he already possesses. He deliberately frames the argument in the context of a Christian meditation which begins with this profound prayer:

> I do not endeavor, O Lord, to penetrate thy sublimity, for in no wise do I compare my understanding with that; but I long to understand in some degree thy truth, which my heart believes and loves. For I do not seek to understand that I may believe, but I believe in order to understand. For this also I believe—that unless I believed, I should not understand.[3]

Indeed he wants his argument to be the philosophical complement to the biblical declaration "The fool says in his heart, 'There is no God' " (Ps. 14:1; 53:1). As a matter of fact Anselm believes that it is actually impossible for the fool to deny the existence of God for how can the fool, he asks, say "in his heart what he cannot have conceived or how could he not conceive what he said in his heart, since 'to say in one's heart' and 'to conceive' are one and the same thing?"[4] The basic thrust of Anselm's reasoning along with his theological commitment are both revealed in this typical passage:

> And this thou art, O Lord our God. Thou dost exist in truth in such a way that thou canst not be conceived as not existing. And that with reason. For if any and every mind were able to conceive of something better than thee then the creature would be rising above the Creator and judging the Creator. This would be most absurd.[5]

In other words, God is *by definition* the unsurpassable one, and since a necessary being surpasses one who is not necessary, God must necessarily exist. For the nonexistence of the unsurpassable one would be a self-contradictory concept.[6] All right-thinking must therefore transpire within the necessary logical framework which assumes there is a perfect being who exists—otherwise one's *thought* of perfection would be greater than the ontological *reality* within which all thinking must transpire. If one's thoughts should prove greater than reality, then there could be no confidence in our thinking. In no other way, according to this argument, may the continuity between a rational thinker, the rational reality in which he lives, and the language with which he expresses his thought be preserved.[7]

The next argument, at least in the order of historical appearance, to be considered is the *cosmological* argument which finds its classical expression in Thomas Aquinas. The ontological argument is clearly rejected by Aquinas who thought it too speculative and merely based upon a logically self-evident linguistic concept of God.[8] Aquinas sought, rather, to base his reasoning on an Aristotelian confidence in the principle of *causality*.[9] His celebrated "Five Ways" to demonstrate the existence of God are based upon the assumption, now seriously challenged, that it is impossible to conceive of the cause-effect series extending into infinite regress. The first way argues from the fact that motion exists to a Prime Mover; the second from causation to a First Cause; the third from contingent beings to a Necessary Being; the fourth from degrees of value to Absolute Value; and the fifth from evidence of purposiveness in nature to a Divine Designer.[10] The third of these is perhaps the most distinctive and contains the essential elements of the cosmological argument:

The third way is taken from possibility and necessity, and runs thus. We find in nature things that are possible to be and not to be, since they are found to be generated, and to be corrupted, and consequently, it is possible for them to be and not to be. But it is impossible for these always to exist, for that which cannot be at some time is not. Therefore, if everything can not-be, then at one time there was nothing in existence. Now if this were true, even now there would be nothing in existence, because that which does not exist begins to exist only through something already existing. Therefore, if at one time nothing was in existence, it would have been impossible for anything to have begun to exist; and thus even now nothing would be in existence—which is absurd. Therefore, not all beings are merely possible, but there must exist something the existence of which is necessary. But every necessary thing either has its necessity caused by another or not. Now it is impossible to go on to infinity in necessary things which have their necessity caused by another, as has been already proved in regard to efficient causes. Therefore we cannot but admit the existence of some being having of itself its own necessity, and not receiving it from another, but rather causing in others their necessity. This all men speak of as God.[11]

This causal type of cosmological reasoning is expressed autobiographically when Germain Grisez, perhaps the argument's leading contemporary defender, shares the following moving reminiscences from his childhood:

It was summer and the ground was warm. The moon had not yet risen; the sky was clear and very black. A little boy lay on the grass in front of his home and gazed up at the stars. He was watching for shooting stars. Earlier in the summer the whole family had watched fireworks set off to celebrate July the Fourth by people from the city. Now there were only shooting stars, but they were not too bad. In between watching shooting stars he scanned the sky, making out the constellations he knew.

A few days later, after dinner, he was standing by the side door of the house, looking at the sunset. "Look, Mama, how pretty the sun is!"

"Yes, the sun is going down, and it is a beautiful sunset this evening." The little boy gazed at the horizon as the edge of the sun sank below it. He thought about the shooting stars.

"Mama, what makes the sun go down?"

"Why, God makes the sun go down."

"But the sun is very big. Why doesn't it fall fast like a shooting star?"

"God doesn't let it fall fast. The shooting stars fall fast but they get all burned up, like the cinders in the fireplace. God wants to keep the sun, so it can come up tomorrow. So he doesn't let it fall fast."

"God must be very big and strong."

"Oh, he is. He is much bigger and stronger than you can imagine."

"Is he bigger and stronger than Daddy?"

"Yes," she laughed, "much bigger and stronger than Daddy."

"Some God."[12]

The child also remembers when his aunt died:

Auntie Min felt cold. She didn't move at all. She didn't wake up. The little boy remembered that Mama had said Auntie Min is dead. He knew what "dead" meant; he had seen plenty of dead flies and dead trees and he once had a pet rabbit which died. Auntie Min was not breathing, Mama had said. God was not there any more. She was cold, like a cinder from the fire which burned in the fireplace yesterday but had been allowed to go out in the evening. God must have stopped thinking about Auntie Min, and she had fallen dead like a shooting star.[13]

The little boy continues to explore the mystery of life and death and wonders:

"Mama, if everyone and all the animals and insects and trees and flowers were dead, God wouldn't be there anymore, would he?"

"Yes, he would. You know he makes them all be, just by thinking. He makes the sun set and lets the shooting stars fall, just by thinking. A long time ago, there were no people or any living things, but God thought and wanted them, and they came to be. A long, long time ago, long before God made living things, there were no stars, there was no sun. The ground and the sky were not here. But God always was, and he thought of all he wanted to be, and everything started and came to be as he wanted it to be."[14]

The child finally musters the courage to ask his mother:

"Auntie Min is living with God?"

"Yes, but in a way we don't understand."

"Is she right here with us too?"

"I think so," she said slowly and thoughtfully. "I don't think Auntie Min is far away from us. But we can be sure she is living with God. She is not sick any more and she is happy now."[15]

Grisez later presents his understanding of the cosmological argument in a more traditional manner when he admits that everyone knows things don't just happen without a cause. Something has to cause them to happen. Everything we know which makes things happen also happens, and would not have happened if something hadn't caused it to happen.[16] The only reasonable explanation for this situation in the cosmos, he ventures, is that there may be something—call it "God" if you like, which makes everything happen.

> God doesn't just happen to make things happen, but he does make things happen, and nothing makes him make anything happen. God himself doesn't happen to be, he has to be; other things don't have to be, they happen to be. God makes other things happen to be, and nothing makes him have to be, except that he's the sort of being who can't help being, even if he happened to want to, which he can't.[17]

In other words, all existing things we observe are contingent, dependent objects, which means they might or might not exist and could conceivably be different than they are in fact. The very existence and individual characteristics of these particular things are, according to our observations from experience, dependent on other things in the universe. Even the universe itself with all its vast incalculable number of dependent things must in turn be unable to account for its own existence. One must consequently acknowledge the existence of a necessary, nonobservable First Cause which is absolutely different from dependent things and which alone is able to explain the existence of the universe. Or one must confess that causal discourse with the universe shall remain forever unintelligible. The crucial issue is therefore, as Frederick Ferré reminds us, whether our demands for intelligibility are conveniently met by the universe.[18] To explore this question in its full metaphysical depth is to realize along with Kant that the cosmological proof is in essence based on the ontological argument.[19]

The *teleological* argument is also founded upon confidence in the principle of causality and in many ways is but a refinement of the cosmological argument. However, it seeks primarily to interpret the patterns of causality *within* the cosmos, particularly where these reflect a certain qualitative, often wonderful, awareness of purpose and beauty, giving rise to the conviction that there must be a supreme Designer. Although the argument has accumulated a great deal of sophistication since the days of William Paley, it is best illustrated by recalling his famous analogy of the watch which is discovered in a lonely field.[20]

We might be able to respond, he reasons, to certain natural objects by comparing them with other things of nature which we may have encountered in the past. However, should we discover a complex instrument which is marvelously suited for telling the time of day, even though we may never have seen a watch before, we would be compelled to compare this object with our broader experiences of purposefulness or design. Because we customarily proceed from things designed by men to the conclusion that they are arranged by someone for some purpose, it seems legitimate to presume that the watch must have been designed by a watchmaker for the purpose of telling time. Even though the watch may not always function perfectly, the absolute rational impossibility of such a phenomenon appearing as a result of mere coincidence still warrants this conclusion. Paley now projects that there are many delicate and awesome arrangements of design in the natural, animal, and human realms which far surpass anything that the human mind could conceive. These evidences of purpose and beauty, he concludes, can only be accounted for if there is a cosmic Designer. This line of teleological reasoning is summarized in a colorful manner more recently by Sir James Jeans when he declares that, in view of all the statistical probabilities, life in this universe as we know it could never have occurred if there were not an omnipotent "cheater" somewhere above the process.

As teleologists we may feel that scientific and mathematical formulations are inadequate to express the truly wonderful intricacies of our world and turn to the poet who helps us realize that

The world is charged with the grandeur of God.
  It will flame out, like shining from shook foil;
  It gathers to a greatness like the ooze of oil
Crushed. Why do men then now not reck his rod?
Generations have trod, have trod, have trod;
  And all is seared with trade; bleared, smeared with toil;
  And wears man's smudge and shares man's smell; the soil
Is bare now, nor can foot feel, being shod.

And for all this, nature is never spent;
  There lives the dearest freshness deep down things;
And though the last lights off the black West went
  Oh, morning, at the brown brick eastward, springs—
Because the Holy Ghost over the bent
  World broods with warm breast and with ah! bright wings.[21]

The teleological proof remains the most popular of the classical arguments, and perhaps the most convincing, no doubt because of its ability to capture an aesthetic response to order in nature which is so closely akin to the sense of order and wonder in religious experience.[22]

The final major rational effort to establish the existence of God to be considered is the *moral* argument or postulate which receives its most elaborate formulation from Immanuel Kant. After having been awakened from his "dogmatic slumber" by David Hume, who suggested that causality might be merely the psychological necessity of our associating certain events in a series rather than an actual cause-effect relationship, Kant endeavors to bring the ontological, cosmological, and teleological arguments down to earth. In his *Critique of Pure Reason* he declares that he shall demonstrate that speculative reason is "as unsuccessful on the one path—the empirical, as on the other—the transcendental, and that it stretches its wings in vain, to soar beyond the world of sense by the mere might of speculative thought."[23]

At the conclusion of his discussions of each of the major arguments, Kant declares: "A Supreme Being is, therefore, for the speculative reason, a mere ideal, though a *faultless* one—a conception which perfects and crowns the system of human cognition, but the objective reality of which can neither be proved nor disproved by pure reason."[24]

In the preface to the second edition of *Critique of Pure Reason*, Kant explains that he had "found it necessary to deny *knowledge* in order to make room for *faith*."[25]

While rejecting the speculative arguments for the existence of God according to his understanding of the canons of *pure* reason, Kant claims to discover the moral necessity for the hypothesis of God in the *practical* reason. He boldly postulates the existence of God from the ethical possibility that men have of seeking the *summum bonum* or highest value. Even though, according to Kant, the will of man cannot possibly correspond completely with the moral law during the limitations of human existence, one cannot escape the practical, rational consciousness of being obligated to seek the *summum bonum*, as prescribed by the moral law. This can have meaning only if there is the possibility of an endless progress toward that complete fitness.

> This infinite progress is possible, however, only under the presupposition of an infinitely enduring existence and personality of the same rational being; this is called the immortality of the soul. Thus the highest good is practically possible only on the supposition of the immortality of the soul.[26]

The existence of God must now be assumed, Kant concludes, because if God does not exist, there can be no ground for believing in either the immortality of the soul or our consciousness of the categorical imperative. This same moral law, Kant argues, must also

> lead us to affirm the possibility of the second element of the highest good, i.e., happiness proportional to that morality; it must do so just as disinterestedly as heretofore, by a purely impartial reason. This it can do on the supposition of the existence of a cause adequate to this effect, i.e., it must postulate the existence of God as necessarily belonging to the possibility of the highest good (the object of our will which is necessarily connected with the moral legislation of pure reason). . . . Now it is our duty to promote the highest good; and it is not merely our privilege but a necessity connected with duty as a requisite to presuppose the possibility of this highest good. This presupposition is made only under the condition of the existence of God, and this condition inseparably connects

this supposition with duty. Therefore, it is morally necessary to assume the existence of God.[27]

The moral argument, in summary, teaches that all men are inescapably confronted by the rational imperative of morality, however diverse the actual content of this concept of obligation may be. This moral consciousness itself may only be considered intelligible provided there remains the possibility for its perfect fulfillment. This cannot, however, conceivably be accomplished in the relatively short span of man's finite life. A belief in the immortality of the soul must therefore be accepted along with its rational corollary, namely, the existence of God who alone can guarantee this immortality. The argument is consequently, as Kant scrupulously maintained, not a rational demonstration for the metaphysical existence of God, but rather a rational extension or postulate which must correspond to man's practical consciousness of moral responsibility. One is not surprised to hear therefore that Kant would follow the academic procession of the University of Königsberg up to the doors of the church—and then quietly slip out of the line and return home another way.[28]

Limitations of the Arguments

Although there are many unique features contained in each of the preceding arguments which must surely involve individual weaknesses and particular strengths, there is good reason for attempting to evaluate them all together. The crucial issue seems to be not so much the relative worth of any single argument but whether it is possible to know God through the reason apart from Christian revelation. The worth of each of these proofs must therefore be determined in the last resort by their ability to speak as a whole and demonstrate the possibility of knowing God in the unity of our experience.

Consider first some of their most significant limitations. Surely a glaring and offensive problem to anyone who feels his religious experience deeply is the abstract form of the arguments and their aura of philosophical detachment. There appears to be an insurmountable gulf between the Thou encountered in personal devotion and the philosopher's arid concepts of perfection, causality, design, and moral imperative. For example, Etienne Gilson calls Descartes' "author of nature," which appears in the conclusion of his reformulation of the ontological argument, a "still-born" God, explaining: "He could not possibly live because, as Descartes had conceived him, he was the God of Christianity reduced to the condition of philosophical principle, in short, an infelicitous hybrid of religious faith and of rational thought."[29]

All of the arguments, according to Paul Tillich, have lost their primary existential orientation. At least they fail to grasp the dialectical depth of personal encounter with God and rely too heavily upon either the internal or structural poles of experience:

> Arguments for the existence of God presuppose the loss of the certainty of God. That which I have to prove by argument has no immediate reality for me. Its reality is mediated for me by some other reality about which I cannot be in doubt, so that this other reality is nearer to me than the reality of God. For the more closely things are connected with our interior existence, the less are they open to doubt. And nothing can be nearer to us than that which is at times farthest away from us, namely God. A God who has been proved is neither near enough to us nor far enough away from us. He is not far enough, because of the very attempt we have made to prove Him. He is not near enough, because nearer things are presupposed by which the knowledge of Him is mediated. Hence this ostensibly demonstrated subject is not really God.[30]

There is furthermore a paradoxical weakness in the basic methodology involved in the arguments in that the stronger the logical or empirical evidences, the more introverted and self-defeating the arguments seem to become. For example, the more completely one understands the concept of perfection, the less he will need a perfect Being above him; the more adequately and exquisitely designed the world is believed to be, the less cause there is to seek a grand Designer or hope for an eschatological fulfillment of divine purpose; the more confidence one has that his ethical consciousness lays upon him an absolute demand, the less obligation he will have to fulfill these commands as though they were divine. There is a danger, therefore, that as the arguments grow stronger in one's esteem, his concept of God may become increasingly more self-contained and could eventually become completely anthropomorphic.

Another problem to which the teleological argument appears to be especially vulnerable concerns the method whereby one takes his thinking in one realm and applies it analogically to another sphere which may or may not be similar. Since all thinking is to some degree analogical comparison there may be no way to avoid this difficulty completely. However, those who would use the arguments need to be careful that they do not press their analogies beyond their experiential evidence. The mere fact that a cause has produced a certain effect often is not sufficient grounds for concluding that the cause must analogically *resemble* the effect as Frederick Ferré illustrates in good humor when he asks: "If the beauty of Helen is great enough to cause the Trojan War, must her form *resemble* the visage of war?"[31] This question becomes quite crucial when one realizes that even though the world may function like a watch, and even have been designed for certain watchlike purposes, there may still be much evidence lacking that the world's designer is in reality like a watchmaker.

There is yet another difficulty, sometimes called "the problem of theism and probability," which calls attention to the fact that the theistic arguments all refer to this one unique universe, yet presume to be able to demonstrate how much better this universe is, assuming that God made and designed it, than it would have been without God's creative hand in the process. This problem is, we believe, not insurmountable because the basic question concerning the possibility of God's existence is not ultimately a hypothetical one regarding our experience in this universe as compared to some imaginable, nonexisting universe, but rather, how to make the best possible interpretative sense of all our experiences in this world here and now. The teleological analogy of a divine cardplayer who distributes the cards not at random but with a selective purpose possesses value as an expression of the fact that men do experience meaning and are conscious at least of immanent design in their world. There remains, however, a crucial difficulty with this statistical argument which R. L. Sturch perceives when he counters that one really ought to know the likelihood of honesty or dishonesty in cosmic card dealers before this analogy is pressed too far. He reasons that if dishonesty is a very uncommon thing the observance of purpose in the universe would mean something quite different than if the dealer were frequently dishonest. He therefore concludes: "We need to know, not only the likelihoods of cheating and random shufflings producing this order of the cards, but also their relative frequency vis-à-vis one another. And how on earth this is to be done with the universe I do not know."[32]

Perhaps the most formidable obstacle of all confronting the arguments is their need to explain how it is possible to move from any finite frame of reference to conclusions of infinite proportions. If, on the one hand, arguments like the ontological and moral are logically self-contained, they must by their very definition be tautological or circular in character; whereas if the cosmological and teleological arguments are empirically based, they must account for their leap from the space-time continuum into the metaphysical realm. The tautological reasoning present within the ontological argument, for instance, was perceived very early in its history when Gaunilon, a contemporary of Anselm, voiced his objection to the argument in his remarkable treatise entitled, "On Behalf of the Fool."[33] He claimed that according to the pattern of reasoning followed in the ontological argument it should be possible to prove that the most perfect of islands must exist somewhere. In his reply, Anselm moves almost to the threshold of empirical experience when he points out that a perfect island is not, like the unique concept of a perfect being, a *necessary* concept for rational thinking. Gaunilon does, however, reveal the subjective weakness inherent in any purely deductive approach.

The empirically oriented arguments also have difficulty here as David Hume illustrates when he reminds the teleologists that even the admission of a purposeful design within the world does not justify the assumption that there is a creator or designer who is transcendent over the world. If you were to see, he reasons, a pair of scales and observe ten ounces on one side which is outweighed by something on the other side, you might have good evidence to assume that the unseen object on the other side weighs more than the ten ounces which you see. You could never, however, legitimately infer that the unseen portion weighs one hundred ounces—and certainly never rationally conclude that it bears an infinite weight.[34]

What confidence can we have—to raise yet another problem—that either the manifold aspects within each of the arguments or the arguments taken all together would give convincing evidence for the same God? Could the argument from design, to choose but one illustration, really be evidence for polytheism rather than monotheism on the basis of the vast number of elements in the universe which give the impression of being designed? This acute difficulty was not overlooked by David Hume who argued that "a great number of men join in building a house or ship, in rearing a city, in framing a commonwealth; why may not several deities combine in contriving and framing a world?"[35] It is quite evident that the assumption of the *unity* within and among the arguments demands as much proof as the *existence* of God! This problem, though significant, need not be conclusive, for both philosophy and theology still work with confidence in "Occam's Razor": "what can be explained on fewer principles is explained needlessly by more."[36]

It must also be asked if the reality which is claimed to be discovered at the conclusion of these arguments is a personal being? Is the God toward which they point more than a perfect being, a causal pusher or puller, a statistical designer, or perhaps only an absolute moral law? To be religiously satisfying, man's understanding of God must be radically personal; and this includes not only his creativity and intellect, but also his holiness, love, and *will* to be gracious. What indications are there from the arguments themselves that if their logically demonstrated being exists, he wishes to communicate with man and is concerned to meet his needs?

However, lest we leave this phase of the discussion with the impression that all the weaknesses mentioned above are so overwhelming as to determine conclusively the irrelevance of the arguments for Christian thought, we need to face the sobering fact that *there is not one single formal problem confronted in these theistic arguments that is not also present incipiently and methodologically in the Christian's claim of knowing God through revelation.* As believers we need to keep in mind that we follow many of these same methods of argument when we respond to revelation with finite concepts or experience some particular divine historical manifestation and then proceed to develop our own theological statements about an eternal infinite God.

Contributions of the Arguments

What may now be said constructively concerning the arguments? There is surely something astounding in the sheer fact that they are still being widely used unconsciously and deliberately in Christian thought today in spite of the ferocious attacks they have received through the centuries from both skeptics and theological critics. It seems safe to say that they are of greater interest in theology and philosophy now than they have ever been in the history of Western thought. Their amazing power to endure resides, no doubt, not in their logical consistency or in empirical data—but in the religious quality of the insights and experiences which lie at their base. For example, is it not the religious awareness that all thought and language transpire in a realm where the thinker is absolutely dependent upon the reality greater than himself which surrounds him that gives the ontological argument its force? In like manner one is conscious of being dependent upon things around him for his very existence. These things contribute also to his sense of value and therefore possess a quasi-religious quality when considered as a whole. Thus the cosmological argument can be understood as a rational projection of a religious awareness that one is absolutely dependent upon a supreme power which holds all things together. Thus the argument often appears convincing on the numinous level even when its logical weaknesses are apparent. H. H. Farmer is quite right, therefore, when he concludes that "the sails of natural theology always need to be in some measure filled with the wind of natural religion."[37]

If the arguments are deemed by some to be of little relevance for a Christian knowledge of God, these interpreters must then seek to account for the near-universal belief in a supreme being which somehow enters human thinking apart from a biblical, christological revelation. If there is indeed no causal, psychical, and structural correspondence between man as man and the cosmos surrounding him which gives rise to such categories as unity, totality, perfection, purpose, and obligation—which all culminate in the equivalent or near-approximation of the concept of God—how then does one explain the origin and persistence of belief in God? According to the biblical revelation, the knowledge of God which exists throughout the human race is accounted for without equivocation by the consciousness of an eternal unseen presence which is mediated to all mankind through God's creation. It is on this basis that Paul considers all men everywhere accountable before God:

> For the wrath of God is revealed from heaven against all ungodliness and wickedness of men who by their wickedness suppress the truth. For what can be known about God is plain to them, because God has shown it to them. Ever since the creation of the world his invisible nature, namely, his eternal power and deity, has been clearly perceived in the things that have been made. So they are without excuse. (Rom. 1:18-20)

There is therefore biblical support for believing that whatever conviction or content is present within the classical arguments must grow out of an ontological dependence of the creature upon the Creator. This dependence inevitably breaks on to the surface of man's consciousness in his concept of God—and moreover in his awareness of obligation toward God. The classical arguments are but formal statements of this knowledge of the divine.[38]

Furthermore, men continue to function within the conceptual *structures* that provide the ontological and cosmological framework for the arguments. That is, we do build our lives confidently upon such categories as perfection, causality, design, and a universal consciousness of moral obligation. Now if these concepts which are used to describe our relationships to the world are themselves valid, indeed absolutely indispensable for an understanding of our experience, do they not at the same time lend credence to the belief that they must transpire within an *ultimate* ontological reference? In other words, if we could account for the presence of meaning in our experience in its total breadth and comprehensiveness without the concept of design, for example, then there would be no legitimate justification for ever postulating that God is a Designer. On the other hand the proponent of the argument from design can only properly be challenged on the level of universal regularities if the challenger can conceive of a universe which would be more perfect in overall benevolence. A world, for example, where disease would not be transmitted by the multiplication of living cells would not permit growth in other more desirable, living organisms. There are to be sure problems with the world as we experience it, but perhaps Robin Attfield is justified when he concludes cautiously: "I would hold, then, that there is a slight presumption at least in favor of belief in the creator's benevolence from a survey of the nature of the material universe."[39] Note carefully that this kind of reasoning is not only assuming a necessary correlation between the thought of perfection and the concept of a perfect being but is actually admitting that one cannot conceive of an *empirical world* more appropriately designed. Until this kind of reasoning can be dismissed as irrational, the classical arguments will continue to give support for belief in God.

There is no intention here to claim a mere linguistic victory over those who reject the arguments, but simply a desire to expose the transcendental dimension of the structures upon which the arguments are framed. For in fact, these structures form the rational scaffolding of every rudimentary claim for understanding, regardless of the verbal designation one may or may not give to the overarching reality which they seem to reflect. John Hick summarizes this conviction quite forcefully in the following passage:

> All of the traditional theistic arguments . . . establish the *possibility* of God by pointing to aspects of human experience which pose problems in reflecting upon which we find ourselves faced with the alternatives of accepting sheer formless and meaningless mystery or the worship-eliciting mystery of God.[40]

Structural Affinities with Biblical Revelation

When we open the Bible to that majestic declaration that God is "in the beginning," we are immediately grasped by the same kind of metaphysical claim of a perfect existing being which also lies at the heart of the *ontological* argument (Gen. 1:1). And even though this biblical declaration may have arisen out of Israel's experience with God in his mighty acts of redemption, it seems safe to assume that no event could have proved revelatory of God in his ultimateness unless it first assumed and addressed the category of perfection. When God reveals himself to Moses in one of the earliest revelations of his nature or being, he declares "I am who I am" (Exod. 3:14). This unheralded declaration of God's *personal* essence and dynamic intention reveals at the same time, in language not too far removed from the ontological argument, the transcendent *being* of God. Unless there were some essential correspondence between the necessary concept of a perfect being, which the ontological argument struggles to represent, and the necessity for acknowledging the existence of Israel's God who manifests himself, the encounter at the burning bush would, I believe, have remained incomprehensible. Whether this be true or not, there can be little doubt that the early Christian missionaries assume a universal awareness of the ontological transcendence of God as they proclaim the gospel. They are confident that even before they arrive their hearers have not been left without a witness; indeed some in the pagan world have already recognized that "in him we live and move and have our being" (Acts 14:17; 17:28). These New Testament equivalents to the Old Testament conviction that "The fool says in his heart, 'There is no God' " can be valid only insofar as the concept of a perfect existing being is both clearly understandable and absolutely necessary for rational thinking (Ps. 14:1; 53:1).

Those of us who rejoice in the biblical revelation may therefore wish to join in Anselm's prayer of thanksgiving which is found at the conclusion of his ontological argument: "I thank thee, good Lord, I thank thee, that what I at first believed because of thy gift, I now know because of thine illumining in such a way that even if I did not want to believe thine Existence, yet I could not but know it."[41]

We might also want to confess with Karl Barth in his commentary on these same words that there is a legitimate correlation between this kind of *ontological reasoning* and the knowledge of God which comes through *grace:*

> God gave himself as the object of his knowledge, and God illumined him that he might know him as object. Apart from this event there is no proof of the existence, that is of the reality of God. But in the power of this event there is a proof which is worthy of gratitude. It is truth that has spoken and not man in search of faith. Man might not want faith. Man might remain always a fool.[42]

In other words, the truth of necessary being speaks, and the ontological argument gives it expression through the philosophical concept of God. Now the Christian faith, employing this same concept of necessary being, declares that Christ is the one who perfectly incarnates the reality and grace of God, and confesses: "Although he was a Son, he learned obedience through what he suffered; and being made perfect he became the source of eternal salvation to all who obey him" (Heb. 5:8-9).

It would likewise be impossible for one to comprehend the biblical meaning of creation, redemption, and eschatological hope without a profound confidence in the concept of causality which pervades the *cosmological* argument. Although it is now possible for higher mathematics to theorize and function using the principle of infinite regress, all existential thought and action are founded upon belief in the reliability of cause and effect as they correspond to some fixed point of reference. If one does not assume this, one's whole life is but a random series of events which at best possess many relative meanings, but no ultimate meaning. This causal framework is, however, integral to the biblical revelation:

> In the beginning God *created*. . . . (Gen. 1:1)
>
> His invisible nature, namely, his eternal power and deity, has been clearly perceived in the things that *have been made*. (Rom. 1:20)
>
> [God is the one] . . . who gives life to the dead and calls into existence the things that do not exist. (Rom. 4:17)
>
> In my Father's house are many rooms; if it were not so, would I have told you that I go to prepare a place for you? And when I go and prepare a place for you, I will come again and will take you to myself, that where I am you may be also. (John 14:2-3)

Little would remain in these passages but sheer mystical longing were there no stable knot in the chain of causality to serve as a juncture for God's creative action. If we are thankful that God has filled the conceptual form of causality with the content of his revelation, we might also appreciate the cosmological argument for striving to make all empirical, contingent relations reveal their limits and encouraging one to search for an adequate First Cause.

In the very beginning when there was only a swirling mass of chaos and "the earth was without form and void," God is the cosmic Designer who says "Let there be light" (Gen. 1:2, 3). And from the dawn of theological thought the ancient biblical poet senses that an awareness of the wonders of God's order in creation is a prerequisite for wisdom:

"Where were you when I laid the
foundation of the earth?
Tell me, if you have understanding.
Who determined its measurements—
surely you know!
Or who stretched the line upon it?
On what were its bases sunk,
or who laid its cornerstone,
when the morning stars sang together,
and all the sons of God shouted for joy?

"Or who shut in the sea with doors,
when it burst forth from the womb;
when I made clouds its garment,
and thick darkness its swaddling band,
and prescribed bounds for it,
and set bars and doors,
and said, 'Thus far shall you come, and
no farther,
and here shall your proud waves be stayed?' " (Job 38:4-11)

The psalmist exclaims in a beloved refrain that "the heavens are telling the glory of God; and the firmament proclaims his handiwork" (Ps. 19:1). He is, to be sure, standing within a covenant relationship to his Creator and singing of God's majesty within a cosmological framework in order to affirm God's redemptive adequacy; he does this, nevertheless, by employing the basic *teleological* and aesthetic categories of the argument from design. Indeed, one of the ways he recognizes the hand of God in his world is by tracing his finite impressions from the heavens and the earth to their larger patterns of purpose until eventually they break in upon a realm of splendor where the only appropriate response is praise. In like manner, the whole redemptive work of Christ could be described as the way God brings men back to him and the design for which they were originally created. This at least is at the heart of Christ's teaching in the Sermon on the Mount when he commands his followers to be "perfect," τέλειοι, even as the heavenly Father is perfect, τέλειός (Matt. 5:48). This means we are to be what God *designs* us to be, even as God is perfectly himself in being God. No one can hope to grow in this regard without that sense of purposeful design and wonder which characterizes the teleological argument.

And finally, whether it be the prophet declaring, "All we like sheep have gone astray; we have turned every one to his own way" (Isa. 53:6), or the psalmist contemplating the omnipresence of his God,

> O Lord, thou hast searched me and known me!
> Thou knowest when I sit down and when I rise up;
> thou discernest my thoughts from afar.
> Thou searchest out my path and my lying down,
> and art acquainted with all my ways (Ps. 139:1-3),

or the searing indictment from the apostle Paul that "all have sinned and fall short of the glory of God" (Rom. 3:23)—the proclamation of the biblical message of salvation is predicated, like the *moral argument*, on the assumption of universal moral responsibility. Certainly the proclamation of the risen Christ goes far beyond the postulates of the moral argument in providing material for an understanding of God, and evidence for hope in eternal life. However, witnesses for Christ, whether in New Testament days or our own, bring no startling alien word of moral obligation from some unknown world, but rather invite men to face realistically the moral demands of which they are, usually quite painfully, already aware. Since the moral argument articulates this universal consciousness of obligation and the need to look beyond this world for its source and fulfillment, it remains valuable for Christian thought and proclamation.

According to George Adam Smith's translation of Isaiah 1:18, the prophet declares: "Come, let us bring our reasoning to a close, saith the Lord."[43] This word is appropriate for our study as well because the classical arguments must all pale before the light of Christ's power, holiness, and love. They cannot be despised, however, until we stop believing that our Lord is ontologically perfect, causally creative, purposefully wonderful, and morally good.

CHAPTER III

The Moving Image of Eternity

If time may be understood according to Plotinus' early picturesque definition as "the moving image of eternity," then the Christian can consider history as the record and interpretation of human movements and their eternal significance. More critically, however, William Dray defines history as one's concern with the *past*, more specifically the *human* past. He explains that natural objects or events have a "history" only as they relate to the story of human beings. Moreover, according to Dray, history is primarily concerned with the *activities* of human beings. If Queen Elizabeth has a sore throat some morning this is a concern for history only if it affects her attendance of a royal council meeting. Furthermore, the activities of individuals are not important in themselves but become subject matter for the historian only when they possess societal significance.[1] Erich Kahler presses the definition of history further into an ontological frame of reference when he describes it as a meaningful happening:

> History is happening, a particular kind of happening and the attendant whirl it generates. Where there is no happening, there is no history. Sheer eternity . . . has no history. And the opposite, that is, sheer happening, a completely chaotic, casual, kaleidoscopic mélange of events . . . does not make history either. To become history, events must, first of all, be related to each other, form a chain, a continuous flow.

> Continuity, coherence is the elementary prerequisite of history. . . . To form a story, the *connection* of happenings must have some substratum, or focus, something to which it is related, somebody to whom it happens. This something, or somebody, to which, or whom, a connection of events relates, is what gives the plain connection of events an actual, specific *coherence*, what turns it into a story. But such specific coherence is not given of itself, it is given by a perceiving and comprehending mind. It is created as a *concept*, i.e., as a meaning.[2]

Even a simple story must therefore, according to Kahler, possess three indispensable ingredients: (1) the connection of certain events; (2) the relationship of this connection to something or someone which accounts for their coherence; and (3) a mind to comprehend this coherence and create the concept which "means a meaning."[3]

Sheer objectivity in history is therefore impossible, not just because of the subjective involvement of the interpreter and his selectivity in what he deems significant for interpretation, but also because of the nature of the historical event itself. History that involves human beings will never be significant merely from some external aspect but will involve an interrelationship between an event and its rational consequences. R. G. Collingwood provides a classic example of this from Roman history:

> The historian, investigating any event in the past, makes a distinction between what may be called the outside and the inside of an event. By the outside of the event I mean everything belonging to it which can be described in terms of bodies and their movements: the passage of Caesar accompanied by certain men across the Rubicon at one date, or the spilling of his blood on the floor of the senate house at another. By the inside of the event I mean that in it which can only be described in terms of thought: Caesar's defiance of Republican law, or the clash of constitutional policy between himself and his assassins. The historian is never concerned with either of these to the exclusion of the other. He is investigating not mere events (where by an event I mean one which has only an outside and no inside) but actions; and an action is the unity of the outside and the inside of an event. He is interested in the crossing of the Rubicon only in its relation to Republican law, and in the spilling of Caesar's blood only in relation to a constitutional

> conflict. His work may begin by discovering the outside of an event; but it can never end there; he must always remember that the event was an action; and that his main task is to think himself into this action, to discern the thought of its agent.[4]

If Collingwood is right in this approach, then it is simply "unhistorical" to pretend that the historian is exclusively or even primarily concerned with external, objective events. This admission on the part of the historian should prove quite helpful to the Christian who seeks to penetrate to the "inside of an event" such as the life of Christ and its significance for the church and the world.

Ontological Perspectives

There are, as might be expected, various models of philosophy of history depending upon the interpreter's point of reference. There are, however, only three major logical possibilities. History may be interpreted as moving toward a given goal or time in a *linear* direction; or continually repeating itself in *cyclical* patterns and periods; or appear purposeless and *chaotic*. The either/or distinction which characterizes any ontological system as being either meaningful or meaningless, is therefore present also in one's philosophy of history. Here it generally takes the form of either an absolutist or relativist posture. If meaning is believed to be present in a pattern of history, there must be some point of stability or certainty from which an interpretation may be established. If, however, there is believed to be no such center, then the historian must be content to describe random human sequences and relationships from within a limited and therefore relativistically oriented perspective. Since no philosophy of history, not even the absolute idealism of Hegel, has ever pretended to possess infinite knowledge, the absolutistic and relativistic designations must be understood modestly as those systems which are either *consciously* metaphysically oriented from some given point or those which are admittedly *merely descriptive* in their approach. Even the Christian interpreter of history must realize, as Alan Richardson warns:

> We do not see history impartially, that is, as God sees it; and the claim of scientific rationalism—whether made by rationalistic theology or by rationalistic unbelief—to give us an undistorted or impersonal vision of the truth of history is but a modern version of the Serpent's lie: "Ye shall be as God, knowing good and evil." (Gen. 3:5, R.V.)[5]

It is doubtful if the concept of world history would ever have arisen if there had been no Judaic-Christian conviction that God himself has become involved in history to accomplish his purposes. In contrast to the gods of Greece, who are either abstract causes or mythical figures who sport with man and his affairs, and the gods of Rome, who are either symbols of human love or insights perceived through the cultic practices of the mystery religions, the God of the Bible is one who acts purposefully in human history. In the Old Testament Miriam shouts after God's deliverance of Israel from the pursuit of the Egyptians: "Sing to the Lord, for he has triumphed gloriously; the horse and his rider he has thrown into the sea" (Exod. 15:21). And in the New Testament Christ teaches that no sparrow falls to the ground without God's knowledge and concern (Matt. 10:29; cf. Luke 12:24). Indeed, according to Paul, it was in history "when the time had fully come, God sent forth his Son" (Gal. 4:4). Moreover the New Testament claims that God has in historical fact raised Jesus from the dead. These biblical convictions have had profound significance for the rise of a historical consciousness in Western thought. Hans-Georg Gadamer states this conviction with justified boldness when he explains:

> Only when Christianity appeared was it possible to consider history as world history. Christianity incorporated the ecumenical tendency of the Roman consciousness of empire and founded (on the expectation of the Kingdom of God) a progressive view of salvation-history. This confidence in salvation-history gave world history its significance for Christianity. Only, then, through Christianity was a theology of history developed and only on this basis could the secularization process arise in later

> centuries. Secularization seeks a unified meaning by internalizing its eschatological expectations. The bringing together of world history with salvation-history forms the basis for the concept of world history and gives it definition and cohesion.[6]

That modern man often secularizes and internalizes his sense of purpose does not alter the fact that historical consciousness even in these forms is originally indebted to Christian revelation for its inspiration. When this is sufficiently acknowledged, the current critial demands for a historical validation of the Christian message can be placed in proper perspective. While there is no desire here to interpret contemporary historical method solely in terms of its origins, there is value in recognizing that the Christian concept of *meaningful duration* lies at the very foundation of modern historiography. It is therefore no mere apologetic rhetoric to ask at the outset, "Shall history judge Christ or Christ judge history?"

The Challenge of Existentialism

The need to find a proper balance between the historicity of Christ and his existential and theological significance is nowhere more clearly illustrated than in the current dialogue between Rudolf Bultmann and his critics. Bultmann says very plainly: "I do indeed think that we can know almost nothing concerning the life and personality of Jesus, since the early Christian sources show no interest in either, are moreover fragmentary and often legendary; and other sources about Jesus do not exist."[7] He believes, no doubt very sincerely, that one must strip the Gospel of its mythological grave clothes in order to understand its message today. Unless the New Testament first-century imagery is "demythologized" the believer in the twentieth century is forced to sacrifice his intellect and claim to believe in a three-storied world of miraculous events and personages which he must deny in everyday life. However, Bultmann does not simply bypass the passages in the New Testament dealing with the supernatural, but endeavors to interpret them existentially. Bultmann therefore considers his task to be the presentation of the myths of the New Testament in such a way as to offer "man an understanding of himself which will challenge him to a genuine existential decision."[8] It is in this manner that he interprets the significance of the resurrection of Christ when he explains: "Christ meets us in the preaching as one crucified and risen. He meets us in the word of preaching and nowhere else. The faith of Easter is just this—faith in the word of preaching."[9]

Easter for Bultmann is not the actual raising of Jesus from the dead, but the rise of the disciples' faith in their Lord. He denies boldly the possibility of knowing whether or not the resurrection really occurred:

> The resurrection itself is not an event of past history. All that historical criticism can establish is the fact that the first disciples came to believe in the resurrection. The historian can perhaps to some extent account for that faith from the personal intimacy which the disciples had enjoyed with Jesus during his earthly life, and so reduce the resurrection appearances to a series of subjective visions. But the historical problem is scarcely relevant to Christian belief in the resurrection. For the historical event of the rise of the Easter faith means for us what it meant for the first disciples—namely, the self-manifestation of the risen Lord, the act of God in which the redemptive event of the cross is completed.[10]

A current crisis the church faces concerns the difficulty the contemporary mind has in accepting the New Testament as evidence for the historicity of the resurrection. Perhaps we can approach this problem more confidently if we realize that the "scandal of the Gospel" comes in different forms and shapes from age to age. For example, in the Middle Ages the point of tension lay in the difficulty one had in believing that a holy and righteous God could indeed forgive a sinner merely through his repentance and trust. It seems that the world with its progress in moral consciousness has learned to accept God as a forgiving being, and even tends to take this for granted, but the current scientific milieu finds it scandalous to think of God's intervening in history and creating life out of death in Christ's resurrection. We must be extremely careful, however, that we neither allow a cultural familiarity with a doctrine to blur its gracious character, nor permit a particular cultural challenge to overwhelm our faith.

Gerhard Ebeling in his *Theology and Proclamation*, which bears the subtitle *Dialogue with Bultmann*, has distilled perhaps as well as any contemporary writer the methodological importance of the historicity of the Christ-event for Christian faith. Ebeling is appreciative of Bultmann's contribution in helping safeguard Christian witnessing from becoming a series of arid documentations of episodes in Christ's life. He is, however, concerned that Bultmann's interpretation of the significance of preaching as a part of the redemptive event itself not be allowed to eliminate the need to deal with the person of Jesus who lies behind the message. He explains that "it is one thing to give a warning against improper attempts to get back behind the kerygma [or message] in order to provide a 'legitimation' for it; it is quite another to stress the necessity of such attempts for the purpose of interpretation."[11]

If, as Bultmann maintains, one can really ascertain nothing authentically historical about the Christ who is proclaimed in the message, it must follow, according to Ebeling, that the relation of Jesus to the message would consist in nothing more than a series of assertions, "for the understanding of which Jesus himself would have no more importance than that of a random and meaningless cipher." Should these conditions prove true, Ebeling concludes in strains that are similar to most of Bultmann's severest critics, the message "would be no more than a mere myth."[12] But this is far from being the case, for one may be sure that the historical Jesus must be distinguished from the biblical message in view of the fact that the *name of Jesus* is an integral part of that which is proclaimed. If there should appear an absolute contradiction or startling misinterpretation of Jesus in the message, then the proclamation itself would also have to be cancelled out as invalid. Bultmann is in danger of doing just this by the way he has allowed the church's preaching to usurp the place of the historical Jesus. In Bultmann's methodology "the difference between the Christological kerygma and Jesus is eliminated with a vengeance." Consequently, Ebeling feels compelled to warn in penetrating manner that if the difference between the historical Jesus and the message of the church disappears we will have to fear that the church has usurped the position of Christ. Moreover we shall eventually have to wonder, in spite of the insistence of the church that Christ is really present in the message, whether "the kerygma has taken the place of something which is absent."[13] Bultmann comes therefore dangerously close to that spirit of antichrist against which John warns when he writes: "Every spirit which confesses that Jesus Christ has come in the flesh is of God, and every spirit which does not confess Jesus is not of God" (I John 4:2-3).

Historical Method

It is now necesary to try to establish some valid methodological approaches and corresponding results which might provide a constructive view of Christ and his resurrection. One must admit at the outset that non-Christian sources throw little if any light on the historical figure of Christ.[14] Josephus, who published his *Jewish Antiquities* around 90 A.D. refers to Jesus only obliquely when he records the trial and stoning of James "the brother of Jesus, who was called Christ."[15] There can be little doubt that the following glowing description of Christ which appears in many editions of Josephus' works is not authentic. Josephus is supposed to have written:

> Now, there was about this time Jesus, a wise man, if it be lawful to call him a man; for he was a doer of wonderful works, a teacher of such men as receive the truth with pleasure. He drew over to him both many of the Jews and many of the Gentiles. He was [the] Christ. And when Pilate, at the suggestion of the principal men amongst us, had condemned him to the cross, those that loved him at the first did not forsake him; for he appeared to them alive again the third day; as the divine prophets had foretold these and ten thousand other wonderful things concerning him. And the tribe of Christians, so named from him, are not extinct at this day.[16]

There is, however, as Maurice Goguel demonstrates, strong internal and external evidence that this segment has been invented or reconstructed by Christian editors.[17] Perhaps the earliest secular reference to Christ comes from the early second century from Tacitus who offers the following explanation for the name "Christian":

> This name originates from "Christus" who was sentenced to death by the procurator, Pontius Pilate, during the reign of Tiberius. This detestable superstition, which had been suppressed for a while, spread anew not only in Judea where the evil had started, but also in Rome, where everything that is horrid and wicked in the world gathers and finds numerous followers.[18]

The Jewish Talmud, while indirectly confirming the historical existence of Jesus, provides no new information concerning him from independent sources. It builds rather on traditions which are later than the New Testament and portrays Jesus as a political extremist, perverter of the law, and magician who is therefore unworthy of the Christians' faith. Although these Jewish and pagan sources are either indifferent or hostile to the Christian portrayal of Christ in the New Testament, there may yet be positive value in these nonbiblical accounts. They at least establish the fact that it never occurred even to the enemies of Christianity in those early years to doubt the historical existence of Jesus. This was, as Günther Bornkamm points out, "reserved for an unrestrained, tendentious criticism of modern times."[19]

Although a linear sense of history progressing toward a meaningful future has always, in varying degrees of consciousness, been present in Western thought due to the influence of the church, it was not until the nineteenth century, when this confidence in meaning merged with rationalism and the development of evolutionary theory, that the modern concept of history in the full critical sense was born. Rationalism encouraged man to be confident in his ability to understand history in terms of his own rational categories and analogies whereas evolution taught him to understand all life in terms of its natural origins. Unfortunately, at least from the church's perspective, modern historical method from the outset was heavily dominated by its early scientific orientation which tended to overlook the significance of intuitive insight, personal involvement, and the creative dimensions of human freedom.

For a time it was thought that through the efforts of men like H. S. Reimarus, David F. Strauss, Bruno Bauer, and E. Renan it might be possible to write a truly historical life of Christ by applying rationalistic and scientific methods to New Testament sources. The results, however, were portrayals of Christ which were little more than the projections of the authors' images of themselves. Albert Schweitzer in *The Quest of the Historical Jesus* demonstrated the futility of these efforts to picture Christ as merely a historical teacher who taught an ethic of love. The Jesus they produced "is a figure designed by rationalism, endowed with life by liberalism, and clothed by modern theology in an historical garb."[20] Whatever else Christ may have been, according to Schweitzer, he was above all a person whom his followers believed to be divine and one who proclaimed the nearness of an eschatological kingdom.

Historical Confidence

Although the New Testament does not present a Jesus who is merely historical, it does nevertheless, as Günther Bornkamm maintains, portray the historical Jesus with "an authenticity, a freshness, and a distinctiveness not in any way effaced by the Church's Easter faith."[21] There is moreover within these New Testament documents a remarkable degree of unity in the midst of diversity in its picture of Jesus. According to C. F. D. Moule, if one asks how this happened "the only answer is that the common factor holding all together is devotion to the person of Jesus Christ—the historical Jesus acknowledged as Messiah and Lord."[22] However, the New Testament not only intends to portray an earthly figure who is believed to be divine, but above all one who in fact is risen from the dead and possesses ultimate eschatological authority. Speaking of the intention of the early disciples to ground their witness concretely in the occurrence of the resurrection of Christ, Jürgen Moltmann explains: "Their statements contain not only existential certainty in the sense of saying, 'I am certain,' but also and together with this objective certainty in the sense of saying, 'It is certain.' "[23] This concern for certainty is perhaps nowhere more clearly expressed than in Luke's prologue to the book of Acts when he claims that the resurrection of Christ has been demonstrated "by many proofs," ἐν πολλοῖς τεκμηρίοις (Acts 1:3).[24] In other words, the assurance that Christ actually rose from the dead and the message of the New Testament are inseparable. T. Müller phrases this conviction quite simply when he concludes: "in the revelation of Christ as historical event, the 'that' and the 'what' fall together."[25]

The modern reader of the New Testament texts cannot of course be an eyewitness of the resurrection of Christ, but it may encourage him to know that even according to the Gospels there were no witnesses of the *resurrection itself as event*—only resurrection appearances of the risen one. In fact, the New Testament does not really make a strong case for the resurrection on the empirical evidence of the empty tomb. Although the Gospel of John tells of "the other disciple, who reached the tomb first, also went in, and he saw and believed"; the empty tomb without an accompanying word from an angel or the Lord himself most frequently evokes perplexity, fear, amazement, and despair (John 20:8). Mary's cry, "They have taken away my Lord, and I do not know where they have laid him," is a typical response before the risen Lord appears (John 20:13). Genuine Christian *faith* cannot be founded on a "faith-easing" empirical fact such as an empty tomb, for at best the fact that the grave is empty tells you only something about the old body and nothing about Christ's resurrection body, which is the essential element in the Easter message.[26] However, *after* the early disciples respond in faith to the risen Christ, the empty tomb provides a tangible counterpart to their encounter with him and strengthens their defense against those who deny the resurrection.

But what about the credibility of those who, according to the New Testament, give witness that the resurrection has taken place? It is on this question that David Hume presented his classical challenge for anyone who claims to have witnessed the occurrence of miracles. He insisted that witnesses to such events could be believed only if these observers were (1) numerous, (2) intelligent, (3) highly educated, (4) of unquestioned integrity, (5) willing to undergo severe loss if they were proven mistaken, and (6) if they presented their claims publicly in a region of the world which was well known and easily accessible.[27] The real crux of his argument lay, however, in the profound and legitimate demand that "no testimony is sufficient to establish a miracle, unless the testimony be of such a kind that its falsehood would be more miraculous than the fact that it endeavors to establish."[28]

This Humean standard for accepting miracles is illustrated humorously but quite accurately by Malcolm Diamond who imagines:

> If a friend told you that he'd seen a violet hippopotamus with orange polka dots flying across the campus, you would not be rationally entitled to believe him unless it were more probable that such an animal actually had been flying across the campus than to suppose that your friend was on drugs and having a bad trip. Clearly, it is the latter possibility that is more likely.[29]

Although this fantasy is intended to disparage the likelihood of there being any reliable witnesses for miracles, it may be that just here the decisive ethical support for the credibility of witnesses to supernatural events comes most clearly into view. For *if* some Christian witnesses were to report such an astounding event, their character, all things being equal and in order, would probably be sufficient evidence that such an event did occur rather than being a delusion or a falsehood. If, therefore, the New Testament documents and the very aura of the continuing Christian community possess a transparent and creative ethical confirmation, the case for the resurrection of Christ is perhaps as nearly established as it can ever be for faith apart from firsthand historical experience.[30] One's historical method should therefore be comprehensive enough to move beyond a total dependency on firsthand experience, for any effort to reconstruct the past will by the very nature of its task have to make value judgments regarding the character and reliability of its witnesses.

One must be willing to allow his total experience of thinking and valuing to provide evidence for the probability that an event has taken place in fact.[31] This means that without taking away from the actuality of the event it might therefore be more accurate to speak of the resurrection of Christ as having been "experiential" rather than "historical." Be that as it may, it is to man's wider experience that one must turn today for a confirmation of the resurrection. Since even an eyewitness account of the resurrection can be trusted only if certain metaphysical points of reference are deemed stable and "meaningfully probable," it seems appropriate that one should be allowed to reason backward from his *experience of meaning* to knowledge of an event which is *historically probable*. With his characteristic brilliance, C. S. Lewis employs this kind of reasoning from meaningful experience to historical confidence in the "grand miracle" of Christ when he insists, parabolically: "We believe that the sun is in the sky in mid-day in summer not because we can clearly see the sun (in fact, we cannot) but because we can see everything else."[32]

Where there is no possibility for a direct experience of a first-century event by a contemporary interpreter, one may be forced to rely on a kind of *reciprocal validation*, or the acceptance of evidence through association with that which one *may* be able to experience firsthand. The same documents which testify concerning the certainty of Christ's resurrection are those which convey his promises concerning forgiveness, a sense of belonging with Christ's people in his church, and perhaps above all, an intuitive inner consciousness of his living presence. If these documents have proven themselves trustworthy and reliable in these existential realms, might we not also feel justified in accepting those associated claims which touch upon issues of facticity, or historicity? This approach to the question of historicity is really in effect merely a reversal of the analogical method of historical reasoning which is most frequently used. For example, if we believe that we can trust the analogical method of historical reasoning which appears to move in a forward direction, would it not also be possible to reason backward toward a confirmation of an original occurrence of an event from that which appears reliable at the end of the chain of reasoning? Regardless of whether we are reasoning forward or backward, we are in essence putting our trust in the causal sequences or causal associations which permit us to move from that which has been experienced or seen directly toward that which appears historically probable. It is this confidence in causality which allows us to make sense of our experience in both its historical and predictive dimensions. The backward method of historical reasoning actually involves more than simply having an experience which resembles one of the themes contained in a document which also, by the way, involves historical claims. For Christian experience is believed to be of such existential *depth* that it can only be accounted for by a creative potency that has itself become historically tangible.

The New Testament accounts of Christ are especially difficult to interpret because they are neither purely objective history nor myth. In their classical literary sense myths are elemental collective insights which are deemed to have universal significance and can only be portrayed in unhistorical dramatic imagery. Hans Frei summarizes the basic characteristics of this complex literary form more precisely:

> Myths are stories in which character and action are not irreducibly themselves. Instead they are representations of broader and not directly representable psychic or cosmic states—states transcending the scene of finite and particular events subject to causal explanation. The deepest levels of human existence, the origin and destiny of the universe, including humanity, are the themes that myths evoke through storytelling. Myths are convincing or true by virtue of their embodiment or echoing of universal experience. "Universal"

> may be too strong a term, but it is not too much to say that a particular myth is external and expressed mirroring of an internal experience that is both elemental within the consciousness and yet shared by a whole group.[33]

While granting that cosmic and eschatological truth cannot be captured fully by a historical narrative and that there is figurative imagery in the resurrection accounts, it should be quite plain that the passion-resurrection stories are not presented by their writers as literary myths. For example, Jesus Christ is the central figure of these accounts and through no stretch of the imagination can he be considered merely incidental to the universal truth depicted. He is not only the symbol of eschatological victory; he is the victor himself! In fact the Gospel narratives are presented to *demythologize* the cyclical, nature myths of the dying and rising gods rather than to promulgate a new myth. What the New Testament does, however, is to link the passion-resurrection narratives so closely with the birth, life, and ministry of Jesus of Nazareth that one is unable to separate the quality of life which Christ lives from the historical claims of his resurrection. There is, according to Frei, a kind of existential-substantial duality or continuity in the New Testament literature concerning Christ. He discovers this, for example, in Luke 24:5 when "the two men" ask the women at Christ's tomb, "Why do you seek the living among the dead?" Christ so embodies life, how can one conceive of him as dead? He also interprets Christ's declaration in the Gospel of John, "I am the resurrection and the life" (11:25) in this same context: "Jesus defines life, he is life: How can he who constitutes the very definition of life be conceived of as the opposite of what he defines? To think him dead is the equivalent of not thinking of him at all."[34] At least it seems reasonable to conclude that whatever knowledge of Christ's resurrection one may possess it must be interpreted within an understanding of his life and creative potential. There can be no legitimate dualistic separation of the Gospels into history and interpretation, for these elements simply do not exist apart from one another in the New Testament—and this alone comprises the basic literary evidence for knowledge of Christ.

If one is willing to allow the form-critical method of research to cast any light on the historicity of the events reported in the New Testament, there is some encouragement to believe the resurrection of Christ occurred because there are so many *independent* accounts given in these documents.[35] This means the hypothesis that there was a deliberate effort to create a belief in the resurrection in order to keep the Christian faith and community alive is not supported by the documentary evidence at hand. While admitting the possibility that the various literary strata dealing with the resurrection may on occasion be late apologetic developments, H. Conzelmann concludes that "form-critical considerations show that the Easter accounts in the Gospels are composed of original single historical reports."[36] Moreover the evidence for the historicity of the resurrection of Jesus is greatly enhanced by the fact that two major separate traditions—that of the empty tomb, and the appearances of Christ—developed alongside one another in complementary fashion in the New Testament. The tradition of the empty tomb can largely be accounted for because of the geographical proximity of the place of the crucifixion and burial to Jerusalem and the surrounding environment where the gospel was first proclaimed. Since the resurrection of Christ was proclaimed shortly after his death, the situation demands that in and around Jerusalem reliable testimony for the empty tomb become an integral aspect in the defense of the gospel. Although this is admittedly an internal evidence, the fact that the tradition appears early and in close association with accounts of the appearances lends support to the belief in the integrity of the reports and the unlikelihood of deliberate collusion. If one may be allowed therefore to assume that the believers' accounts of the empty tomb were distributed not long after the resurrection was believed to have taken place, then the Jewish explanation that the body of Jesus had been stolen and the grave was in fact empty is also complementary evidence for Christ's resurrection. For the Jews would have had everything to gain by being able to go to Christ's grave and produce his body.

Even if one allows that the appearances are reported in language within the context of the term "vision" this concept really only describes something about the subjective response of one's experience and does not necessarily determine the presence or absence of any objective content which might occasion the response. For that matter, the appearances could not possibly be explained on the basis of the mere psychological expectancy of the disciples for they were originally, in the context of their apocalyptic tradition, only expecting a general resurrection at the end of the world. Moreover, their spirits were too low at the time of the crucifixion to expect Jesus' resurrection at this time. The trustworthiness of the biblical testimonies regarding the appearances is, it seems, further enhanced by the number of these appearances, their temporal distribution, and their close proximity to the church's early proclamation of the gospel. For example, the appearance to five hundred brethren at one time on a mountain in Galilee cannot be a later development of the biblical tradition because Paul, whose writings are believed by nearly everyone to be of early origin, made a very deliberate point that some of these witnesses were still alive and could therefore attest the truth of his proclamation.

While the *independence* of the Christian testimonies when viewed from a form-critical perspective make it difficult to believe there was a collusion or deception on the part of the New Testament writers, the passages nevertheless give strong evidence for having originated from a *common source*. For example, Paul's declaration of the resurrection in I Corinthians 15 and the witness of Simon Peter in the house of Cornelius according to Acts 10:40ff. appear to have a common source tradition. Gerhard Delling explains:

> In every form of expression in Acts the witnesses of the appearances of Jesus are referred to as witnesses of his raising: God had raised him, and of this (to this) we are witnesses: 2:32;

> 3:14; cf. 5:32. In more exact formal terms, it is also possible to say that God raised him on the third day and made him visible not to his "people," but to the witnesses previously chosen by God, that is, to us, who ate and drank with Him, after he had risen from the dead (10:40f.). In this somewhat fuller statement from Peter's sermon in the house of Cornelius, one can see that the author is just as capable as Paul of placing side by side the raising on the third day and the appearing before chosen witnesses. This does not imply the literary dependence of the sermon at Caesarea on I Cor. 15; rather, the similarity goes back to the common tradition, with regard to the substance of what is said. At the same time it is clear that the testimony to the resurrection by the twelve in Acts is important in the same way as [for] Paul: whether it is "Luke" or Paul, they proclaim the same risen Jesus (I Cor. 15:11).[37]

Granted that a common literary source does not prove that an occurrence lies at the base of a narrative, it does nevertheless commend the writers of these documents for their endeavors to report accurately, without fanciful additions, what they had either seen or believed had actually transpired. On the plane, therefore, of literary independence of witnesses and evidence of a common source, the New Testament documents seem as reliable as any other writings from a comparable historical period and literary type.

Modern historical methodology is founded largely on the confidence that a past event can only be known by comparing it analogically with contemporary events which can be known with some certainty through direct experience or participation. This analogical method with its obvious phenomenological bias is represented by Ernst Troelsch who insists:

> Agreement with normal, usual, or at least variously attested, happenings . . . as we know them, is the mark of probability for happenings which the critic can recognize as really having happened or can leave aside. The observation of analogies between past events of the same kind makes it possible to ascribe probability to them and to interpret the unknown aspects of the one on the basis of the known aspects of the other. The omnipotence thus attaching to analogy implies, however, the basic similarity of all historical events, which is not, of course, identity . . . but presupposes that there is always a

> common core of similarity, on the basis of which the differences can be sensed and perceived.[38]

Alas, what does this method do if allowed to run its full course with such basic Christian affirmations as the creation of the world in the beginning, the final eschatological culmination of all things, and the resurrection of Jesus Christ from the dead? To what events may these event-claims be compared for analogical support? The confidence to believe an event like the resurrection of Christ from the dead can come, not from an analogical determinism, for in fact there is no event which *could* compare with it analogically, but rather from the creative potential of that historical claim, i.e., what it causes to happen in the future. This of course does not mean that any claim whatsoever will be allowed to stand, but that any claim which is sustained by subsequent events should be given serious historical credence. In other words, the concept of history must be expanded from being merely a reconstruction and interpretation of what *happened* in history to include that which *makes history*. Since the belief in the resurrection of Christ from the dead has created the church and continues to provide eschatological hope, it should be understood as a *historical event*. Perhaps, therefore, that early counsel of Gamaliel when he applied the category of causal creativity and historical durability to the claim of the apostles that Christ has been raised from the dead is far more valid as a historical principle than was ever dreamed. He concludes wisely: "If this plan or this undertaking is of man, it will fail; but if it is of God, you will not be able to overthrow them. You might even be found opposing God!" (Acts 5:38-39). Whether one is willing to move from an effect, such as the existence of the church, to a belief in the historicity of its founder's resurrection is surely a matter where varied intelligent interpretations are possible. However, if one attempts to explain the rise and continuance of the church on the basis of an early misunderstanding, one should prepare to defend an *ontology* which can sustain creative living and profound hope on the basis of that which has no foundation in reality.

History and Eschatological Expectation

In a fictitious and sometimes humorous but provocative dialogue between Karl Barth, Rudolf Bultmann, Wolfhart Pannenberg, and Jürgen Moltmann concerning the historicity of the resurrection of Christ, Daniel L. Migliore creates a theological fantasy in which Karl Barth extends a preaching invitation to the others. They are to declare on what biblical text they would preach their next Easter sermon. Barth himself answers first:

> For my part, I would like to preach on the text in which the angel announces to the disciples at the tomb, "He has risen. He is not here" (Mark 16:6). I think I would emphasize that an angel brought this message, that it was revelation, and that above all else it was good and joyful news.
>
> Bultmann: I have always been especially attracted to the Gospel of John. I think I would preach on the word of the risen Lord to Thomas: "Have you believed because you have seen me? Blessed are those who have not seen and yet believe" (John 20:29).
>
> Pannenberg: I would want to preach a sermon emphasizing the centrality of the fact of the resurrection for our faith. A good text would be the Pauline claim: "If Christ has not been raised, then our preaching is in vain and your faith is in vain" (I Cor. 15:14).
>
> Moltmann: My choice for an Easter text is perhaps a little unexpected, but that is surely appropriate for the subject matter. I would preach on the text from the Apocalypse: "Behold, I make all things new" (Rev. 21:5).[39]

Migliore thoughtfully allows the reader to draw his own conclusion regarding the theological significance of this imaginary dialogue. The lesson however seems to be clear that there is not just one but many biblical methods by which the resurrection of Christ as event and meaning is demonstrated to the believer. There is—as Barth stresses—a transcendental dimension wherein revelation itself appears to minimize the significance of eyewitness accounts by stressing God's supernatural presence in his

Word. And yet there are times when—according to Bultmann's insight—the accent falls biblically upon the necessity of an existential response which issues in a redirection of life toward venture, risk, and hope. The absolute necessity of the occurrence of Christ's resurrection—as Pannenberg explains—is without question the foundation of New Testament faith. Moreover, the capacity of Christ's resurrection to create history—as Moltmann perceives—is also employed by the New Testament to give support to the belief that it has occurred. These and many other approaches, some of which are incorporated in the presentation above, may be held in the unity of faith as long as one remains true to the reality that "Jesus is Lord!" (I Cor. 12:3). Rejoice then because the promise that "he who raised Christ Jesus from the dead will give life to your mortal bodies also through his Spirit that dwells in you" is negotiable, not only for the early eyewitnesses, but for all who encounter the risen Christ in the presence of his Spirit (Rom. 8:11).

Although different interpreters will recognize many shades of historicity present in the Christ-event, it seems reasonable to expect that each should allow his confidence in the historical nature of the event to find corresponding or analogous expression in his presentation of the Christian message. In other words, the degree to which Christ and his resurrection are deemed to be "actual" should determine the degree of expectation that God will "actually" accomplish his purpose in history and eschatology. This correlation can be illustrated rather simply. Suppose someone borrows a hundred dollars. There are several kinds of encouragement which the borrower can give to the one who loaned the money. He can merely say the words, "I promise that I will repay the debt." This is *verbal*, propositional assurance. Or the debtor may conduct himself in such a trustworthy manner that he evokes the hope in the lender that he may one day be paid back. This is *existential* assurance. If, however, the debtor not only says he will pay the debt and lives worthily but *in fact* pays half the debt and promises soon to return the full amount—this is *historical* assurance. This is just admitting that, whether we have the right to ask it or not, we usually expect to receive evidence for our expectations in the very same ways in which these expectations are to be relevant and fulfilled. Extended theologically the illustration of the debtor can mean that when we read an apocalyptic passage in the New Testament we have a *verbal* assurance that one day we will rise from the dead. As we live in the consciousness of God's presence and love in light of that Word and in the fellowship of the church, we gain an *existential* assurance that we will one day live with Christ. If, however, we know that *in fact* Christ has been raised from the dead, we possess a *historical* assurance that involves not just mind, emotions, and will, but our tangible, *historical bodies* as well!

Christian communication may, therefore, in keeping with its historical rootage, function on the hermeneutical principle that the nearer one comes to announcing what God has actually done in Christ in language that corresponds to the Christ-event, the nearer one comes to the central theme of biblical revelation and the more hope and expectancy we may have that God will do again in the hearer redemptively and existentially what he did when men first encountered the historical Christ. In other words, the event of Christ's coming is theologically central, and it is this historical substance which gives revelational weight to the teachings of Christ and the instructions and exhortations which are found in the larger corpus of New Testament writings. Quite legitimately, then, the Christian message will include much more than mere recitations of objective accounts of historical events. However, it must be underscored that in affirming a Christological fulcrum for New Testament faith, the objective criterion for validating divine authority in Christian witness will be the degree to which the message—including announcement, explanation, application, and exhortation—analogically approximates and expresses the divine will which was present in the initial impact of God's breaking in upon *human history* in Christ.

What then can be concluded concerning a Christian philosophy of history? Since the Christian believes that God has come into history in Christ, he holds that God is

Lord of history and the master of all its temporal manifestations. This means also that each moment, as Herbert Butterfield used to say, is "equidistant from eternity" and that time is meaningful, moving, segmented eternity. Moreover, in light of Jesus' resurrection from the dead and the assurance he gives the believer not only for his own personal future but for the fulfillment of God's purposes in history and the cosmos as well, history must be viewed according to a linear model. Creation, incarnation, resurrection, and eschaton are the pivotal, temporal points which provide the paradigms upon which history may be experienced as *meaningful*. The fact that Christ has been raised from the dead and transcends history teaches that history can never exhaust the meaning of eternity. A Christian philosophy of history therefore is not primarily concerned with history, in the sense of its "happenedness" but with *lived* history—and this particularly as it is shaped by life with Jesus Christ. In a very compact and yet moving statement Erich Dinkler recognizes this transcendental dimension when he summarizes the New Testament view of history:

> It views the past as the place where there is not yet faith in Christ and consequently, no salvation: where thus man lives in disobedience and consequently, in the aeon of death. The present begins there where man understands himself through Christ and knows himself to be free. This means, however, that past and present are not historical, but soteriological quantities. Past and present are not to be divided as objective time sequences, but exist side by side. As long as men close their eyes to faith in Christ they allow the past aeon of death to exist beside the new aeon of life.[40]

The Christian consequently approaches history, indeed lives within it, with the conviction that his own personal life and the historical moments which surround him are moving toward fulfillment. He need not fear the meaningless determinism of cyclical repetitions nor the void of an irrational chaos, but can put his hope in the one who is so vibrant with life that even when he confronted death, "it was not possible for him to be held by it" (Acts 2:24).

CHAPTER IV

Christ—The Clue to Reality

Christian philosophy endeavors with a staggering audacity to penetrate being or reality in its wholeness. This is the special concern of ontology, or metaphysics. It seeks to discover what reality is in its totality as compared or contrasted to a mere function, appearance, linguistic symbol, or partial manifestation. Expressed classically, it wonders with Martin Heidegger, "*Why is there something rather than nothing?*" It then proceeds to probe what that reality would be if all misconceptions and accidental properties could be stripped away.[1] It is as though, to use Malcolm Diamond's imagery, one were immersed in an "Infinite Sea of Being" which is ultimate reality itself without surface or shore. One has no alternative but to recognize through faith that particular segment of reality which illuminates the nature of the whole and provides the resources which are needed to participate in it most effectively.[2] This ontological quest for an understanding of reality is illustrated somewhat humorously but perceptively in Margery Williams' delightful children's story, *The Velveteen Rabbit or How Toys Become Real:*

> The Skin Horse had lived longer in the nursery than any of the others. He was so old that his brown coat was bald in patches and showed the seams underneath, and most of the

> hairs in his tail had been pulled out to string bead necklaces. He was wise, for he had seen a long succession of mechanical toys arrive to boast and swagger, and by-and-by break their mainsprings and pass away, and he knew that they were only toys, and would never turn into anything else. For nursery magic is very strange and wonderful, and only those playthings that are old and wise and experienced like the Skin Horse understand all about it.
>
> "What is REAL?" asked the Rabbit one day, when they were lying side by side near the nursery fender, before Nana came to tidy the room. "Does it mean having things that buzz inside you and a stick-out handle?"
>
> "Real isn't how you are made," said the Skin Horse. "*It's a thing that happens to you.* When a child loves you for a long, long time, not just to play with, but REALLY loves you, then you become Real."
>
> "Does it hurt?" asked the Rabbit.
>
> "Sometimes," said the Skin Horse, for he was always truthful. "*When you are Real you don't mind being hurt.*"
>
> "Does it happen all at once, like being wound up," he asked, "or bit by bit?"
>
> "It doesn't happen all at once," said the Skin Horse. "*You become. It takes a long time. That's why it doesn't often happen to people who break easily, or have sharp edges, or who have to be carefully kept.* Generally, by the time you are Real, most of your hair has been loved off, and your eyes drop out and you get loose in the joints and very shabby. But these things don't matter at all, because once you are Real you can't be ugly, except to people who don't understand."
>
> "I suppose *you* are Real?" said the Rabbit. And then he wished he had not said it, for he thought the Skin Horse might be sensitive. But the Skin Horse only smiled.
>
> "The Boy's Uncle made me Real," he said. "That was a great many years ago; but once you are Real you can't become unreal again. It lasts for always."[3]

Even the child, it is assumed, will recognize that his concern for the reality of that which is concrete and particular must be set within a comprehensive context of that which is real everywhere and always.

Now the Christian faith, according to Alfred North Whitehead, "has always been a religion seeking a metaphysic"[4] and the maturing Christian will want to explore and articulate the ontological implications of his faith.[5] If, for example, a meeting with Christ occurs—either in an initial New Testament sense or through secondary channels in a contemporary moment—which functionally produces an existential consciousness of liberation that we dare to call "forgiveness of sins," what confidence may we have that the experience is real and not only apparent, enduring and not just exuberance of mood, an encounter with life that touches the whole of our concern and not merely one atomistic fragment? These are surely questions which admit varying degrees of solution; yet they are genuine experiential issues which call for a recognition of ontological depth if they are to retain their functional effectiveness. This necessity which Christian faith has for confronting the comprehensive context of ontology is portrayed convincingly by Gerhard Ebeling in his essay entitled "Theology and Reality" when he affirms:

> Theology has to do with reality as a totality—not with the sum of all the realms of reality and all the ways in which reality encounters us. . . . However much theology is based upon the testimony of Christian faith, it has yet to make good faith's claim by bringing to expression what unconditionally concerns every man in his totality.[6]

Christian faith, therefore, cannot be content to deal exclusively or even primarily with manifestations and functions, but must concern itself with ontology—that is, with the question concerning the correspondence between the function or expression of a thing and its reality. Where shall one go for a Christian solution to these issues?

What About Natural Theology?

In recent decades Protestant theology has been chastened by Karl Barth for its surrender of the sovereign Word of God to the human criteria of natural theology. Remember how he thundered "one cannot speak of God by simply speaking of man in a loud voice."[7] During Barth's day the church desperately needed his injunction that Christian proclamation "as it takes place in preaching and sacrament, presupposes that neither the nature of the object nor the situation or desire of the speaker are, or can become, so clear to any man as to put him in the position of making a judgment as to its truth." There is, he goes on to add, only one criterion for interpreting revelation and that is the Word of God itself. "This criterion we cannot handle. It is the criterion which handles itself, and apart from that is in no man's hands. The other criteria we can handle by recollecting and expecting this criterion. But only its own judgment holds as absolutely binding and inviolable."[8] Barth's resounding *Nein!* to natural theology is, moreover, still as appropriate as ever: (1) wherever the human ego insists on reigning supreme through pride in its own spiritual affinity with the ultimate source of its existence and knowledge; or, (2) where man endeavors to establish his own conceptual patterns as the content-norm for an understanding of God; or, (3) when he just quite simply defies the demand for a repentance that could make available the divine resources which he needs. However, at the same time there remains the challenge which T. F. Torrance dares to suggest with reference to his beloved teacher when he writes that today "if we are to take as seriously as Barth himself did the relation between the incarnation and the creation in God's creative and redemptive interaction with the world, then a closer relation must be established between natural theology and revealed theology."[9]

In other words, as long as Christian theology maintains: (1) that men are universally responsible for a knowledge of God which is available to them apart from special acts of revelation;[10] (2) that the incarnation contributes to an understanding of the unity of truth which makes this space-time order an intelligible universe; and, (3) that the God who is believed to hold all created things together is essentially *one*—then it is reasonable to conclude with Torrance that natural theology must be intimately correlated with Christian theology in such a way that the structures of both natural theology and Christian theology will change. Natural theology will change because it will be able to see what God's revelation has done in space and time, and positive theology will change because it will need to integrate its message to the whole natural realm.

Only through such a total reorientation will it be possible "to overcome the dualisms that have undermined theology from below, and fragmented it in the tragic manner of modern times."[11] These are strong words. It is doubtful if many are ready at this time to speak so favorably of this old arch enemy, natural theology, as long as it is not willing to remain in the formal outercourt of the Gentiles and insists on handling even the content of revelation within the Holy of Holies. Nevertheless, the prospects of implementing Torrance's concern in the realm of positive Christian theology is not nearly so frightening when there is a clear understanding of the basic distinction, which Torrance himself cherishes, between *revelation as the divine self-giving*—over which man has no control—and *theology as the human ideational response* to that revelation. This latter can and must change from age to age in order for one to interpret the Word of God with the greatest possible assurance and cultural integration for each contemporary generation. The way is now open to explore how a philosophical concern for ontology can contribute to an understanding of the Christian faith.

No Escape from Ontology

To begin, it should be acknowledged that wherever understanding is sought, man as existing individual—or in religious terms—man as creature, seems to have *no possibility of escape from an ontological frame of reference*. It is in this vein that Willard Quine assumes, "Ontological statements follow immediately from all manner of casual statements of commonplace fact,"[12] and Paul Tillich concedes, "Every epistemological assertion is implicitly ontological."[13] It is therefore more than semantically relevant to realize that even the denial of the possibility of ontology is an ontological interpretation of reality. For even if we could retreat into a rigid individualism, we would do well to understand that we draw limits only at the frontier of our claim to knowledge, not necessarily on the nature of reality itself. Gabriel Marcel comes boldly to this issue when he concludes: "The *cogito* merely guards the threshold of objective validity, and that is strictly all; this is proved by the indeterminate character of the *I*. The *I am* is, to my mind a global statement which it is impossible to break down into its component parts."[14] He reasons still further that

> to withdraw into oneself is not to be for oneself nor to mirror oneself in the intelligible unity of subject and object. On the contrary . . . here we come up against the paradox of that actual mystery whereby the I into which I withdraw ceases for as much, to belong to itself. "You are not your own"—this great saying of St. Paul assumes in this connection its full concrete and ontological significance.[15]

There is furthermore an experiential basis for the necessity of ontological categories to be found in the fact that man refuses to be satisfied with a merely functional, fragmentary interpretation of his experience. Tillich expresses this insight well when he says "the concept of true being is the result of disappointed expectations in our encounter with reality."[16] It would seem, then, that the very structures of experience, such as man's perennial struggle between form and vitality, to cite only one example, are constituted to arouse in him an intuitive impression of an ontological oneness or wholeness which lies behind the fragmented pattern of his dealings with men and things. This, of course, does not mean that a unified reality is "there" to be found and explained, but one may so *interpret* his experience and thereby offer a plausible theory for the almost universal appearance of such an expectation. In other words, the Christian thinker can assume philosophically an "ontological anemia" in man which expresses itself in concern to know and participate in that which is real and ultimate in much the same manner in which theologically he posits the belief that all men are sinners and need God.

Another existential encouragement for recognizing the need for an ontological response can be seen in the fact that man relates to his world as though he believed in the logos-quality, or rational cohesion, of his environment. In an effort to make conceptual room for an ontological

Christology, T. F. Torrance reasons that when man raises the question concerning the rationality of the universe, he not only must depend upon its intelligibility to determine the answer, but he must assume it even to be able to place the question. It is not possible to ask a meaningful question of one's environment and at the same time to call in question the category of meaning itself and presume to stand outside the realm of intelligibility. If this is attempted, the result can only be a surrender, sooner or later, to irrationality. "Before the question as to the relation between our knowing and ultimate rationality we cannot but stand in awe and acknowledgment, and can ask our questions rightly only within the actuality of that relationship."[17] In other words, the intelligibility of human discourse and the rational interest which man has toward the understanding of his place and destiny implies, if it involves any meaning at all, an ontological congruence between reality and experience.[18]

Thus far, effort has been made to say only that meaningful experience makes ontological *questions* unavoidable and that there are some rational reflections which support the belief that positive ontological insights are *possible*. What can now be said about ontological conclusions and the decisive matter of their verification?

Validating an Ontological Claim

One may in epistemological faith hold an interpretation of a thing, person, concept, or spiritual entity to be ontologically valid to the extent to which the "reality" creates in one's experience the conditions which appropriately correspond to one's conceptual understanding of that which is claimed to be "real." Although continual reformulation of the ontological categories and restructuring of the experiential channels of encounter with the "real" will be necessary, such an "ontological-existentialism" could help avoid the dangers of a merely speculative approach to reality. It might also guard against a positivism or a functionalism which is reluctant to recognize an ontological realm. It remains to be seen how this thesis is relevant to a Christian ontology.

Like its philosophical counterpart, the need for Christian ontology arises from one's unfulfilled expectations of experience; however, in Christian experience these expectations have been intensified by one's encounter with Christ through scripture. The Christian is therefore encouraged to develop an ontology not only because his or her natural experience seems to awaken intimations and longings for an understanding of the whole, but also because the functional, fragmentary experiences which he or she has with Christ through the scripture seem to call for a unified interpretation of Christ's relationship to reality as a whole. For example, the experiences one has with Christ through the various Christologies of the New Testament—such as adoption (Heb. 3:2), virgin birth (Matt. 1:18-25), obedience (Rom. 5:18-19), incarnation (John 1), and resurrection (Rom. 1:4)—seem literally to demand that a systematic Christology be formulated so that the meaning of these particular encounters is not lost in functional relativism. This is no doubt Barth's concern when he writes: "In seeking to understand I must advance to the point where it is well nigh only the riddle of the *substance* that confronts me, and really no longer the riddle of the *text* as such."[19] It might therefore even be possible to paraphrase Tillich's statement mentioned earlier by suggesting that the theological desire for a comprehensive ontology is at least in part the result of disappointed expectations in one's encounter with the unreconciled phenomena of scripture. Fortunately, there are more positive bases for Christian ontology which can be seen in the implications of redemption itself. Hugh Montifiore illustrates this principle well when he is willing to move from the functional effects of Christ to his ontological significance. Speaking of the significance of the life, death, and resurrection of Christ, he concludes that he enabled man

> to accept himself and thereby to enter into a right relationship with God and with his fellow men, and so to fulfil the purpose

> for which he was created. It is because Jesus achieved this that his disciples began to recognize in him One who in some way was to be identified with him who brought the Jews out of Egypt and who fashioned the stars and the earth.[20]

In other words, it is the disciples' dissatisfaction with a merely existential understanding of Jesus which leads them to their ontological declarations concerning his being Christ and the Son of God.

A Christological Focus for Ontology

Whatever ontological dimension is biblically and appropriately ascribed to God, is, according to some major strata of biblical revelation, applied with equal weight to the person of Christ. Do not certain prominent strands of scripture[21]—even though they are not identical in either analogy or meaning, and surely must have arisen out of a functional crucible of experience—indicate an intention by the writers to acknowledge an ontological reality which transcends the immediate encounter? A representative systematic response to the "trans-functional" language which characterizes these scriptural patterns is provided by Emil Brunner in his interpretation of the Christological hymn in the second chapter of Philippians. He attempts to deal with the redemption provided by Christ by recognizing both its historical occasion and eternal origin. The source of Christ's coming is from eternity, and the willingness of the Son to be sent belongs to the realm of mystery. This means that not only the one who sends is God, but also the Son who comes is God. Brunner then proceeds to summarize the ontological implications of Christ's coming clearly but not at all too sharply, declaring:

> To regard this as a "speculative" idea means that one is still held in the grip of historical positivism; that one has not yet discovered the dimension of faith. If *this* is empty speculation—as quite naturally it must seem to unbelief—then the whole of the Christian religion is speculation, everything, that is, that goes beyond the ascertained facts of history. But faith only begins where the historical perception ceases.[22]

With strikingly similar force Gerhard von Stammler in his splendid treatment of the role of ontology in theology warns that the interpreter who surrenders his task in face of the difficulties of ontology "proves only, that in that moment he feels no authority of the Spirit."[23]

At this juncture the relationship between the philosophical questions sketched early in the chapter and an ontological approach to Christology can come more distinctly into view. Heinrich Ott helps to link the two areas together when he explains that the problem which besets all theology is "whether the subject-object pattern provides a suitable ontological framework for an adequate presentation of a real redemptive history."[24] Theology, therefore, inherits the philosophical question: Is there a structural schema in *reality itself* which must be assumed before it is possible for us to have confidence that our concepts and language can truly grasp and represent reality? This issue is related to Christology by R. H. Fuller in his interpretation of the second chapter of Philippians. He admits it is possible to argue that this ontic language is merely the translation of functional Christological themes into Greek categories. But this is not the whole truth. "For it is not just a quirk of the Greek mind, but a universal human apperception, that action implies prior being—even if, as is also true, being is only apprehended in action."[25] Reliance on this subject-object structure of reality and experience enables Karl Barth to amplify his understanding of "Christological revelation" into a theological model of "Christological Being." Observe how he moves methodologically from revelation to ontology when he explains that the uniqueness of Christ's revelation and reconciliation for us is "the analogue of what God is in His Being antecedently in Himself, the Son of the Father, beside whom there can as little be a second, as there can be a second God alongside of the one God." In other words, "We have to take revelation so utterly seriously that in it as the act of God we have to recognise immediately His Being as well."[26] And is it not also the correlation of subject-object which permits Wolfhart Pannenberg in *Jesus—God and Man* to espouse a resurrection Christology which is retroactive ontologically? He believes that the profoundest elements in both Greek and Hebrew thought concerning the nature of truth permit an ontological understanding of Christ which is confirmed with his resurrection:

> Jesus' essence is established retroactively from the perspective of the end of his life, from his resurrection, not only for our knowledge but in its being. Had Jesus not been raised from the dead, it would have been decided that he also had not been one with God previously. But through his resurrection it is decided, not only so far as our knowledge is concerned, but with respect to reality, that Jesus is one with God and retroactively that he was also already one with God previously.[27]

These above-mentioned Christologies stem from a variety of biblical emphases and even involve different balances in methodological approach, however, they indicate a willingness to build upon the subject-object structure which is present in Christian experience in a way that can provide a solid foundation for a Christian ontology.

If Christology is not to be constructed on an anthropological foundation but rather upon revelation, and if there really is a biblical need for an ontological position which takes its point of departure not exclusively from the acts of Jesus but from the person interpreted through his acts, then an interpretative scandal is bound to appear when the theological effort is made to show the relation of the divine to the human. It is tempting to say with Oscar Cullman that "Christology is the doctrine of an 'event,' not the doctrine of natures."[28] But it may be wiser to admit that the ultimate issues of the interplay between God and man on any level, whether "event" or "natures," shall always involve a relationship which defies definition and at the same time precludes the submission of either one of the elements to the other. On this very point James Barr observes that the current hostility between ontological and event-centered Christology is not only the result of the historical-critical method of exegesis but also stems from an interpretation of revelation that has been far too confident of its understanding of the nature of "history."

> Thus it is natural for many of us to come to think of "natures" in the sense of the old Christology as a "speculation" while at the same time treating so grossly uncertain a concept as Heilsgeschichte (i.e., "salvation history" or the revelational significance of history) as if it was some kind of firm ground. This in itself is no decisive argument; but it is not without importance.[29]

The principle, therefore, seems tenable that as long as it is maintained that salvation is from God and not man, the gospel will contain an offense to man that will demand his faith. Moreover, the content of that faith will need to include not just a functional but a Christological perspective which will center in Christ's *person* and will involve ontological affirmations.

The incarnational model of Christology, which includes the life, teaching, death, and resurrection of Christ, because of its creative comprehensiveness is extremely well qualified to provide a Christian paradigm, or focus, on reality. Why, one may ask, have those levels of scripture been chosen which present, or at least allow, a transcendental Christology to become the foundation of Christian ontology? To this it may be answered that within the experience of the church these scriptures have been superior in creative force to the other biblical motifs for engendering vital Christian experience. Furthermore, the incarnational model based on these biblical themes is capable not only of conveying its own distinctive contribution, but also of containing the other facets of Christ's person and work most comprehensively. It is here that a systematic concern for creativity and comprehensiveness overtakes in theological significance the biblical interest in the chronological appearance of a concept. The issue here is simply: Where does one find that content within scripture which is, conceived both individually and collectively, the most existentially creative? Once this is established, the concepts which describe that creative source must be expressed comprehensively and systematically.

If an incarnational Christology can be given normative theological status, on the grounds of its creativity and comprehensiveness as proposed, it may serve as the primary model for picturing the rational framework that God intends man to have concerning the relation between creation and redemption. This relationship is examined with penetrating depth by T. F. Torrance in his recent work, *Space, Time and Incarnation.* Due to the inherent cohesion of this argument and precision of his language, certain stages of his thought deserve to be presented in progression and fullness. He portrays the Incarnation

> as the chosen path of God's rationality in which He interacts with the world and establishes such a relation between creaturely being and Himself that He will not allow it to slip away from Him into futility or nothingness, but upholds and confirms it as that which He had made and come to redeem. Thus while the Incarnation does not mean that God is limited by space and time, it asserts the reality of space and time for God in the actuality of His relations with us, and at the same time binds us to space and time in all our relations with Him. We can no more contract out of space and time than we can contract out of the creature-Creator relationship and God "can" no more contract out of space and time than He "can" go back on the Incarnation of His Son or retreat from the love in which He made the world. . . . That is the infinite freedom and the unique kind of necessity that hold between God and the world, which not only preserve its contingence but which so ground it in the being and rationality of God as to provide for us in our creaturely existence an intelligible medium and an objective basis for all our relations with God. . . . In this way the Incarnation together with the creation forms the great axis in God's relation with the world of space and time apart from which our understanding of God and the world can only lose meaning.[30]

It is therefore in the historical incarnation of Christ that the Christian finds the objective ground and rational paradigm for his understanding of creation, redemption, and the meaningfulness of reality as a whole.

How Man Becomes Real

Consequently it is only when we are rightly related to reality through our creator and redeemer that we can be truly confident of our own personal reality. Paul Holmer is right as far as he goes when he declares that "the meaning of saying that Jesus is God is that in that historical person from the town of Nazareth I find the possibility which I am willing to actualise."[31] Genuine involvement, however, in this kind of existential "possibility" can only be redemptively *and* functionally effective if one can follow Jesus of Nazareth into an ontological relationship which is not just apparent but reliable, enduring, and comprehensive. The reader will remember that it was previously concluded that whatever interpretation of ontological reality is chosen, its validity can only be sustained through the capacity of the concept to engender in one's experience the conditions which correspond most appropriately to the fuller understanding of that category (*cf.* page 111). The endless definitional cycle which characterizes every epistemological statement can be broken out of only if the ontological concept has the creative capacity to make contact with experience and *empower* man to realize his potential for authenticity. This is essentially what transpires biblically when that Word which was in the beginning with God and in reality "was God" became flesh enabling those who received Him "to become children of God" (John 1:1, 12). Paul Lehman expresses this same theme ontologically when he explains: "In Jesus of Nazareth the face of reality has changed and with this change, the experience of reality, the perspectives, terms, signs, and symbols by which the new reality is apprehended and interpreted have changed also."[32] An ontological belief in a Christ who is indeed God, not only in his revelation but also in his being, must therefore be capable of creating in experience a quality of life which corresponds to that which the Christian holds as theologically valid in his understanding of God as real. The functional relevance of this conviction is summarized concisely by Gerhard Ebeling when he concludes that to the ultimate question of what is real, the most adequate theological answer "will be to point to Jesus, of whom we confess that in him God became Man in order that we through him may become real."[33]

CHAPTER V

Where Your Treasure Is

Even though we may feel that we possess an appropriate method for knowing reality and understanding its Christological center, we must still explain why we *value* certain portions of that reality more than others. This is the task of axiology.[1] The problem is illustrated poignantly by Jean Paul Sartre who tells about a student of his who came to him one day for help in determining a priority of values. During the German occupation of France in the Second World War the young man was trying to decide whether to stay by his mother who was grieving over the loss of her older son and quarreling with her husband who was inclined to be a traitor to his country, or leave France by the underground and seek to join the Free French forces of resistance in England. On one hand he felt his mother would probably die without his support and on the other he felt his country desperately needed his allegiance. Both options are ambiguous: the mother might live with her son gone, and the boy might never reach his military companions; one value centers around a particular individual and the other around a collective unit; one kind of morality is based on sympathy and devotion and another on freedom, revenge, and survival. Sartre describes the situation and his existentialist solution:

> He had to choose between those two. What could help him to choose? Could the Christian doctrine? No. Christian doctrine says: Act with charity, love your neighbour, deny yourself for others, choose the way which is hardest, and so forth. But which is the hardest road? To whom does one owe the more brotherly love, the patriot or the mother? Which is the more useful aim, the general one of fighting in and for the whole community, or the precise aim of helping one particular person to live? Who can give an answer to that *à priori*? No one. Nor is it given in any ethical scripture. The Kantian ethic says, Never regard another as a means, but always as an end. Very well; if I remain with my mother, I shall be regarding her as the end and not as a means: but by the same token I am in danger of treating as means those who are fighting on my behalf; and the converse is also true, that if I go to the aid of the combatants I shall be treating them as the end at the risk of treating my mother as a means.
>
> If values are uncertain, if they are still too abstract to determine the particular, concrete case under consideration, nothing remains but to trust in our instincts.[2]

The Christian would surely encourage Sartre's student to search the scriptures and pray about this decision until he receives assurance from the Lord that his priorities are arranged properly and that he could proceed confidently with a certain course of action. Sartre would no doubt respond by asking how this procedure differs from following one's instincts, since all philosophical and doctrinal values are uncertain and susceptible to ambivalent motivations and interpretations. The fact is, however, that both the instinctive and structural approaches are needed together and both are quite inadequate when isolated from one another. This dialectical tension can be explained more fully when one explores the method by which a value claim is established on a revelational foundation.

Self-Validation and Categorical Verification

The belief in revelation is confronted on the one hand with an affirmation that revelation is self-authenticating and beyond questioning, and on the other hand with an imprisoning, self-contained system of standards which dares to prescribe the categories through which divine revelation and its corresponding scale of values *must* come. The difficulty arising from a self-validational stance is that every revelational claim made on this basis alone should unquestionably be allowed to stand on an equal level of credibility and worth with any other such claim. If, however, there is a conviction concerning the superiority or uniqueness of a revelation, as is the case with the Christian faith, this means that certain categories of evaluation are intrinsically present and objectively discernible when the Christian revelation is compared with conflicting or competing claims.

This is, of course, no new problem, for in historical Christian theology it is a perennial one which found its classical expression in the medieval church in the conflict between the intellectualism of Thomism and the voluntarism of Scotism. The debate at that time centered on the question of whether the will of God was worthy because it was *worth* willing as an expression of the rational values which were present inherently and structurally in the universe, or because *God willed* it and voluntarily endowed his will with his own worth. This question, far from being an archaic theological issue, continues to have systematic and apologetic relevance in that the apparent failure of Christian theology to solve this paradox once and for all is a stumbling block for those who see this as evidence that the claim to know God is logically contradictory and self-defeating. Notice, for instance, how Bertrand Russell attempts to hide between these antitheses while criticising the Kantian form of the moral argument for the existence of God when he declares tauntingly:

> If you are quite sure there is a difference between right and wrong, you are then in this situation: Is that difference due to God's fiat or is it not? If it is due to God's fiat, then for God himself there is no difference between right and wrong, and it is no longer a significant statement to say that God is good. If you are going to say, as theologians do, that God is good, you must then say that right and wrong have some meaning which is independent of God's fiat, because God's fiats are good and not bad independently of the mere fact that he made them. If you

> are going to say that, you will then have to say that it is not only through God that right and wrong came into being, but that they are in their essence logically anterior to God.[3]

Unfortunately, Russell fails to point out that any statement of value that seeks to rise above a mere functional, descriptive observation confronts the same chasm between inherent worth and structural expression.

Could not examples of this intuitive-structural correlation be selected throughout the scriptures? Notice how the prophet defies all human standards and valuations when he thunders on behalf of his God: "For as the heavens are higher than the earth, so are my ways higher than your ways and my thoughts than your thoughts" (Isa. 55:9). *And yet* he goes on to exult in the promise by which this same transcendental word is to be validated through the *faithfulness* of God who will not suffer his word to return empty but like rain sent from heaven shall accomplish that purpose for which it is intended: "For you shall go out in joy, and be led forth in peace" (vv. 11-12). There can be little doubt, moreover, that the New Testament enjoins the followers of Christ to become like their Lord in obedience to the will of God and love toward fellowmen which surely can come about only as one lives in the presence of God and derives strength through his Holy Spirit. So it is that James Stewart expounds on the sovereignty of the Spirit because "the wind blows where it wills" (John 3:8):

> Just as it is impossible to control the wind or dictate to it its direction, so no man, no Church, can domesticate the Spirit of God or delimit His sphere of operation. . . . But God is forever upsetting our neat logical schemes and discomfiting our tidy regulations. . . . "The wind bloweth"—not where we timidly suggest or dogmatically demand that it should. . . . Don't try to tame that intractable wind.[4]

But how is it possible, it may be asked, to understand what is involved in receiving the Spirit of God? Cannot this noble theme, when left unqualified, mean anything, everything, or nothing at all? Gratefully, therefore, the interpreter welcomes the biblical insight that the Holy

Spirit has a Christological orientation, may be recognized through creative Christ-centered directives within the Christian community, and enables men to proclaim the gospel effectively throughout the world. In fact, the New Testament on occasion actually provides a table of certain basic qualities such as "love, joy, peace, patience, kindness, goodness, faithfulness, gentleness, self-control" (Gal. 5:22), which may serve not only as spiritual performance indicators for testing the Spirit's presence in man but also as illuminating and normative axiological categories for an understanding of the nature and function of the Holy Spirit. The contemporary interpreter's task, however, is not completed with a mere cataloging of selected Christian virtues, even though they are biblically derived, for he still has a responsibility for clarifying and to some extent defending why just these attributes are acceptable and determinative for a description of the Godlike life. Moreover, he must proceed to show in relevant language what it means today to possess or to lose the Spirit of God. Listen again, therefore, to Stewart preaching on "take not thy Holy Spirit from me" (Ps. 51:11):

> I would put it like this. To be aware of and obedient to the inner voice that speaks in conscience, to be alert and sensitive to the mind of Christ. . . . To have a faith that takes God at His word, to have a hope that looks beyond the darkness to the dawn. . . . To realize that the common ways of life are continually being interpenetrated by another dimension, the dimension of the Eternal—this it is to have the Spirit.

On the other hand:

> To be unresponsive to the still small voice, . . . and weary of the irksomeness of Christ. To grow skeptical about faith, disillusioned about hope. . . . To feel that the struggle between good and evil is not worth the battle; to find your spiritual zest and idealism smothered by the dust and dreariness of life, replaced by moral lassitude and inertia and debility; to stop caring for religion, to find prayer weariness—this is to lose the Spirit.[5]

The absolute necessity of recognizing the axiological structure of a revelational claim is perhaps nowhere more clearly apparent than in the hermeneutical arc which moves from (1) the acceptance of the resurrection of Christ as an event, to (2) the recognition of the historical and conceptual milieu within which it is believed to have transpired, and (3) on beyond into a recognition of the values which it is supposed to conserve. What could possibly be more self-evident as a paradigm of divine revelation than the coming back to life of a particular historical figure—yet what could possibly be in more need of ethical qualifications and theological perspective than such an occasion so infinitely fraught with ambivalent potential? Even Wolfhart Pannenberg (who has perhaps come as near as anyone in the entire history of Christian theology to saying that the actuality of the resurrection of Christ is demonstrable through historical method alone and its meaning evident from the event itself) has found it necessary to rely on the Jewish messianic and apocalyptic expectations and the continuity of Israel's religious traditions to provide the appropriate categories for understanding the redemptive significance of the resurrection:

> If the resurrection or the appearances of the resurrected Jesus were only brute facts without inherent significance, then, certainly, the origin of faith would not be understandable from this event. But that event had its own meaning within its sphere in the history of traditions: the beginning of the end, the confirmation and exaltation of Jesus by God himself, the ultimate demonstration of the divinity of Israel's God as the one God of all men. Only thus can Jesus' resurrection be the basis of faith.[6]

It seems reasonable to conclude, then, that one of the larger purposes, if not the primary one, for God's providential patience with man through the ages, and particularly his election of the children of Israel as bearers of his covenant, was to provide the categories of meaning and value through which the infinite worth of his Son, the supreme gift, could be received and understood.

To Sartre's student, therefore, one can say that instinctual, intuitive impressions about values are indispensable indeed and may in the last analysis be the determining factor which tilts a decision one way or another. However, these impressions should never be trusted apart from a recognized standard or norm whose structures can be formulated in axiological categories. These categories discussed below are admittedly functional and provisional; nevertheless, they help articulate the actual standards employed to make a value judgment, or better still, in the case of Christian revelation—to locate the place and the person where one believes the highest value resides. Once this locus has been established in the person of Christ as revealed in the scriptures, then the instincts and intuitions can be guided toward the higher alternatives. It is interesting to note that Sartre assumes two relatively high values as alternatives for his student: the boy can either take care of his mother or fight for the freedom of his country. These particular options are surely not sustained, without contradiction, by the instincts alone! At no point does Sartre advise the young man to encourage his mother into prostitution or to betray his country for a profit. Where does an existentialist get such high alternatives? Perhaps as many have observed before, the atheist "lives by a borrowed light." No, the Christian counselor would not direct the young man to either alternative, but he is confident that the will of God as man's highest good can be found in a sensitive response to God's revelation in Christ. This revelation will, it is believed, be ontologically life-affirming, finitudinally and moralistically realistic, cosmologically extensive, psychically integrating, communally inclusive, intrinsically rational, and eschatologically enduring.

Categories of Valuation

1. While it is imperative never to lose sight of the conviction that the Christian respondent has no desire, nor indeed possibility, to dictate to God how his revelation must come to him in order for it to be acceptable, there is,

nevertheless, some merit in realizing that when it comes, it is in fact esteemed to be of divine worth through its promise of being *ontologically life-affirming*. If Gabriel Marcel is allowed to assume that "the fact that suicide is always possible is the essential starting point of any genuine metaphysical thought,"[7] may not one be allowed to assume that the conviction that life itself is grounded in reality, which is in essence *good*,[8] is the essential starting point for any genuine *axiological* thought? Marcel believes that the ground for all value and hope resides in what he calls the center of the ontological mystery. This allows one to assert that there is "at the heart of being, beyond all data, beyond all inventories and all calculations, a mysterious principle which is in connivance with me, which cannot but will that which I will, if what I will deserves to be willed and is, in fact, willed by the whole of my being."[9] He presses his point further and somewhat defiantly, even in the face of life's extremities:

> To hope against all hope that a person whom I love will recover from a disease which is said to be incurable is to say: It is impossible that I should be alone in willing this cure; it is impossible that reality in its inward depth should be hostile or so much as indifferent to what I assert is in itself a good. . . . I assert that a given order shall be re-established, that reality is on my side in willing it to be so. I do not wish: I assert; such is the prophetic tone of true hope.[10]

To this kind of ontological affirmation the Christian thinker may add biblical themes concerning God as creator of a world which he deemed "good" (Gen. 1:4, 10, 12, 18, 21, 25), the cross-resurrection as the victory over sin and death, and the presence of God's Spirit in the fellowship of the church as a pledge of everlasting life. These are the motifs which most effectively embody and convey the conviction that God, as he is known and proclaimed in the church, is *worthy* of trust and love. John the Baptist illustrates this same issue rather conclusively when he instructs his disciples to ask Christ, "Are you he who is to come, or shall we look for another?" Then Jesus replies, "Go and tell John what you hear and see: the blind receive their sight and the lame walk, lepers are cleansed and the deaf hear, and the dead are raised up, and the poor have good news preached to them" (Matt. 11:3-5). No better reason can be given in any age for following Christ and allowing all of one's values to find their ultimate axiological standard in him.

It will by the very nature of the question remain open for the future to determine, but one could well defend the axiological thesis that no consistently life-denying metaphysic—and this would include a theology of the cross alone—can continue to claim the hearts of men. As indispensable as the cross is for man's salvation, it must be understood as only an interim stage on the way to the resurrection and a triumphant affirmation of the redeemed life. Is it not, therefore, both providentially and axiologically "necessary that the Christ should suffer these things and enter into his glory?" (Luke 24:26).

2. Lest one, in the light of the above principle, become presumptuous regarding his personal value and creative potential, it must be acknowledged immediately that revelation is in fact accepted only when it is deemed to be *finitudinally and moralistically realistic* with reference to human nature and its capacity. Even on the natural level of human existence we must recognize our limitations before the claims of a supernatural revelation can be entertained. If we long for God but are unwilling to admit our own weakness and need, revelation can never be for us. When, however, we recognize the demands the absolute lays upon our finite sinful life, the very demands laid upon us can actually become an evidence of the truth of revelation. It is at just this sensitive point that the shattering demand of the cross becomes axiologically relevant. The cross of Christ is a stumbling block to the Jews and foolishness to the Greeks (I Cor. 1:23) largely because it forces us to acknowledge our sin and inability to redeem ourselves. Therefore at the heart of every revelational claim there lies the need for us to recognize that we do not ultimately belong to ourselves—"you are not your own" (I Cor. 6:19). Furthermore, we will remain incapable of realizing authentic existence until we are reclaimed by that power, not of ourselves, which

enables us to have peace. Augustine's admission that "our hearts are restless till they rest" in God speaks eloquently on behalf of the axiological premise that before any gift of God's love finds reception in the heart, there comes first, like the portents of that first day of creation, the stirring of God's Spirit on the chaotic waters of human restlessness.[11] Whether it be the princely prophet Isaiah crying from his spirit-seared lips "Woe is me! For I am lost"; a timid and bewildered apostle like Philip pleading "Lord, show us the Father"; or even an arrogant but stricken fanatic by the Hebrew name of Saul imploring "Who are you, Lord?"; revelation must eventually be received in that moment of surrender wherein all pretense of self-sufficiency is renounced and one is conscious of nothing save the proffered grace and potential strength of Christ (Isa. 6:5; John 14:8; Acts 9:5). The maxim which Goethe once voiced in his classic novel, *Wilhelm Meister*, is as crucial for the recognition of lasting value as it is for finding one's personal identity: "A man is never happy till his vague striving has itself marked out its proper limitation."[12]

3. And now to proceed "one giant step" further. An axiological claim, to be really existentially convincing and ethically compelling, needs to be *cosmologically extensive*. If, for example, it were ever possible, to use the psalmist's imagery, to ascend to the highest heaven or make one's bed in Sheol or even to "take the wings of the morning and dwell in the uttermost parts of the sea" and discover there a place in extended space where God does not dwell and where there were no holy obligation or any binding, sacred relationship, then the very notion of divine revelation or ultimate value will have collapsed (Ps. 139:8, 9). The concept of revelation itself will have become a mere functional proverb as a result of its spatial limitations and relativity. There is that, however, about the self-transcending ego which Gabriel Marcel calls its "global" quality. The ancient Preacher long before him recognized this dimension when he perceived that God "has put eternity into man's mind" (Eccles. 3:11). This capacity refuses to allow any temporal or spatial barriers to be erected against man's contemplation of deity.

Nowhere has the human quest for a consciousness of personal destiny in the midst of an infinity of possibilities and cosmic breadth been expressed more sublimely than in Pascal's haunting refrain:

> When I consider my brief span of life, merged in eternity before and after, the little room I fill and can even see, engulfed in the infinite immensity of spaces which I know not and which know not me, I fall into fear, and wonder to find myself here rather than there, for there is no reason why here rather than there, why now rather than then. Who has set me here? By whose order and direction have this place and this time been assigned to me? "The remembrance of a guest that tarrieth but a day."
>
> The eternal silence of these infinite spaces fills me with fear.[13]

Unless there is a presence which extends throughout the cosmos itself, sustaining the transcendental aspirations of man, there is really no solid foundation for his values and hopes, particularly as these relate to his eschatological future. The universe would be a closed spatial shell indifferent to man's highest goals, and human freedom would be merely an illusion.

A clear example of the way God's revelation converges upon man's awareness of his cosmic and eternal dimensions is the vital role which apocalyptic language plays in the biblical revelation. This linguistic dimension prevents the message of the New Testament from becoming merely a history, an ethic, or an existential challenge. With Jürgen Moltmann we can be grateful that: "The New Testament did not close the window which apocalyptic had opened for it towards the wide vistas of the cosmos and beyond the limitations of the given cosmic reality."[14] Cannot this, therefore, be just that unique and legitimate function of symbolical language that only by this means is it possible for one to perceive the cosmic value of revelation? The Bible therefore offers a vision for spiritual sight which opens out onto the far reaches of cosmological grandeur and redemptive design. This cosmic panorama signifies for the believer today what it meant for the witnesses of old—nothing less than the complete redemptive adequacy of an almighty God and the supreme value of his revelation.

4. Far from transpiring in an ethereal vacuum, revelation enters existentially into the total life of man and provides him with an object of worship and ultimate concern which may become *psychically integrating*. The identity and integration of a personality is largely determined by the integrity and durability of the object of loyalty which provides the person's basic psychic orientation. True psychological well-being is possible only where one is thoroughly committed to a value which is personal in nature, worthy in itself, and enduring. The basic question on this level of inquiry is just what kind of encounter with reality is required before man can arrange his emotional drives, centers of consciousness, and interest into a truly stable pattern of self-realization. Well does this writer remember the impact on his life and thought which his esteemed professor of Christian philosophy, Emile Cailliet, made that day in Princeton when he told of the noble longing of the old Stoic philosopher, Epictetus. As he came to the end of his days the philosopher implored his disciples:

> Show me a man moulded to the pattern of the judgments that he utters, in the same way as we call a statue Phidian that is moulded according to the art of Phidias. Show me one who is sick and yet happy, in peril and yet happy, dying and yet happy, in exile and happy, in disgrace and happy. . . . Do me this kindness, do not grudge an old man like me a sight I never saw till now . . . show me the soul of a man who wishes to be at one with God, . . . one who . . . desires to change his manhood for godhead. . . . Show him to me. Nay, you cannot.[15]

And then, with a pathos befitting the tragedy of the disappointment, Cailliet sadly explained that the philosopher's request was made only a few decades after Christ's appearing.

According to the scriptural revelation, God offers, through a living relationship with his Son, a richness and depth of personal existence which is called variously a way of wholeness, the abundant life, salvation, and a legacy of peace.[18] There is hope, therefore, that man "the monster of uneasiness" may grow in Christ toward that maturity wherein motives are cleansed and intellect and will increasingly unite around an absolute loyalty to the will of God. An unknown poet portrays Christ's psychical creativity more adequately than any definition or piece of prose when he announces:

> Thou shalt know Him when He comes,
> Not by any din of drums,
> Nor the vantage of His airs,
> Not by anything He wears;
> Neither by His crown,
> Nor His gown
> But His presence known shall be
> By the holy harmony
> Which His coming makes in thee.

5. While the divine communication and self-giving must certainly be appropriated individually before it can be determined that revelation has taken place (at least there appears nothing in the biblical heritage which has not passed through a personal crucible), the overall direction toward which revelation moves is the creation of a human community designated collectively as the people of God, the church. The revelation which makes this new corporate relationship possible can be recognized through an additional distinctive mark: it is *communally inclusive*. Any revelational claim which implies that it can remain an exclusive personal possession and neglects the need for all men to be reconciled to one another must be deemed axiologically inferior to the offer of a universal community founded on love.

One of the clearest ways in which the revelation of God in Christ authenticates itself existentially in the life of Christians is through the awareness that we have been granted liberty to love not only God as the giver of life but also our neighbor as ourselves (Luke 10:27). The axiological significance of the phrase, "as yourself," is perceived by Søren Kierkegaard when he argues: "Should the commandment to love our neighbour be formulated in another way than by the expression *as thyself*, which can be handled so easily and yet has the tension of all eternity, the commandment could not master our self-love so effectively." The meaning of loving one's neighbor as himself, he insists, cannot be distorted but judges "man with the insight of eternity."[17] The remarkable element in this teaching is the way in which it so clearly draws the implication that since the command of Jesus cannot be experientially avoided, it may therefore be assumed to come from an eternal source. However that may be, one feels biblically justified in naming that commitment to an ever-increasing communal unity, which should distinguish the followers of Christ, as one of the indispensable categories by which a revelatory value is recognized. "Love is of God, and he who loves is born of God and knows God. He who does not love does not know God; for God is love" (I John 4:7-8). In a manner that does not escape, I believe, the leavening influence of a Christian personalism, the Jewish theologian Martin Buber commends the importance of human community for realizing divine values:

> Man wishes to be confirmed in his being by man, and wishes to have a presence in the being of the other. The human person needs confirmation, because man as man needs it. An animal does not need to be confirmed, for it is what it is, unquestionably. It is different with man; sent forth from the natural domain of species into the hazard of the solitary category, surrounded by the air of chaos which came into being with him, secretly and bashfully he watches for a Yes which allows him to be and which can come to him only from one human person to another. It is from one man to another that the heavenly bread of self-being is passed.[18]

How much more should the Christian, because of his belief that Christ died for every man, realize that his values are esteemed and valid to the extent that they reflect a communal consciousness and responsibility.

6. Perhaps enough has already been said about the role of reason in *receiving* knowledge claims about God, but it also needs to be stressed that one *values* God's revelation in large measure because it is *intrinsically rational*. It is the

task of philosophical theology, as Wolfgang Weidlich explains in his essay, "Questioning the Philosophical Theology of Radical Questionableness," to explore the categories which are most adequate for evaluating an existential sense of truth and value. Toward this goal he offers a lucid and valuable contribution when he concludes that for a basic experience of life to be able to claim a durable sense of worth, "the *logical quality which is capable of becoming an axiom* must be at hand in order that this basic experience can understandably enter concepts at the point of philosophical-theological thinking and not remain in pure 'primal feeling.' "[19] H. Richard Niebuhr also recognizes the role which rationality plays in assessing the value of revelation when on a more distinctly Christian plane he defines revelation as "the intelligible event that makes all other events intelligible."[20]

To be sure, there is, in the scandal of grace, an affront to man's rational pride which demands of him a surrender to the sovereignty of God's revelation. Paul explains to the Corinthians: "When I came to you, brethren, I did not come proclaiming to you the testimony of God in lofty words or wisdom. For I decided to know nothing among you except Jesus Christ and him crucified" (I Cor. 2:1-2). However, he goes on to add in this same chapter an emphasis which can be easily overlooked—yet "we do impart wisdom, although it is not a wisdom of this age" (v. 6). The mind of man could never imagine nor produce the gospel of Christ for it is "superior to human wisdom, nobility, and plausibility; yet it has a wisdom, nobility, and persuasiveness of its own, which it derives from God."[21]

Something of this pattern of divine wisdom and interior logic can be seen in the following selected biblical passages. Notice the logical force of the arguments:

> "Ah Lord God! It is thou who hast made the heavens and the earth by thy great power and by thy outstretched arm! Nothing is too hard for thee!" (Jer. 32:17)
>
> "I am the Lord your God, who brought you out of the land of Egypt, out of the house of bondage.

"You shall have no other gods before me." (Exod. 20:2-3)

If Christ has not been raised, your faith is futile and you are still in your sins. . . . we are of all men most to be pitied. (I Cor. 15:17, 19)

If one is tempted to disparage this kind of biblical reasoning, let him consider for a moment what value he could find in texts which, though they might claim to be from God, would read like this:

I am your God! I have no power,
  but you must worship me.

I am your God! I have never done anything for you;
  nevertheless, you owe me everything.

Christ has not been raised,
  but your faith in his resurrection is valid,
  your confidence in his ability to forgive sins is warranted,
  there is much hope for your own resurrection.

The very effort which is made to share the gospel clearly and enable men to understand it provides convincing evidence, as Gerhard Ebeling testifies, for the inherent rationality of the Christian message:

Faith is in fact not, as fear, an immediate utterance of life but rather, in any case in its Christian understanding, directed toward mediation. It arises from the hearing of the message (Rom. 10:17), is related to speech, to tradition, to communication, to recounting, and for that reason is inseparable from understanding. Compared to fear, which is the epitome of irrationality, faith belongs to rationality.[22]

Although it is impossible to move through reason alone from the need of man to an omnipotent God who is at the same time a gracious redeemer, there is a certain reasonableness in effect when we encounter an absolute moral claim upon our life through an event such as the cross of Christ. We can with Paul quite rationally and coherently conclude that this kind of graciousness requires of us nothing less than our full commitment to Jesus Christ as our reasonable, λογικήν, logically appropriate, worshipful response (Rom. 12:1).

7. Finally, if man is indeed as Jürgen Moltmann defines

him, "an open question addressed to the future of God," then it seems fitting to expect that revelation would offer values that are *eschatologically enduring.*[23] Against those who object that any faith which looks forward to an eschatological verification must be forfeited because of its nonexperimental, futuristic character, John Hick counters with a fascinating parable of the two who journey together on a road. One believes that he moves toward the Celestial City while the other is equally convinced there is no such place awaiting him. During the course of the journey, Hick concedes, the ultimate issue which distinguishes the two men has not yet become an experimental one; however, when they come to the end of the journey it will then be determined that one of them has been right all along and the other wrong. While the issue by its very nature could not have been decided during the journey, it has nevertheless the character of a verifiable proposition. The matter cannot be resolved by saying that the two merely have different impressions while traveling together, for in fact, one will be proven right and the other wrong about the actual existence of a Celestial City. Therefore, according to Hick: "Their opposed interpretations of the situation have constituted genuinely rival assertions, whose assertion-status has the peculiar characteristic of being guaranteed retrospectively by a future crux."[24] The Christian believes that to a certain extent the eschatological future toward which he moves has already appeared proleptically in the person of Christ and the event of his resurrection. God has decisively begun to recreate the lives of believers and through them to reshape the course of human history. As the creative vitality of this movement endures or diminishes through history and into whatever the eschatological future may hold, so will the confidence in its revelational source and axiological value be confirmed or invalidated.

The apostle Paul confesses his eschatological hope without reservation when he shouts "Lo! I tell you a mystery. We shall not all sleep, but we shall all be changed. . . . 'Death is swallowed up in victory. O death, where is thy victory? O death, where is thy sting?' " (I Cor. 15:51, 54-55). While this faith is assuredly based on Paul's certainty of the resurrection of Christ, the victory of which he speaks will remain by its very transcendent nature a futuristic projection until confirmation is given through an ethical demonstration in the life of the believer in the form of an existential *victory over sin*. "The sting of death is sin, and the power of sin is the law. But thanks be to God, who gives us the victory through our Lord Jesus Christ" (I Cor. 15:56-57). It is, consequently, the responsibility of those who confess that Jesus Christ is risen from the dead not only to wait confidently and patiently for the future but to demonstrate as far as possible the *validity* of this claim through a life characterized by conquest over sin and a victorious freedom from the fear of death. Perhaps it will even be possible to face the unrelenting fiend as though through Christ it has become a friend. Such is the trust of John Bunyan as the gates of heaven swing wide for companions gone before, and he dreams:

> that all the Bells in the City rang for joy, and that it was said unto them, Enter ye into the joy of your Lord. . . . the City shone like the sun; the Streets also were paved with Gold. . . . And after that they shut up the Gates. Which when I had seen, I wished myself among them.[25]

Regardless of whether or not one's faith is strong enough to share Christ's victory in such a dramatic form, the axiological issue seems beyond dispute that wherever the *enduring* gift of life with him is found—there the search for God and ultimate value is at an end.

Whether it be through the flickering lamps of an orderly but fragmented natural world providing its bounty through the regularity of its seasons; or the poignant whispers of a restless conscience; or the commendable striving of a noble mind for philosophical and aesthetic excellence; or the radiance of God's own presence with his chosen through the events and encounters of the indispensable biblical revelation—God has not only refused to "leave himself without witness" (Acts 14:17) but has also through the striving of his Spirit created and preserved the *axiological categories* through which we may know him when he comes.

CHAPTER VI

The Futurity of Beauty

The aesthetic perception of beauty has long evoked in man the feeling of being drawn from the present moment toward a *future* which offers promise of higher value.[1] The actual consciousness of temporal sequence may be imperceptible, but who has not, through an encounter with beauty, become aware of a dissatisfaction with the world as it usually appears and felt at the same time a dim premonition of the possibility of its recreation along the lines of one's dreams? This intimation of being called by beauty[2] to participate in a realm of wholeness still unknown is movingly but disturbingly portrayed by C. E. M. Joad when he laments that there is

> no sky in June so blue that it does not point forward to a bluer; no sunset so beautiful that it does not awaken the thought of a greater beauty. The soul is at once gladdened and disappointed. The veil is lifted so quickly that we have scarcely time to know that it has gone before it has fallen again. But during the moment of lifting we get a vision of a something behind and beyond which passes, before it is clearly seen, and which in passing leaves behind a feeling of indefinable longing and regret.[3]

Although every awareness of excellence seems destined to confront this chasm between expectation and realization, ideal and form, the discrepancy between the realms can be an indication not only of one's distance from his goal but of the inescapable presence of a more enduring good. Perhaps there is reflected here, even within the created order, a fragmentary knowledge of man's divine origin which he has never totally lost and the hope of a destiny which the crushing demands of life cannot destroy. The lure of beauty may, therefore, possess an inherent eschatological quality that reflects and anticipates a kingdom of joy which shall be more fully revealed and established in days to come. Surely one who discovers a futuristic propensity in aesthetic experience need not disparage the intense delight in the satisfaction of the moment. However, I personally believe the enjoyment and contemplation of beauty in all its intended richness can never be attained where this futuristic dimension is not perceived.

The Objectivity of Beauty

Any attempt to define beauty is certain to bring disappointment because of the sheer breadth of the concept and the vitality of the creative energy which moves it toward expression. However, an effort must be made at least to trace a conceptual outline of its features or discern an intelligible pattern within its countless manifestations in order for the emotions it calls forth to find their integral place among the rational relations of human discourse. It is quite possible that beauty first stimulated artistic insight in man, as Alfred North Whitehead imagines, because cravings generated by the physiological functionings of the body were accompanied by the psychical need for reenaction. Man desires through some manner of symbolic presentation to protest the mere factuality of his existence. This he does by freely and dramatically portraying the past and the future so as to relive and project emotionally the truly vivid moments of his struggles with the threatening necessities of life. The arts, in their elemental force, permit the strength of the initial creative trauma to be felt again but, fortunately, after the crisis is past. The threat is over and thus the joy can be experienced intensely. Originally this intensity arose from the tension in the situation itself;

but art has transcended the compulsion of its origin: "If Odysseus among the shades could hear Homer chanting his Odyssey, he then re-enacted with free enjoyment the perils of his wanderings."[4] However valid this particular hypothesis regarding the source of beauty in experience may be, a certain amount of objective content must be assumed to be present in beauty if an aesthetic judgment is to be meaningful at all. This, of course, does not mean that every aesthetic evaluation will be valid and rewarding, but that each can be meaningful only so far as it assesses the worth of its object realistically and without illusion.

It would be difficult to improve here on the logic of Immanuel Kant, who, though his stress falls overwhelmingly on the importance of the subjective categories of response, sees nevertheless the necessity for positing an objective and moral referent in aesthetic judgment:

> Now I say, that which is beautiful is the symbol of moral good, and it is only in this regard (a relation which is natural to every man, and which also every man assumes in others as an obligation) that it pleases, with a claim for agreement of everyone else in a manner whereby this disposition becomes conscious of a certain ennoblement and exaltation above the mere sensibility of pleasure which is received through sense impression.[5]

A responsibility is, therefore, laid on men collectively and, as far as it is conceivable, universally, to discern and acknowledge beauty as the creative ground and structural basis for the symmetry, brilliance, and purity of being which become tangible in beautiful forms. In its highest manifestations beauty often reflects a numinous quality closely akin to that which men experience religiously as "the holy." It is in this sense that Martin Heidegger, in an early essay, "The Origin of the Work of Art," speaks of aesthetic sensitivity in terms of consecration, reasoning that

> to consecrate means to make holy in the sense that the holy is revealed in tangible presentation as a holy thing and God is called forth in the openness of his presence. To consecration belongs the celebration of the worth and splendor of God as

> appreciation. Worth and splendor are not characteristics beside and behind which there yet stands God externally, but in the worth, in the splendor God becomes present. In the reflection of this splendor radiates, that is to say, becomes illumined, everything which we call the world.[6]

The consciousness of beauty thus understood awakens feelings of both security and discontent. For a moment one enjoys a sense of well-being because he believes he catches a glimpse of reality as it truly is and human existence as it ought to be, but soon he becomes uneasy and knows that he is at least partially responsible for arranging his own life in harmonious form and re-presenting his vision to the world.

The Unity of Beauty

That which one perceives as beauty is brought to formal expression in the different arts through selected media which are interrelated but which, nevertheless, betray a certain uniqueness which accounts for their particular employment.[7] In *sculpture*, line and color are involved, but its outstanding feature appears to be its isolation of an image into a massive spatial compactness; *architecture*, insofar as it expresses a beauty beyond mere utility, organizes space in such a manner as to give a linear focus of symmetrical unity to that which before was only bare openness; *painting*, in its endeavor to reproduce its impressions on canvas, works with a definite limitation of area and surface dimension but strives to allow almost unlimited imagination to become embodied in color and perspective; standing midway between prose and music, *poetry*, like painting, knows also the freedom of the imagination but, being a verbal art, has greater capacity to convey the conceptual and tonal qualities of a trans-sensuous ideal in language; *music*, which is possibly the most potentially creative of the arts because in actuality it need not re-present anything and is only indirectly related to things in space, creates audible harmonies and contrasts which, if they in fact correspond to anything at all, mirror the sequences of nature and man in their temporality; *drama* and *prose* both possess the means to address issues of value, or lack of it as the case may be, by portraying life existentially in its personal interconnections in the context of its origins and limits—that is, as it may be viewed in its totality.

While recognizing that beauty may be experienced and reproduced in an infinite number of cultural and communicative patterns, the *unitary principle* which endeavors to penetrate to a common creative and ontological source explains most satisfactorily the qualitative kinship between the forms.[8] Otherwise, how can we account, asks Teilhard de Chardin

> for that irresistible instinct in our hearts which leads us towards unity whenever and in whatever direction our passions are stirred? A sense of the universe, a sense of the *all*, the nostalgia which seizes us when confronted by nature, beauty, music—these seem to be an expectation and awareness of a Great Presence.[9]

Even Jean Paul Sartre, whose passionate concern with the here and now of existence appears devastating to any comprehensive interpretation of reality, realizes that the artist must recognize the universe in its totality and strive toward a recreation of the world which is surrounded on all sides by infinity. According to Sartre, a work of art is never limited to the external expression or object produced by the artist:

> Just as one perceives things only against the background of the world, so the objects represented by art appear against the background of the universe. . . . If the painter presents us with a field or a vase of flowers, his paintings are windows which are open on the whole world. We follow the red path which is buried among the wheat much farther than Van Gogh has painted it, among other wheat fields, under other clouds, to the river which empties into the sea, and we extend to infinity, to the other end of the world, the deep finality which supports the existence of the field and the earth. So that, through the various objects which it produces or reproduces, the creative act aims at a total renewal of the world.[10]

Far from being a thing of pure facticity, then, beauty is best comprehended and integrated within the larger spectrum of human experience when it is considered as a worth which offers itself to rational beings to be esteemed and preserved for continued enjoyment and enrichment. This can take place only within a universal structure where the excellence of that which is given and the appreciation of the one perceiving are believed to coexist in a common field of intellectual value. The need to assume this analogical relationship between the two spheres is stressed by Robert Leet Patterson when he declares cryptically, "Beauty in a mindless world would therefore be as much a contradiction as a shield with only one side."[11] However, a mere rational concept of the unity of aesthetic experience between the one interpreting and the object observed taken alone is not capable of providing adequate criteria for the categories of value. Unless the comprehensiveness of the experience is related to an originative mind whose worth is in essence *good*, aesthetic judgments remain suspended in the void or at best isolated from the highest personalistic values known to man.[12] The contemplation of the beautiful and its accompanying awareness of aesthetic obligation leads one to believe, therefore, that there exists a common ethical ground from which they both arise and within which a comparative estimate of their worth has relevance. Without this supposition both the desire for sharing inspiration, which lies at the root of creative effort, and the conviction one has of participating in personal communion through works of beauty would be incomprehensible.

When beauty is believed to reflect the true nature of being, and this is understood to be grounded in value that is personalistic and essentially good, then a genuine appreciation of beauty can and should be distinguished from that which is merely enjoyable and gives pleasure. The *true* experience will enrich the beholder and contribute to the fullness of his own personal being. There is, however, always a latent danger in aesthetic experience that it will degenerate into a mere "aestheticism" where one seeks to retreat into the ornamental excitement of the moment and remain there in noncommital suspense, avoiding the claims of responsible selfhood. It is precisely this kind of escapism that betrays the shallowness of the familiar phrase "art for art's sake." Surely the maxim has a valid role to play in order to prevent art from becoming prostituted by sentimentalism, propaganda, and commercialism; however, it would be well to remember that according to this formula, art can easily lose all value reference and become merely art for the artist's own self-expression even though his understanding and values may not be *worth* expressing. The appropriate response to beauty, therefore, asks that we commit ourselves responsibly in singleness of purpose to that which we have been granted to discern of the divine unity and design underlying all things. When one understands and truly surrenders to this demand there can be no desire to substitute the appearance for the reality. For as Jacques Maritain uncompromisingly maintains, it is only with God that a man can "give himself totally *twice at the same time*, first to his God and second to something which is a reflection of his God."[13]

Beauty and the Future

If beauty may be assumed to have an integral relation to truth, then it must exist in relation to the dysteleological and tragic aspects of human existence. While the enjoyment of beauty involves a necessary selectivity and at times near isolation of the pleasing characteristics of the world, the experience invariably transpires in the presence of offsetting proportions, common hues, and threatening forces. The artist must wrestle with these unbalanced and often chaotic aspects of his world and create a work which serves as a symbol of conquest over them and possibly even as a pledge of a world beyond. This capacity to face without evasion the harsh and unpleasant chords of life and modulate them into a hymn of triumph is clearly illustrated in the music of Mozart. With a persuasiveness convincing one that more than a matter of personal taste is involved, Karl Barth commends the relevance of Mozart for Christian theology because the composer was permitted in purity of heart to behold something of the total goodness of creation and its eschatological goal. But Barth reminds us this was 1756–1791, the time when God was being attacked on all sides for the Lisbon earthquake! Nevertheless, Mozart possessed the peace of God which enabled him to face the problem of evil with a joy transcending the critical and speculative reason which merely judges or condones.

> He had heard, and causes those who have ears to hear, even today, what we shall not see until the end of time—the whole context of providence. As though in the light of this end, he heard the harmony of creation to which the shadow also belongs but in which the shadow is not darkness, deficiency is not defeat, sadness cannot become despair, trouble cannot degenerate into tragedy and infinite melancholy is not ultimately forced to claim undisputed sway.[14]

Such heights of ecstasy can be sustained as enduring value only if there is in fact at the foundation of all existence an ontological reality which is interested in and capable of securing such values. When, however, aesthetic experience begins to point beyond itself to a higher, transcendental realm, it may give ontological, even eschatological confidence for the fulfillment of the values it represents.[15]

On the other hand, what about that dominating segment of contemporary art which is apparently preoccupied either with despair or the absence of meaning in modern life such as is represented in Jackson Pollock's "art of the broken center," the cacophonous elements of "Woodstock," and the banal masterpieces of Campbell soup cans by Andy Warhol? Although many, the writer included, enjoy these expressive sensations for the moment, is it not possible to see at least a shadowy outline of purposeful awareness in the colors, shapes, and sounds that *do not appear* but are only left vacant or remain silent? Perhaps Picasso alludes to something like this in his oft quoted remark, "Art is a lie that makes us realize the truth." And it may even be as Paul Tillich dares to suggest: "Whoever can endure and represent his finitude, demonstrates also that he participates in endlessness. . . . And whoever can endure and represent meaninglessness demonstrates that he has experienced meaning."[16] In other words, an honest aesthetic confrontation with life, even if this should demand of the disappointed a stark portrayal of the fragmentation and awful infinality of nature and human experience, may serve to indicate the direction from which the solution of life's deeper issues must come.

Unfortunately there is a limitation inherent in aesthetic experience which prevents man from being satisfied with it as the bearer of the solution to his need for ultimacy. This inadequacy is due not solely to the fact of man's finitude, for this, of course, is an inescapable aspect of any human experience including the religious. The inadequacy is also due to the need for aesthetic insights to find relationships of meaning which are capable of rational expression in a comprehensive world-view. If the ability to perceive and express that which lies beyond linguistic concepts is a virtue of aesthetic experience (and this pertains also to the verbal arts), then it must be recognized at the same time as a most vulnerable characteristic where categories of interpretation are sought. Karl Jaspers writes convincingly of art's eventual dependence upon verbal and reflective conceptualization when he concludes:

> Even when it is perfected art does not remain untouched by philosophical consciousness, but is assimilated into it; the uncommitted nature of enjoyment is broken through, the release received only as anticipation and again placed in question; music, transcending everything which is expressible presses at the end again to words, all contemplation of art to thought.[17]

Since aesthetic experience transpires in a world interlaced with manifold structures of meaning and there appears to be no prolonged escape from responsibility, there always remains, no matter how ineffable the ecstasy of soul, the task of understanding what one feels. There may be no immediate necessity for communicating the content of this enjoyment to others, but the arranging of impressions within cognitive patterns, even though this takes the form of negative evaluation or unconscious compartmentalization, is a continual and unavoidable process. If, however, it is seen that aesthetic experience occurs in a rational world, as a necessary and therefore moral component of response to environment, and yet there is no language or frame of reference within aesthetics which is capable of relating it to other areas of comprehension, then one must look outside of it for criteria to determine its significance. Many have known the disillusionment of which Augustine spoke when he described that period in his life in which he understood and enjoyed the brilliance of the great works of the liberal arts but still felt himself to dwell in the shadows and confessed: "I took delight in them, but knew not whence came whatever in them was true and certain. For my back then was to the light, and my face towards the things enlightened; whence my face, with which I discerned the things enlightened, was not itself enlightened."[18] Aesthetic experience, therefore, seems certain to arouse expectations which it cannot ultimately fulfill; for the realm of beauty alone, however, intense the impression, can never really satisfy a contemplative mind. There remains always a need to hear an interpretative word, to address some responsible spirit, and perhaps even encounter someone who can give intelligible integration to those sublime sensations which often come in beauty's wake.

The Beauty of the Lord

It would, indeed, be presumptuous and misleading to give the appearance of being able to proceed lightly from the aesthetic experience of beauty to a teleological theism, and more particularly the transcendentalism of the Christian revelation, for there is no such way of direct transition. There is, however, enough correspondence between the personalistic outline of aesthetic *limitation* and the positive radical personalism of the Christian interpretation of reality to warrant venturing in that direction. The correlation between the capacity for aesthetic experience and an awareness of that which is holy encourages one to assume that both streams of experience could well converge in a confrontation with the person of Christ. Rudolf Otto gives this theme considerable, and at times controlling, emphasis in his classic *Idea of the Holy*. He maintains that everyone in an a priori sense is capable of being aesthetically receptive to beauty but that what is mere receptiveness or appreciation in most men emerges on a higher level from the artist as invention, creation, and the originality of genius. This latter stage is an endowment and is not derivable from the first, for there is more than a difference in degree involved. A similar stratification, according to Otto, is observable in religious experience, for most men have only a predisposition for recognizing and responding to religious truths for themselves. A higher plateau, however, does exist which, like its aesthetic counterpart, is not evolved from the lower level of sheer receptivity and this, in the realm of religion, is represented by the prophet. The prophet in the field of religion corresponds, therefore, to the creative artist in the sphere of aesthetics, for he is the one whom the Spirit endows with true discernment and the gift of creative energy. Now in words which themselves partake of the numinous about which he writes, Otto presents the climax of his argument in these concluding lines of his work:

> Yet the prophet does not represent the highest stage. We can think of a third, yet higher, beyond him, a stage of revelation as underivable from that of the prophet as was his from that of common men. We can look, beyond the prophet, to one in whom is found the Spirit in all its plenitude, and who at the same time in His person and in His performance is become most completely the object of divination, in whom Holiness is recognized apparent.
>
> Such a one is more than Prophet. He is the Son.[19]

Judgments of *beauty* arise from impressions that are conditioned by nature and culture. The basic form of these judgments comes through a highly personal and selective impression of that which in aesthetic faith is believed to possess worth. In like manner, a Christian estimate of *goodness* arises in the midst of natural and historical phenomena through a discerning and evaluating selectivity which leads to the conviction that there is ultimate value in Jesus Christ. The Christian may say, therefore, that in this one whom he believes to be the

Son—the goodness and intelligibility of God made comprehensible—he has discovered the logos-quality of eternal reality, and every claim of worth or meaning, including the aesthetic, must be evaluated and interpreted for him as far as possible by the absolute standards implicit in the life and work of this person.

The parallel between aesthetic and religious experience extends even further in that both realms, particularly in their highest expressions, witness to the rationale of existence and intensify the feeling of distance between what life should be and the way it actually exists. In this regard art and religion, in fact, share a common concern for fulfillment and redemption. For example, the essence of beauty, according to Jacques Maritain, is most fully grasped when it is apprehended not as final realization and perfection but as anticipation and desire. He gives eloquent testimony to the aesthetic significance of these receptive attitudes in his unexcelled *Creative Intuition in Art and Poetry* when he explains:

> Beauty does not mean simply perfection. For anything perfect in every respect in its own genus—anything "totally perfect" on earth—is both totally terminated and without any lack, therefore *leaves nothing to be desired*—and therefore lacks that longing and "irritated melancholy" . . . which is essential to beauty here below. It is lacking a lack. A lack is lacking in any totally perfect performance (with all due respect to Toscanini). A totally perfect finite thing is untrue to the transcendental nature of beauty. And nothing is more precious than a certain sacred weakness, and that kind of imperfection through which infinity wounds the finite.[20]

The Christian faith maintains in strikingly similar fashion on the religious plane that there must be a realistic acknowledgment of the limitations and failures of personal behavior and the self-destructive quality of evil embedded in the very structures of human life and society. This realism is precisely what is given men to know through the cross of Jesus Christ. For the cross, as Roger Hazelton points out, is not only an event in history where the Christian believes something of ultimate redemptive significance took place, but also a symbol demonstrating what many contemporary theologians are recognizing as "the cruciform nature of human existence itself." Here one truly learns that the fulfillment of life can be found only on the other side of being willing to lose it in self-surrender and in a confidence that the excruciating incongruities of history will eventually be overcome.[21] It appears, therefore, reasonable to suppose that on the aesthetic level beauty in its incompleteness and positive aspirations corresponds analogously to the Christian understanding of the cross and resurrection. While the aesthetic and religious spheres do not invalidate one another, nor dissolve into a third which is neither, they are manifestations of a common creative origin and offer compatible models for dealing with life in its depths of despair and hopes for the future.

Only in the beauty and holiness of God the creator and redeemer have men an adequate image of what the world is intended to be, and at the same time secure ground for believing in what it may become through the Spirit and the grace of Christ. Francis of Assisi came very close at times, I believe, to perceiving the pristine beauty of creation which God originally intended for us all. Francis' devoted disciple and first biographer, Thomas of Celano, asked:

> What gladness thinkest thou the beauty of flowers afforded to his mind as he observed the grace of their form and perceived the sweetness of their perfume? For he turned forthwith the eye of consideration to the beauty of that Flower which, brightly coming forth in springtime from the root of Jesse, has by its perfume raised up countless thousands of the dead. And when he came upon a great quantity of flowers he would preach to them and invite them to praise the Lord, just as if they had been gifted with reason. So also cornfields and vineyards, stones, woods, and all the beauties of the field, fountains of waters, all the verdure of gardens, earth and fire, air and wind would he with sincerest purity exhort to the love and willing service of God. In short he called all creatures by the name of brother, and in a surpassing manner, of which other men had no experience, he discerned the hidden things of creation with the eye of the heart, as one who had already escaped into the glorious liberty of the children of God.[22]

As though inviting one to the very threshold of creation's first morning, the apostle Paul identifies the initial creative word with which God thrust the universe into existence as being essentially that same transforming energy which surges in the life of the believer through the presence of Christ, exclaiming, "For it is the God who said, 'Let light shine out of darkness,' who has shone in our hearts to give the light of the knowledge of the glory of God in the face of Christ" (II Cor. 4:6).

Furthermore, God is glorious in such a way in Christian experience that the beauty of his purpose for life breaks in upon man, awakening not just feelings of mystery and awesome responsibility, but surprising him with grace and above all, joy. Karl Heim, in his summary of biblical eschatology, stresses that both the Old and New Testaments employ words not only of power and blessedness, but also of brilliance and glory. There is consequently strong encouragement to believe

> the thirst for beauty will be satisfied. Every really great piece of music, every great work of art therefore is the morning light of eternity, a first dawn of the perfecting of the world. Immortal works of music, classical works of art are like the fir trees on the slopes of the mountain, whose tops are already in the light of the approaching morning while the valley is still covered in mist.[23]

One can hope that every such aesthetic intimation of a destiny beyond this world may one day be fulfilled. Then all who have known the beauty of God's creative and eschatological design will sing in radiant joy: "Worthy is the Lamb who was slain, to receive power and wealth and wisdom and might and honor and glory and blessing!" (Rev. 5:12).

CHAPTER VII

The Sound of Meaning

The biblical declaration, "In the beginning was the Word," may be not only a Christological confession but also an ontological description of reality itself as *primal language* (John 1:1). Being in its primordial context appears to surround man with structures of meaning or intelligibility which press upon him in varying degrees of intensity and call for communal association and expression through symbolic forms. In this ultimate sense, language may be understood as the logos-quality of reality *at the point of its communicativeness*. It is, therefore, not a creation or possession of man but the gift of rationality from the surrounding world which *possesses him*. One can invent artificial vocables or signs but these are used intelligently only when they are employed within some previously articulated pattern or transpire within established coherent linguistic relationships. Hans-Georg Gadamer introduces this characteristic of primal language clearly when he explains:

> Language is by no means simply an instrument or a tool. For it is in the nature of the tool that we master its use, which is to say we take it in hand and lay it aside when it has done its service. That is not the same as when we take the words of a language, lying ready in the mouth, and with their use let them sink back into the general store of words over which we dispose. Such an analogy is false because we never find

> ourselves as consciousness over against the world and, as it were, grasp after a tool of understanding in a wordless condition. Rather, in all our knowledge of ourselves and in all knowledge of the world, we are always already encompassed by the language which is our own.[1]

This transcendental dimension of language, however, could never be comprehended or utilized apart from its tangible expression in *formal language*. Here the hidden structures of meaning are recognized and then embodied in the particular sounds, sights, and shapes of human communication. Formal language may, therefore, be defined as *the intelligible employment of arbitrary sensible signs* (these may be either audible, visual, kinetic, or certain patterns of silence[2] in a given context) *by which man in a community of association or agreement represents his understanding of reality to himself, God, and others self-consciously and overtly.*

If one allows the above description of language with its transcendental reference to stand, it will follow that language is unique to man. Although the empiricists believe that language is simply a learned, or an acquired, natural response which any creature with a high intelligence could develop, the rationalistic or personalistic view, which says that man has an inborn capability for language making him qualitatively different from the animals, possesses the greater weight of experimental evidence. For instance, the high level of ape and chimpanzee intelligence, and their capacity for learning would lead one to expect these creatures to have developed at least the rudiments of language. This has, however, not proven to be true. Extensive experiments and careful observation have revealed that animals may be capable of very complex signal responses, but these invariably function within the very narrow range of reward conditioning and survival techniques. Moreover, when man has sought to provide the higher animals with the more sophisticated tools for expressing themselves, it is discovered that they have nothing to communicate and surely do not possess the capacity to speak self-consciously *about* what they may be saying. However all children, even those of low intelligence, learn to communicate in ways virtually identical to their respective models. Every child seems to master almost unconsciously a complex set of grammatical laws that govern an infinite set of possible sentences and subsystems of communication. This is amazing because the child masters it on the basis of indirect and fragmentary evidence, and at an age when he is hardly attempting to think logically or analytically. "There is," therefore, as Ronald Langacker concludes, "absolutely no evidence to indicate that anything even remotely resembling the complex system of rules and abstract underlying representations of a human language can arise in other species."[3]

While the meaning-laden character of reality is not only valuable but the ground of all valuing, the accumulated or deliberately selected signs of formal language are axiologically neutral. There is no inherent reason why any particular form or cipher should represent any given thought, fact, or combination of circumstances. Both the intelligibility and value of any particular sound, name, word, or constellation of linguistic symbols are dependent upon one's association with a given reference. This principle is clearly underscored by the experience of Helen Keller who was a partially blind, deaf, and mute child when she had her first encounter with language. Notice in the following moving account from Helen's teacher that at first the signs seem arbitrary to Helen yet she perceives the necessity of making certain associations with the signs if she is to experience meaning.

> I must write you a line this morning because something very important has happened. Helen has taken the second great step in her education. She has learned that everything has a name, and that the manual alphabet is the key to everything she wants to know.
>
> . . . This morning, while she was washing, she wanted to know the name for "water." When she wants to know the name of anything, she points to it and pats my hand. I spelled "w-a-t-e-r" and thought no more about it until after breakfast . . . [Later on] we went out in the pump house, and I made Helen hold her mug under the spout while I pumped. As the cold water gushed forth, filling the mug, I spelled "w-a-t-e-r" in

> Helen's free hand. The word coming so close upon the sensation of cold water rushing over her hand seemed to startle her. She dropped the mug and stood as one transfixed. A new light came into her face. She spelled "water" several times. Then she dropped on the ground and asked for its name and pointed to the pump and the trellis and suddenly turning around she asked for my name. I spelled "teacher." . . . All the way back to the house she was highly excited, and learned the name of every object she touched, so that she added thirty new words to her vocabulary . . . [The next morning she] got up like a radiant fairy. She has flitted from object to object, asking the name of everything and kissing me for very gladness. . . . Everything must have a name now. . . . She drops the signs and pantomime she used before, as soon as she has words to supply their place, and the acquirement of a new word affords her the liveliest pleasure. And we notice that her face grows more expressive each day.[4]

Is it not also apparent here in this kind of germinal linguistic experience that formal expression is needed not merely to enable one to receive and initiate communication but also to bring one's own thoughts into perspective and make them recognizable to the understanding? Maurice Merleau-Ponty perceives this vital function of language when he asserts that speech is not purely for purposes of mediation, nor is a word for a speaker merely the "translation of an already completed thought," but rather that "which only truly completes thought."[5]

Because of the transcendental nature of human personality, man is never free from the tension between primal and formal language. He must, on the one hand, avoid the temptation to allow an experience to carry value significance for him without relating that experience to a conceptual, verbal expression of its meaning; on the other hand, he must avoid making any linguistic medium of expression the final standard by which the value of an experience is determined. This dialectical polarity can be practically illustrated. If one should claim that he has experienced something of ecstatic intensity and ineffable significance, but feels he can never relate this experience to any verbal conceptualization, we would be tempted to believe nothing of any real importance has transpired. If, however, one claims that he has had a meaningful experience which could be exhausted by a rigid definition or linguistic formula, we would have every right to question the depth of meaning conveyed through that experience. Far from disparaging the possibility of meaningful experience, this paradoxical linguistic phenomenon reveals that one cannot respond appropriately to ultimate reality by either noncommitment or total self-possession but only through dynamic personal trust.

Indeed, the fact that language can develop and be employed as a means of communication between persons may be an encouragement to believe that man inhabits a personalistically oriented cosmos which is positively interested in making such communication possible. Charles Hartshorne even goes so far as to suggest that theism itself is just the full elucidation of the categorical meanings of unavoidable linguistic terms. Hartshorne thinks that such terms as "causality," "matter," "good," "mind," and "private" cannot be understood as having any clear, unparadoxical meaning apart from the concept of God as depicted by theistic metaphysics. For example, in the case of privacy, he asks, what sense does it make to talk of one's feelings as being either like or unlike another, since an objective comparison between them can never take place? Hartshorne replies that it makes no sense at all—unless all private states are directly known by God who actually does make the comparison in question.[6]

However convincing this line of argument may be, the conclusion seems valid that communication between persons can only be pursued within an ontological realm where personalistic structures have some control over the material and psychical conditions of human existence, and where the surrounding environment is capable of sustaining the personalistic quality of a word until it is received by the one to whom it is addressed. Unless we can assume we are speaking through a sphere constructed to receive and transmit personal impressions which others can receive in a manner corresponding to our original intention, we may be conscious of producing sounds and sensations, but this can hardly be called language. And while it is not possible to prove the existence of a personal God from the fact of human language, linguistic experience may strengthen the confidence that ultimate reality is interested in communication between persons and may be at the same time seeking to convey its own message to man. At least it seems valid to conclude that men continue to speak of God simply because existentially *they must*. There appears to be no escape. Even for the one who wishes to deny the existence of God, there remains the necessity of telling what should be involved in a legitimate refusal to speak of him. It seems that regardless of what one thinks about the ontological status of God, deity must at least be conceived as the one about whom man *cannot be silent*.

All formal language, from all that can be known about its origin and development, appears to have a natural, objective, or nonsymbolic foundation, or referrent, to which its symbols initially correspond. However, linguistic references to that which is basically tangible must remain grossly inadequate for capturing the fullness of God's being and one's intimate personal relationship with him. This inherent limitation may partially account for the divine reticence in biblical revelation to allow visual imagery—whether it be the particular graven form of idols, some holy place, or even a parabolic image—to overshadow the immediate sovereignty of God's *spoken* word. Very early in the biblical account, God warns his people against the projection of his personal presence into any kind of pictorial representation:

> "Then the Lord spoke to you out of the midst of the fire: you heard the sound of words, but saw no form; there was only a voice. And he declared to you his covenant, which he commanded you to perform, that is, the ten commandments; and he wrote them upon two tablets of stone. And the Lord commanded me at that time to teach you statutes and ordinances, that you might do them in the land which you are going over to possess.
>
> "Therefore take good heed to yourselves. Since you saw no form on the day that the Lord spoke to you at Horeb out of the midst of the fire, beware lest you act corruptly by making a graven image for yourselves." (Deut. 4:12-16)

The significance of this admonition, according to T. F. Torrance, is that revelational language is not essentially illustrative, for visual imagery inclines one toward the worship of the creature rather than the creator and is always a prelude to idolatry. God's word is more distinctively *evocative:*

> The Bible certainly uses many dramatic and vivid images, but these are employed as pointers to realities beyond themselves, and are not thought of as imaging them. They are symbols but not myths, they are signitive but not eidetic images. Or, to express it in another way, the connection between the sign and the thing signified is the Word: it involves an acoustic and not a mimetic relation.[7]

God intends, therefore, that he never be portrayed in a static form which one might substitute for his personal word of invitation and command. He does provide, however, enough intelligible substance in his historical redemption and biblical revelation to enable man to know him as person and expect his immediate presence to accompany a faithful interpretation of his Word.

Analogical Language

All language, according to its classical description by Thomas Aquinas, may be employed univocally, equivocally, or analogically.[8] (1) When language is used *univocally*, two or more linguistic concepts (these may or may not be conveyed through identical words) refer to two or more sets of circumstances in an identical sense. If modern examples might be allowed, the word "living" may be employed with reference to both a man and a flower to mean that both are organically or biologically animate and neither is "dead." (2) Language used *equivocally* refers to two or more situations where there is surely no identical correspondence but a vague, misleading, and at times even contrasting or contradictory relationship involved. One could speak, for example, of having "made a *living*" while he "*lived* in a certain city," and then use the same language to exclaim dramatically about having "truly *lived*" during a favorite pleasure. (3) Although all language is to a degree analogical in that it seeks to point toward that which must be recognized in relation to something else, language which is used *analogically* is that employment of words or symbols which reflects a high degree of correspondence or conceptual *proportionality* between two or more objects of reference. If man is spoken of as a "living," spiritual, personal being, it may, therefore, be analogically meaningful to speak of God as a "living," spiritual, personal being. There is, according to this representation, no univocal identification of man and God, neither is there an equivocal confusion or disparity, but a common field of reference which makes the linguistic comparison meaningful.

More recently analogy is defined as that "method of predication whereby concepts derived from a familiar object are made applicable to a relatively unknown object in virtue of some similarity between the two otherwise dissimilar objects (called analogues)."[9] Actually, the use of language analogically is an effort to reflect that process of thinking which recognizes the need to reconcile man's factual, temporal limitations with his consciousness of self-transcendence. Erich Przywara expresses this conviction succinctly when he declares that the principle of analogy is "in effect a denial that man's existence is his essence."[10] The analogical method is of paramount significance for the Christian who believes not only that man is created by God to be a self-transcendent being, but that the creator also grants man revelation which allows him to know and speak of God's transcendent being. The analogical method of formulating theological language may, therefore, be understood as *that way of giving expression proportionally or correspondingly to that which has through faith been discerned of the knowledge of God. That which is known of God is now expressed through linguistic forms where it is believed true and valid knowledge is conveyed, and at the same time, the limitations of human language are acknowledged and the transcendent character of the divine subject is preserved.* It may be helpful at this juncture to amplify this principle by considering how it can be more directly correlated with Christian theological language.

Theological Implications

1. The mere formulation and multiplication of various analogies concerning the concept of God should never be allowed to put language in the position of being a *creator* of divine knowledge. All knowledge of God must be based upon that kind of experience which could be legitimately expressed univocally. There is always a danger in the analogical approach to language that one will speak comparatively of two subjects which have no legitimate correlation or correspondence. In this case, one's linguistic association of concepts or events becomes mere verbal trickery or manipulation. The Christian, however, believes that he has immediate experience with God of such self-validating clarity and intensity that it permits him to project this knowledge through faith toward that which has not yet the evidence of direct encounter. He maintains not that complete comprehension is possible through this method, but rather that any valid experience with God can only be interpreted through analogies which point beyond themselves to one who transcends finite existence.

2. It may be at just this point of willingness to employ analogical language that one confronts the vital threshold between sheer facticity and the transcendental dimensions of faith. At the very beginning of Christ's ministry he stressed the need for going beyond the bare literalism of his teaching when he explained to Nicodemus, "Truly, truly, I say to you, unless one is born anew, he cannot see the kingdom of God." The disappointing literalistic response is, "How can a man be born when he is old? Can he enter a second time into his mother's womb and be born?" (John 3:3, 4). Later Christ gave great offense to those in his crowd who were unwilling to comprehend the spiritual symbolism of total identification with him when he proclaimed, "He who eats my flesh and drinks my blood has eternal life" (John 6:54). Even the crisis which was eventually to

culminate in his crucifixion was precipitated by those who heard his declaration, "Destroy this temple, and in three days I will raise it up," for they perverted it into a threat of political anarchy (John 2:19; Mark 14:58). Now on the more positive side, it is with such analogical qualifiers as "eternal," "only begotten," and "Lord" that the true significance of Christ can be comprehended. The divine energy in his presence which is perceived by his followers explodes the traditional univocal language and transforms it into that dynamic analogical imagery which is more appropriate for conveying the truth about his person. Thus it is only when an encounter, mediated by the historical Christ but not revealed "through flesh and blood," results in the confession that he is "the son of the living God," that the disciple truly becomes a believer and the Christian church is born (Matt. 16:16-17).

3. All normative Christian knowledge of God and, consequently, every appropriate linguistic response to him is derived not from an "analogy of being" but from an "analogy of grace." The major stream of Roman Catholicism, going back to Thomas Aquinas, believes that it is possible to analyze the nature of being as such—that is, man's rational and causal relations with the world—and find there sufficient correspondence between man and God to claim a natural knowledge of the divine. However, Protestant theology in the main stresses the priority of man's knowledge of God which is received from one special segment of being, namely, the being of God as he is present in Christ. Any effort, therefore, to discover and describe the nature of God through an analysis of natural or human analogies is destined to fail as A. M. Hunter warns when he tells the painful story of a certain prodigal son. A young man who found himself "in a far country" away from home was counseled by a minister in that region to return to his father and he "would kill the fatted calf for him." When, however, the minister saw the young man sometime later he inquired how he had been received, whereupon the boy replied that his father had "nearly killed the prodigal son!"[11] This account seems both humorous and pathetically true to life, and its central

thrust is worth remembering: one does not come to a knowledge of God by assimilating and projecting even the most noble human qualities and ideals into a concept of deity, but normatively, through a faithful response to God's gracious revelation in Christ.

4. The strength or validity of a theological analogy is determined primarily by the extent to which the analogy participates in the historical occasion which gives it birth and in the subsequent existential encounter with God which it makes possible. A Christian analogy possesses theological value not because of the number of people who subscribe to it, nor its inherent facility for relevance or communication, nor its possession of certain aesthetic qualities, nor even from its ethical sublimity, but rather through its historical reliability and existential creativity. For example, the analogy of God as a "living" Lord has its foundation in the actuality of the historical event of the raising of Jesus from the dead. This event, according to the New Testament, has transpired in a literal sense and is reported univocally. The event has, moreover, chosen and perhaps even created the very form of linguistic response which God deems necessary to communicate knowledge of its occurrence and importance. The analogy, "living," and its family of qualifiers, such as "risen," "resurrected," "victorious," and "triumphant" receive their potency from their association with the original resurrection event and their capacity to point others toward the possibility of encountering Christ's living presence. Without this historical-existential coalition the analogy "living Christ" would hang suspended in midair and at best reveal an extraordinary religious imagination or literary hypothesis.

5. In order for the analogical method not to become the basis for a self-contained philosophical determinism, there must be enough freedom or openness in one's world-view to admit the possibility of a new and unique event which has no exact analogical counterpart in past or present experience. A. M. Farrer's premise, "About that which is simply unique, there can be no discourse," is surely correct at the point of need for a common field of intelligibility before knowledge can be received and conveyed.[12] Even

so, the practice of comparing event with event should not be elevated into a metaphysical principle which determines what can or cannot take place. In other words, the status of analogical language must never be allowed to usurp the place of ontology. Linguistic method must be content to fulfill its function as an interpreter of the linguistic pattern of reality—not to create it or circumscribe it deterministically. Without this flexibility an event such as the resurrection of Christ would be a priori inconceivable.

6. One needs also to ask if there is a literary locus which might serve as the chief point of reference for normative theological analogies. For the Christian this can be none other than the biblical revelation because of its historical proximity to the Christ-event and the existential encounter which is made possible through its language. Scripture is the God-given collection of historically occasioned analogies which God elects as his linguistic instruments to provide knowledge of him. This does not mean, however, that one is permitted to use the biblical theological language, even though one believes it to be divinely inspired, in a merely univocal sense. To do so would relegate such biblical analogies as "shepherd," "king," "redeemer," and "savior" either to a nontranscendental identification of God with man or an anthropomorphic projection of man to God.

7. Since the Bible in its wholeness contains a broad spectrum of analogies which neither singularly nor collectively are capable of exhausting the ultimate meaning of God, then no one analogy, not even a biblical one, should be allowed to dominate one's Christian theology. Even though one must always work either consciously or unconsciously within the limitations of a theological model, the model must always remain responsive to the manifold concerns of the biblical revelation. It is, moreover, not possible to establish an adequate statement concerning God's being and purpose merely by intellectually balancing the conceptual content of these linguistic categories. In a very constructive sense, knowledge of the dynamic personal nature of God can be found only

"somewhere in between" the rational compatibility and paradoxical antitheses of these biblical analogies. One must compare analogy with analogy, scripture with scripture, and trust the living Christ to guide sensitively and wisely toward that particular aspect of divine revelation which is needed today. The movement of God's Spirit may swing from accent to accent like a pendulum, prompting a recognition of some crucial need in the historical and theological condition of the times. On occasion, to cite a few examples, one will need to give alternating priority to the following theological themes and their complementary analogies:

No one can come to me unless the Father who sent me draws him. (John 6:44)	*and*	Let him who desires take the water of life. (Rev. 22:17)
There is therefore now no condemnation. (Rom. 8:1)	*and*	Take up your cross daily and follow me. (Luke 9:23)
The church is the body of Christ. (Col. 1:24)	*and*	The church is at Corinth. (I Cor. 1:2)
The Father knows what you need before you ask him. (Matt. 6:8)	*and*	Pray constantly. (I Thess. 5:17)

It is the Christian interpreter's responsibility, therefore, to live devotionally within these polar tensions and also to anticipate theologically any possible excess or abuse which might result from current trends—and, where necessary, initiate corrective change.

Communication and Relevance

It can now be asked, "What role should the category of *relevance* play in the function of language?" Christian communication can only rightfully claim authority for the contemporary situation if the central redemptive event of Christ was responded to meaningfully in the past by men whose capacities and basic struggles in life correspond essentially to those of men today. A biblical message therefore does not become relevant just because a preacher understands his audience and uses their language, all of which is necessary, but primarily because those addressed are, in a rich ontological sense, *already present in the passage*. The practice of grounding Christian witness firmly in scripture moreover provides the interpreter with much more than confirmation regarding the constancy of human nature through the centuries. A biblical text also reveals the direction in which God's action entered the situation in the past and, because of God's constancy, creates the expectancy of his redemptive action in the present. One needs, therefore, as Heinrich Ott has said, the guidance provided by a scriptural passage because the essence of a text is just this: "that it springs from the heart of a situation in which the gospel has already brought matters to a final issue."[13]

The linguistic interpreter, therefore, strives to remove any conceptual hindrance which would prevent the revelatory events already present in scripture from breaking through to man in self-confirming witness. For a biblical passage not only reveals God's word to man but shows the kind of human response which God expects from man. Appropriate listening to the Word of God involves drawing near to those rational categories and patterns of obedience which enabled the biblical participants and writers to know God's will in the initial setting. In a very real sense we lay our minds and hearts beside these who have gone before in order to learn what kind of persons are pleasing to God. It is wonderful indeed to find these thought-forms and patterns of obedience already formed and made visible in the Word of God. Thus the problem of relevance in a Christian understanding of language, far from being solely a matter of style of presentation, touches profoundly upon the theological content of that which is communicated and the attitude in which it must be received. If the gospel were to consist intrinsically of religious concepts, humanistic projections or certain ethical attitudes or practices which a speaker seeks to persuade his hearers to accept, then the matter of relevance in presentation would become more controlling than it actually is in Christian communication. The message must surely be communicated in an excitingly relevant form to meet basic human needs; however, the believer does not have the ultimate burden of *making* the gospel relevant for this has already been accomplished.

The primary function of Christian language, it may therefore be concluded, is to conduct those to whom it is addressed into the original encounter from which the scriptures were congealed, in the hope that the spiritual affinities between the biblical and contemporary situation will coalesce in a gracious illuminating moment. Sigmund Freud tells about a small girl who was having trouble going to sleep at night. She calls to her nurse in the next room, "Speak to me, nurse, I am afraid." The nurse answers, "What difference would it make, for you can't see me?" whereupon the child replies simply but profoundly, "When someone speaks it becomes brighter."[14] The Christian believes not only that God speaks and there is light, but also that the eternal, creative "Word became flesh" and is, moreover, "the light of the world" (Gen. 1:3; John 1:14, 8:12). Wherever this *Word* is truly proclaimed and received the world indeed becomes *brighter*!

PART II

EXPLORING THE FRONTIERS

CHAPTER VIII

Christianity and Converging Faiths

Before entering into dialogue with some of the major religions of the world[1] it will be helpful to clarify the concept of religion. The word itself is of uncertain origin and the experience of religion appears to be so spontaneous and universal that its presence and meaning are almost taken for granted by the respective adherents. At least, according to Emile Cailliet, there appears to be no word for religion among the ancient Hebrews, Greeks, Hindus, Germans, or Celts. And he believes that in spite of the fact that many translate θρησκείας as religion in Acts 26:5 and James 1:26-27, "it is fair to say that the word 'religion' is foreign to the New Testament."[2] While the Bible seeks to refute false beliefs and practices and meet all man's religious needs, it never really defines the concept. Not until the Christian proclamation encounters the threat of a comprehensive world-view does the need arise for the church to define the nature of religion.

Definitions of religion now range all the way from A. N. Whitehead's cryptic saying that "religion is what the individual does with his own solitariness,"[3] to H. H. Farmer's insistence that the Christian religion rightly provides the normative categories for determining the nature of religion itself. The Christian apprehension of God structurally involves (1) an ontological other, (2) an axiological other, (3) an inherent personalism, (4) absolute demand, (5) absolute succour, (6) empowering indwelling, and (7) a numinous feeling tone.[4] Any definition of religion appears therefore to be responsible for describing the form or structure of religious experience while at the same time being broad enough to allow the various religions to fill these structures with their own understanding of the content of that experience. This crucial distinction between form and content is described well by G. Mensching when he explains:

> We define therefore religion as an experiential encounter with holy reality and as the answering action of the one who is existentially conditioned by the holy. This definition, in which the basic element which is contained in every religion—encounter with the holy and answer of man—are distinguishable, contains this basic element only for the purpose of a formal description of the structure of the relationship to the holy, which can be filled in historical reality with many different contents.[5]

One of the most helpful definitions to appear in recent days is offered by Frederick Ferré who says in a Tillichian vein that religion is man's "way of valuing most comprehensively and intensively."[6] Although one need not be restricted ultimately to this phenomenological plane, Ferré's description does at least insist on the necessity of correlating one's understanding of religion with experience. This simple designation will, then, with the important distinction between form and content noted above, serve functionally as the basic definition of religion within which this investigation will proceed.

No effort will be made here to explore the question of the *origin* of religion for it is believed that the essence of religion may be understood, as G. Dawes Hicks has said, not by "peering into its cradle and seeking oracles in its infant cries," but rather by empirically recognizing its universal existence and seeking to know the truth or falsity of its transcendental references.[7] Moreover, the origin of religion cannot be allowed to determine its value for the simple reason that we have no knowledge before the time when men responded to their environment with a feeling of numinous awe transcending mere fear or ecstasy. If one does not already know in some experiential sense what religion is, no amount of historical or anthropological probing will ever be able to account for the phenomena. John Oman is wise to warn that "if we do not know already what religion is, we can no more hope to reconstruct a living religion out of a mere welter of facts than if we had never seen a tree to reconstruct it out of sawdust."[8]

Religion is simply a given fact in human experience which, interpreted phenomenologically, reveals two essential polarities, as Heinz von Zahrnt describes so forcefully:

> *Negatively* the experience of a distress, a suffering in life, as it is, a chaffing at the reality at hand, in other words, the disappointment, that the world is not whole, but full of unwholesomeness, that it is wicked—and man himself is the same. As *positive*, basic experience religion includes that demand for overcoming this unwholesome situation, the expectation of that which is better, the longing after a fullness and wholeness, in other words, the hope that the world not remain in wickedness, but may become whole—and man himself in like manner. . . . It is, as though man had somewhere, one time received a kind of promise and waits now, indeed seeks and pursues after it, that it may be redeemed and be fulfilled.[9]

Some might believe from these paradoxical phenomena that there is a good possibility for uniting all religious experiences and consequently all cultural expressions of religion around a common center of human value. Upon closer examination, however, it is readily apparent to the perceptive observer that such categories as wholeness, promise, and expectation are intended to be much more than mental or conceptual projections.[10] At least it must be admitted that when a Christian, a Hindu, a Buddhist, or a Muslim gives formal and cultic expression to these categories, they most assuredly mean for them to refer to realms which are comprised essentially of quite different ontological content.

Comparative Ontologies

R. Puligandla sets forth the basic issue at stake here in his provocative essay, "Could There Be an Essential Unity of Religions?" when he contends:

> The truth or falsity of any religion is inextricably bound up with the truth or falsity of some ontology or other, and it is the uniqueness of one ontology that bestows upon a religion its uniqueness. Put differently, associated with any given religion, there can be exactly one ontology and vice versa. A religion cannot be unique if it is, or could be, associated with more than one ontology.[11]

Let us therefore endeavor to describe briefly the peculiar ontological elements of Christianity, Hinduism, Buddhism, and Islam at the point of their (1) view of gods, God, or ultimate reality; (2) basic understanding of man; (3) central ontological focus where one's basic understanding of reality may be perceived most clearly; (4) concept of redemption or the solution which is proposed for man's struggles within the human situation; and finally, (5) essential eschatology or interpretation of ultimate destiny.

Christianity

1) Christianity believes that God alone is ultimately real and that everything that exists in spatial and temporal manifestations has its creative ground and sustenance or continued existence in God himself. God as Father, Son, and Holy Spirit is both absolute in his oneness and distinctive in his triune being. He has through his creative word brought everything that exists in the created, cosmological order into existence out of nothing and granted it a relative independence outside himself.

2) Man, though created in the image of God with the capacity to reflect God's glory and enter into personal relationship with him and his fellowmen—is nevertheless a creature. According to the biblical tradition, this transcendental creature has asserted himself in willful rebellion against his creator, and until he is restored by Christ to personal communion, remains in a state of estrangement from God, himself, and his fellowmen.

3) The central clue or focus by which we are able to understand the essential nature of reality is found in the Christian faith in God who gives himself to be known in the *person of Jesus Christ* as He is recognized through the presence of the Holy Spirit. While the Christian knows

Christ through the Holy Scripture, it is essentially in the person of Christ himself that one truly *encounters* God and begins to understand how in Christ "all things hold together" (Col. 1:17).

4) Salvation, at least in the Protestant tradition, is essentially a personal relationship between Christ and the believer, which is possible because of God's offer of grace and man's reciprocal trust. Because of the epistemological and ethical distance between God as creator and man the creature, and God as holy and man the sinner, this redemptive union can only be accomplished through God's grace. And since this salvation is essentially an eternal personal relationship, it may be realized only through the believer's trust. Although divine strength to meet suffering and death are provided, the external circumstances which threaten one's earthly happiness or well-being may or may not be altered according to the sovereign will of God.

5) The eschatological destiny of man in Christian thought is determined largely by its understanding of God and man as personal. In light of God's personal offer of grace through Christ it seems appropriate to conclude that it is only through a personal response in faith that man could be prepared for fellowship with God throughout eternity. Most classical Christian eschatologies, therefore, accept the awesome responsibility of declaring the possibility of eternal separation from God when his grace is rejected. On the other hand, the Christian believes he has evidence for eternal life because of God's personal redeeming love for him and the resurrection of Jesus Christ.

Hinduism

Hinduism arose in northern India so long ago as to be virtually without traceable historical origins. Furthermore it is so many-sided and all-inclusive as to be at times almost indistinguishable from culture itself; however, its most recognizable ontological features are as follows:

1) *Brahman* is the Hindu name for ultimate reality, the supreme soul of the universe, which is at once beginningless and endless, unchanging and eternal, and completely

beyond description, defying all predication. Brahman is not to be considered as the creator of the world as the following passage from the Upanishads clearly demonstrates:

> This whole world is *Brahman*.
>
> He who consists of mind, whose body is life, whose form is light, whose conception is truth, whose soul is space, containing all works, containing all desires, containing all odours, containing all tastes, encompassing this whole world, being without speech and without concern.
>
> This is my self within the heart, smaller than a grain of rice, than a barley corn, than a mustard seed, than a grain of millet or than the kernel of a grain of a millet. This is myself within the heart, greater than the earth, greater than the atmosphere, greater than the sky, greater than these worlds.
>
> Containing all works, containing all desires, containing all odours, containing all tastes, encompassing this whole world, without speech, without concern, this is the self of mine within the heart; this is *Brahman*. Into him, I shall enter, on departing hence. Verily, he who believes this, will have no more doubts.[12]

There are, to be sure, theistic or personalistic elements within this monism which give particularity to the religious quality of Hindu experience. The one who is worshiped in the temple is not the Brahman of abstract thought but the threatening, near-demonic goddess Kali, the dynamic yet ascetic Siva, the glorious and gracious Vishnu, or the loving and invincible Krishna. In practice modern Hinduism contains many gods ranging from the simple provincial deities with their animistic heritage to the more personalistic cultic gods which are approached through elaborate images, idols, and ritual. However, all Hindu worship, it must be remembered, takes place within the monistic premise that Brahman is all. It is not the creator of all things, but *is in its very essence all things*, whether they be material objects, men, or gods.

2) Man, or *Atmán*, along with the material world about him, is a manifold conglomerated collection of changing finite phenomena. "This entire apparent world, in which good and evil actions are done . . . is a mere illusion . . . and does in reality not exist at all."[13] The apparent

tangibility of man and his world, one is told, is due to his viewing reality, not as it should be in a spiritual unity, but as a duality. The belief that man himself and the surrounding external world are real is due to *maya*, which is commonly understood as illusion. Its central meaning, however, is that Brahman is able to express itself in many different forms.[14] Atmán, which is not to be confused with the empirical ego, is the innermost, true being of man and is like Brahman, eternal and unchanging. The Hindu uses many images to portray this identity, but perhaps none is more effective than the comparison of Brahman to the air outside of a jug and Atmán to the air which is inside.[15] Suffering and the need for salvation occur, consequently, through the ignorance of one who cannot understand this ontological identity of Brahman and Atmán.

3) The conceptual thesis concerning the identity of Brahman and Atmán is the central ontological affirmation of Hinduism. The individual's realization of this principle provides its experiential counterpart. This conviction has important practical implications for the devout Hindu as seen in a contemporary commentary on the Bhagavad Gita. Eknath Easwaran makes the following application:

> Yesterday when I was taking our dog Muka for a walk I saw a jackrabbit in front of us seated on the road, full of confidence that no one at Ramagiri would harm him. But seeing Muka, he became unsure and gave a couple of leaps, getting out of our way. Muka looked up at me as if to say, "Why does he have such abnormal legs? Why are the back two so much longer than the front ones?" Muka looks upon his four legs of equal length as normal, and he measures the world from this point of view; anything not conforming to his dimensions is abnormal. The jackrabbit is no different. Looking at the world from his vantage point, he would have said, "What strange legs your dog has—all equal lengths. How does he manage to hop?" Of course, from our point of view the rabbit's legs are just right for a rabbit and Muka's are just right for a dog.
>
> Similarly, most of us live with people who have different opinions than ours. Everyone has different dimensions, and each walks or jumps forward in his own way; yet there is a common core in all of us.[16]

4) Absolute freedom and salvation, *moksha*, is obtained by the conceptual understanding and experiential realization of the identity of Brahman and Atmán. Since man's greatest burden is not original or existential sin but rather ignorance of the true nature of his own identity with Brahman, salvation can occur only by overcoming this ignorance through a proper understanding and appropriation of this truth. *Moksha* is available to man through his own efforts and involves the possibility of his perfectability here and now in this life. Once one realizes his Brahman consciousness, he will no longer be deluded by maya and will transcend all suffering and need.

It is here that the practical significance of yoga is seen in the Hindu religion. Yoga is the name for the spiritual discipline which is required to reach this goal of identification. The word itself means yoke or union; it is therefore a method of training or discipline designed to lead one to union or integration with Brahman. There is a Karma Yoga which stresses the significance of good works or actions. The essental quality of these works is that they be self-less. Jnana Yoga is for intellectual persons and stresses the path to oneness through knowledge or contemplation. Bhakti Yoga is the simplest and most popular form of yoga and places its primary stress on emotion or devotion. This is probably the closest of all the yogas to Christian worship; in fact, according to most Hindus, Christianity is simply one of the Bhakti paths.

5) Since both human existence and history are products of *maya*, any question concerning eschatology and the future would seem to have little real significance for Hinduism. It does, however, teach that the individual, empirical soul, or *jiva*, is responsible for good works which, according to the doctrine of *karma*, will be rewarded with an exact equivalent of merit or demerit according to the nature of the deed. The soul is then subject to reincarnation or *samsāra* in keeping with the merit which was obtained in the previous life. The Upanishads show how closely the doctrine of karma and reincarnation are linked together in Hindu thought:

> If the buddhi [the faculty of the mind which makes decisions], being related to a distracted mind, loses its discrimination and therefore always remains impure, then the embodied soul never attains the goal, but enters into the round of births. That is to say, the life of samsāra.
>
> But if the buddhi, being related to a mind that is restrained, possesses discrimination and therefore always remains pure, then the embodied soul attains that goal from which he is not born again.[17]

The eschatological goal of Hindu religion is seen therefore as our escape from the cycle of rebirth and the world of demons, sin, ignorance, caste, and *karma*—and the absorption into Brahman to whose essence we already belong.

Buddhism

Buddhism originated historically as an effort to reform Hinduism by rejecting its more speculative philosophical orientation and giving greater attention to the existential and ethical responsibilities of man as he confronts the problem of suffering. It possesses, nevertheless, these distinctive ontological elements:

1) Ultimate reality is understood from within the same Brahmanistic perspective which characterizes Hinduism. However, in Buddhism, this ultimate reality while still being one is in all its component parts in a continual state of change and process, and is frequently described as being little more than a dynamic atheistic void. Any concerns for the beginning and end of the world and time are just idle speculations. Moreover, such questions are a serious hindrance to the urgent task of discovering the enlightenment which enables one to confront suffering and yet live in peace.

During his lifetime Siddhartha Gautama Buddha (ca. 563–483 B.C.) discouraged his followers from deifying his person; however, with a sublime irony his disciples through their adoration deified the very one who denied the existence of God. Now a Buddhist is taught to pray:

> Oh, thou, the Buddha, the supremely awakened one, the most honored one, here are we gathered in thy presence with deepest reverence and adoration in our hearts. We place our whole trust in thee, in thy teaching and in thy order, and we do earnestly

resolve to be good Buddhists, and follow the holy path thou hast shown us, so that we may, like thyself, attain the happiest and the most peaceful realm of Nirvana. *Namu-Amida-Butsu.*[18]

2) Man cannot really be said to "exist" in Buddhism for according to the anattā doctrine there is nothing that can be called the self in the sense of an unchanging, abiding substance. This is illustrated in the famous story of the chariot where a man named Nagâsena seeks to convince King Menander that selves do not really exist. On one occasion, according to this tradition, the venerable Nagâsena addressed the King:

"How then did you come, on foot, or in a chariot?"

"I did not come, Sir, on foot. I came in a carriage."

"Then if you came, Sire, in a carriage, explain to me what that is. Is it the pole that is the chariot?"

"I did not say that."

"Is it the axle that is the chariot?"

"Certainly not."

"Is it the wheels, or the framework, or the ropes, or the yoke, or the spokes of the wheels, or the goad, that are the chariot?"

And to all these he still answered no.

"Then is it all these parts of it that are the chariot?"

"No, Sir."

"But is there anything outside them that is the chariot?"

And still he answered no.

"Then thus, ask as I may, I can discover no chariot. Chariot is a mere empty sound. What then is the chariot you say you came in? It is a falsehood that your Majesty has spoken, an untruth! There is no such thing as a chariot!"

When he had thus spoken the five hundred Yonakas shouted their applause, and said to the king: "Now let your Majesty get out of that if you can?"

And Milinda the king replied to Nâgasena, and said: "I have spoken no untruth, reverend Sir. It is on account of its having all these things—the pole, and the axle, the wheels, and the framework, the ropes, the yoke, the spokes, and the goad—that it comes under the generally understood term, the designation in common use, of 'chariot.' "

"Very good! Your Majesty has rightly grasped the meaning of 'chariot.' And just even so it is on account of all those things you questioned me about—the thirty-two kinds of organic matter in a human body, and the five constituent elements of being—that I come under the generally understood term, the designation in common use, of 'Nâgasena.' "[19]

Man is, it seems, but the name that is given to the place where certain aggregates of existence flow together as matter and energy into particular shapes or forms.

3) The ontological center of Buddhism is found unquestionably in the belief that all suffering is due to desire. This is the major thesis of Gautama Buddha's First Sermon at Benares:

> The Noble Truth of suffering is this: Birth is suffering; aging is suffering; sickness is suffering; death is suffering; sorrow and lamentation, pain, grief and despair are suffering; association with the unpleasant is suffering; dissociation from the pleasant is suffering; not to get what one wants is suffering—in brief, the five aggregates of attachment are suffering.
>
> The Noble Truth of the origin of suffering is this: It is this thirst (craving) which produces re-existence and re-becoming, bound up with passionate greed. It finds fresh delight now here and now there, namely, thirst for sense-pleasures; thirst for existence and becoming; and thirst for non-existence (self-annihilation).
>
> The Noble Truth of the Cessation of suffering is this: It is the complete cessation of that very thirst, giving it up, renouncing it, emancipating oneself from it, detaching oneself from it.
>
> The Noble Truth of the Path leading to the Cessation of suffering is this: It is simply the Noble Eightfold Path, namely right view; right thought; right speech; right action; right livelihood; right effort; right mindfulness; right concentration.[20]

The Buddhist word for suffering is *dukkhá* which includes the concepts of pain and sorrow but also implies the idea of impermanence or lack of wholeness. There can of course be a legitimate desire which is distinct from anxiety. This is called *chanda*, and it may appear in such natural occasions as when one walks down the street and desires to put one foot down in front of the other. On the other hand, there is the desire which is coupled with anxiety, greed, fear, envy, or anger. This is called *tanha* and should be avoided because it brings suffering.

4) Salvation, as anticipated above, is possible in Buddhism only through the renunciation of all anxious desire, and this includes even the desire for that which is good for oneself. The supreme example for this is found in the Buddha himself who, according to one prominent tradition, upon realizing that he was approaching the

threshold of total release or *nirvana*, deliberately withheld himself from this experience in order to be able to show others around him in the world of suffering the way to peace.[21] The kind of salvation experience toward which Buddhism aspires as well as the role which is played by Gautama in this experience is illustrated dramatically but authentically in the conclusion of Hermann Hesse's novel *Siddhartha*. The setting is in the Far East where two lifelong friends, now grown old, meet again, perhaps for the last time. Siddhartha has found peace, but Govinda has not and asks his friend to give him something to help him on his way for it is often hard and dark. Siddhartha looks at his friend with a deep, penetrating compassion—and suddenly Govinda no longer sees the face of his friend.

> Instead he saw other faces, many faces, . . . a continuous stream of faces . . . which were yet all Siddhartha. He saw the face of a fish, of a carp, . . . of a newly born child, . . . of a murderer, saw him plunge a knife into the body of a man; at the same moment he saw this criminal kneeling down, bound, and his head cut off by an executioner. He saw the naked bodies of men and women in the postures and transports of passionate love. He saw corpses stretched out, still, cold, empty. He saw the heads of animals—boars, crocodiles, elephants, oxen, birds. . . . Each one was mortal, a passionate, painful example of all that is transitory. Yet none of them died, they only changed, were always reborn, continually had a new face: only time stood between one face and another . . . and over them all there was continually something . . . stretched across like thin glass or ice, like a transparent skin, shell, form or mask of water—and this mask was Siddhartha's smiling face. . . .
>
> Govinda bowed low. Incontrollable tears trickled down his old face. He was overwhelmed by a feeling of great love, of the most humble veneration. He bowed low, right down to the ground, in front of the man sitting there motionless, whose smile reminded him of everything that he had ever loved in his life, of everything that had ever been of value and holy in his life.[22]

5) The future toward which the Buddhist moves is much the same as that of the Hindu, although there appears to be a much more elaborate setting forth of what absorption into

Brahman means in the experience of *nirvana*. The word nirvana itself means a "blowing out" and is used to describe the obliteration of all consciousness, particularly all conscious desire. The Buddha claims to have dwelt in this contentment after his Enlightenment:

> Nibbana have I realized, and gazed into the mirror
> of the Dhamma, the Noble Truth,
> I am healed of my wound;
> Down is my burden laid; My task is done;
> My heart is utterly set free.[23]

He taught his followers the significance of this experience in one of the most important statements available on Hindu and Buddhist eschatology:

> Monks, there exists that condition wherein is neither earth nor water nor fire nor air: wherein is neither the sphere of infinite space nor of infinite consciousness nor of nothingness nor of neither-consciousness-nor-unconsciousness; where there is neither this world nor a world beyond nor both together nor moon-and-sun. Thence, monks, I declare is no coming to birth; thither is no going [from life]; therein is no duration; thence is no falling; there is no arising. It is not something fixed, it moves not on, it is not based on anything. That indeed is the end of Ill.[24]

Nirvana is therefore surely not to be conceived as a futuristic state of existence resembling the Christian concept of heaven. On the experiential level it is rather a psychological condition of peace in which the self-asserting ego has been annihilated and one is liberated from those cravings which make human existence a self-defeating circle of assertion and anxiety. On the ontological plane it is to be viewed more as a realm of meaninglessness and personal oblivion.

Islam

1) Islam, with its heritage in the Judaeo-Christian tradition, believes that all reality is grounded ultimately in the one sovereign personal being of God who has created the world and granted it relative independence. Muhammad (570–632 A.D.) endeavored to counteract what he believed to

be polytheistic and idolatrous trends in Judaism, the threat to God's oneness inherent in the Christian doctrine of the Trinity, and the rampant and demoralizing polytheism in his own contemporary Arab religion. His stress was therefore overwhelmingly on the *unity* of God. He writes in the Koran: "Allah (Himself) is witness that there is no God save Him. And the angels and the men of learning (too are witnesses). Maintaining His creation in justice, there is no God save Him, the Almighty, the Wise" (Koran 3:18). This concern of Islam for the oneness of God is nowhere more clearly observed than in that venerated passage from the Koran where God directs Muhammad to say, "God is one God; the eternal God, he begetteth not, neither is he begotten: and there is not any like unto him" (Koran 112).

2) The Islamic doctrine of man is couched within the Judaeo-Christian teaching that man is created for the purposes of God and possesses the capacity for self-transcendence and an inescapable responsibility toward God and one's fellowmen. In effect, however, the freedom of man in this relationship is often overshadowed by Islam's emphasis upon the sovereignty of God. For example, the Koran declares: "He whom Allah sendeth astray, for him thou canst not find a road" (Koran 4:48). Thus there frequently appears no reluctance on Muhammad's part to ascribe certain human actions as the direct result of God's decree and yet there are many times when the freedom and responsibility of man are maintained without question. This dialectical tension has led D. B. MacDonald to write that evidently Muhammad "never thought about predestination and free will, whatever later traditions may have put into his mouth; he expressed each side as he saw it at the moment, and as the need of the moment stood."[25]

3) In keeping with Muhammad's obsession for the unity of God, he makes no claim of deity for himself; however, it seems accurate to say that the *apostolate* or instrumentality of Muhammad in being the mouthpiece for Allah to produce *the book* of the Koran provides the central ontological foci for Islam.[26] Once when Muhammad had withdrawn into a cave for spiritual retreat during the

month of Ramadan, he reportedly fell asleep or into a trance whereupon he had a vision of Gabriel who said:

> "Read!"
> Mohammed replied, "I cannot read." This was repeated three times, whereupon Mohammed asked, "What can I read?" The voice replied:
> "Read: In the name of thy Lord who createth,
> Createth man from a clot.
> Read: And thy Lord is the most bounteous
> Who teacheth by thy pen,
> Teacheth man that which he knew not."[27]

According to this tradition, Gabriel proceeded to authorize Muhammad as the messenger of Allah and empowered him to write the words which were dictated to him directly from a book kept in heaven. Hence, this sacred book of Islam is called the Koran, Al-Qur'an, "The Reading," the reading of one who before the revelation was unable to read.[28]

The Koran, according to Islam, is in no way the word of man. Consequently, the Koran is held in such reverence that it is only with reluctance and apology that a devout Muslim will allow it to appear in any language other than Arabic. Notice how Muhammed Pickthall introduces his English translation of the Koran with such reservation:

> The Book is here rendered almost literally and every effort has been made to choose befitting language. But the result is not the Glorious Koran, that inimitable symphony, that very sound of which moves men to tears and ecstasy. It is only an attempt to present the meaning of the Koran—and peradventure something of the charm—in English. It can never take the place of the Koran in Arabic, nor is it meant to do so.[29]

This kind of awe before the book has almost elevated the popular expression "the Koran cannot be translated" into a doctrinal article of faith. One is not surprised to learn that every Muslim should wash his hands before reading the Koran. It appears, therefore, to be no exaggeration to conclude that "Koranology" functions for Islam in much the same way that Christology does for Christianity.[30]

4) Although salvation in Islam, in keeping with the very meaning of the word Islam, "peace" or "surrender," inherently involves man's submission to the sovereign will of God, there is a surprising, at times almost dominating, emphasis upon the necessity of good works. The responsibility of man for his own salvation is set forth clearly in the basic "five pillars of Islam" which are found in the Koran:

1. Every Muslim must declare aloud "the witness," i.e., "I bear witness that there is no god but God, and that Muhammad is his messenger," at least one time in his life very slowly, with deep meaning, and full understanding. Most devotees repeat it many times each day.
2. Regular patterns of prayer five times daily while facing Mecca, the holy city.
3. Almsgiving, approximately 2½ percent of all one's income and permanent annual worth, to the poor.
4. Fasting, particularly during the month of Ramadan, which commemorates the giving of the Koran during this time of year.
5. Pilgrimage to Mecca is expected at least once from every believer who is physically and financially able to make the journey.

A sixth pillar is sometimes added by those who believe a holy war should be pursued as the will of God.

5) There will be a final day of judgment, consummation of history, and the assigning of heaven and hell to all persons in light of their acceptance or rejection of the message of God and their accompanying good or evil deeds. The Muslim is assured that Allah will watch carefully that no one will be treated unjustly. The prophets will be called upon to give account of their faithfulness in proclaiming the messages of warning that they were given. No one will be able to blame the jinn, those devils who tempt to idolatry, nor anyone else for his unbelief. There will be no mediation, of a father for his son or a brother for his brother. Even the hope that has grown up in some traditions that Muhammad might intercede for one "in whose heart there is only a speck of goodness," is not sustained by the Koran. There is, according to Tor Andrea's

summary of Islam's eschatological teaching, "only one hint that 'with Allah's permission' mediation may be possible, and in this case the angels are apparently thought of as the mediators."[31] The pattern of work-righteousness on this day of judgment is clearly visible in the concrete images which depict Allah as weighing the good and bad works on a delicate scale of balance that is accurate even to the weight of a grain of mustard seed.[32] Those whose good works outweigh the evil will inherit a garden filled with sensual pleasures and unspeakable delight:

> in gardens of pleasure, . . . and gold-weft couches. . . . Around them shall go eternal youths, with goblets and ewers and a cup of flowing wine. No headaches shall they feel therefrom, nor shall their wits be dimmed! And fruits such as they deem the best, and flesh of fowl as they desire, and bright and large-eyed maids like hidden pearls, a reward for that which they have done.[33]

And the evil ones will reap an undying existence in hell where there is neither rest nor hope but unspeakable pain.

A Christian Response

There has probably never been a time in history when so much pressure has been placed upon the Christian believer to surrender his faith to a religious syncretism based upon common cultural ideals. Intercontinental communication is greater than ever and expanding business and travel encounters are literally forcing the religious communities of the world to become respectfully conscious of one another. All of this not only involves a quantitative intensification of cultural and geographical exchanges but a certain qualitative change of outlook. For the first time in the existence of the human race there is a real possibility of *one world history*. It seems appropriate now as never before to ask, "Should not all the world religions be combined into one in order not only to conserve the highest values they enshrine but also to avoid the exclusivistic claims of any one?" In fact, Arnold Toynbee's plea for the unification of the major world religions sounds tremendously appealing to this age when he claims to have discerned the essential elements of man's collective religious experience in the following beliefs:

1) Man himself is certainly not the greatest spiritual presence in the Universe.
2) There is a presence in the Universe that is spiritually greater than Man himself.
3) In human life, knowledge is not an end in itself, but is a means to action.
4) Man's goal is to seek communion with the presence behind the phenomena, and to seek it with the aim of bringing himself into harmony with this absolute spiritual reality.
5) A human self cannot be brought into harmony with absolute reality unless it can get rid of its innate self-centeredness. This is the hardest task that Man can set himself.
6) Absolute reality has both an impersonal and a personal aspect.
7) The personal aspect of Absolute Reality must be good as well as omnipotent.[34]

In light of such challenges, the Christian church may now confront its greatest strategical threat and, if faith and conviction are strong, its greatest opportunity.

Consequently, the first thing to be done before a Christian can proceed to a meaningful response to the various options provided by the world religions is to explode the myth that they are all teaching essentially the same truth. To begin with, all of the religions considered do not point to the same understanding or conception of the highest good. For Christianity and Islam this would obviously be God or Allah whereas Buddhism places its central emphasis upon the eternal Brahman quality that is man, and Hinduism points mystically toward a supreme universal impersonal substance. There is furthermore a vast difference concerning what these religions say is morally good. Fatalism, as seen in Islam's god who "sendeth astray" according to his sovereign will, can hardly be assimilated into the Christian's concept of God as self-giving, agape love. There is also a basic distinction in the way these religions view the nature of the material world. The Hindu and Buddhist outlook upon the natural world as illusory is diametrically opposed to the Christian concept of the world as God's creation. And, moreover, it cannot be overlooked that neither Hinduism nor Buddhism has any real place for personal communion with God or petitionary prayer. Any religion which offers only the formal possibility of praise and thanksgiving to the neglect of confession, repentance, and supplication can only invalidate the worth of the individual and reveal its ontological distance from the personalistic structure of Judaism, Islam, and especially Christianity. This tension between personalism and impersonalism may also account for the conflict on the practical level when the Hindu and Buddhist strive for ultimate absorption into the supreme reality while the Christian and the Muslim maintain uncompromisingly the distinction between creator and creature and believe tenaciously that human personality will endure throughout the eschatological future. It must, therefore, be admitted that, no matter how sincere the motive for trying to discern a common content within these major representative religions, any effort to blur their basic ontological differences must be dismissed as either shallow semantic confusion or deliberate misrepresentation.[35]

Neither should the Christian believer be easily misled to think that the major non-Christian religions are syncretistically tolerant of other faiths, whereas the Christian religion is distinctively characterized by its claim to possess the final and exclusive way of salvation. The fact is that any movement which is indeed a *religion* and concerns itself with essential issues will by its very nature claim to provide the *only* method by which one should respond to ultimate reality. This is as true for the eclectic and inclusivistic Eastern religions as it is for the acknowledged exclusivism of the Christian revelation. Hans Küng is one of the few contemporary interpreters who recognizes that every religion which claims to deal with ultimacy must contain this characteristic:

> Eastern religions like Hinduism and Buddhism, predominately mystically oriented, for which the experience of absorption is central, also represent in their own way an absolute claim to

> exclusiveness: unlike the prophetical religions (Judaism, Christianity, Islam), for which the event of revelation and God's authority are central, the very fact that they do not exclude other religions involves a claim to include them all.[36]

Hinduism tends to absorb all other religions, and Buddhism, with its claim for a superior doctrine of salvation, merely tolerates other approaches. Both religions, however, assume by their eschatologies that anyone in error now will eventually come to the right perspective. Consequently, the task remains to determine which one of the world religions best *sustains* its claim for exclusive truth.

There are, however, at the same time certain recognizable themes within these religions considered with which the Christian can identify constructively. For example, there is a parallel between the mystical orientation of the Eastern religions and the Christian's participation with ultimate reality through his personal encounter with Christ. While the status of the individual in Eastern mysticism ranges from a total absorption in Brahman which leaves no trace of individuality, to a state where both unity and diversity somehow merge into one and remain distinct, Christianity overwhelmingly stresses the identity and distinctiveness of the individual in his relationship to God as personal. Yet there is concurrently in Christianity an undeniable emphasis upon the need and value for the individual to lose himself in surrender to the will and purposes of One who is transcendent. The Christian may therefore welcome the Eastern concern for the transcendental unity of all reality and nevertheless continue to maintain the ontological identity and enduring quality of the individual in Christian experience. These values of both the transcendental and personal dimensions are perhaps nowhere better conserved and expressed than in Paul's mystical confession: "I have been crucified with Christ; it is no longer I who live, but Christ who lives in me; and the life I now live in the flesh I live by faith in the Son of God, who loved me and gave himself for me" (Gal. 2:20).

Furthermore, the intensity and breadth of the Hindu

contemplation of the ultimate unity and inner cohesion of all reality could encourage the Christian to reexamine how all things cohere in Christ. The self-denying commitment of many Buddhists with their understanding of the roots of selfishness and the potential of the human will might cause Christians to ask if they really understand the meaning of self-denial, sacrifice, and the cross. They might also wonder if they have truly sought to confront the suffering of others with the compassion of the Buddha, not to mention the example of their own Lord. And does not the absolute demand of Islam to abhor polytheism and idolatry in all their forms challenge the spirituality of Christianity to its very depths?

In an article in *Psychology Today*, Harvey Cox seeks to interpret the results of three years of informal study of dozens of the Eastern cults made by some of his students at Harvard Divinity School. Dr. Cox's findings reveal many reasons why young Americans are turning to the Eastern religions; some believe they have found a home in these ancient faiths because quite simply they have found human *friendship*. There is also a conviction among them that the East offers a kind of *immediacy* which they have not been able to find in the more elaborate worship patterns of the West. They find there also a note of *authority*, usually in some gifted person, which they had not experienced before. A few confessed that the religious style of the East seemed more natural, artless, and *spiritual* to them than the conglomerated, materialistic cultural expressions of the West. Their feelings are conveyed with poignant candor when they say that Western civilization is spiritually bankrupt. It is dominated by technology, power, rationalization, and money. We need to learn from the Oriental peoples who have never been spoiled by machines and science, and have remained faithful to the simplicity of their ancestors. "Western religion has invalidated itself," they lament. "Now only the East is possible."[37] Regardless of how accurate one feels these criticisms of Western culture and religion are (and few would deny they contain some truth), it would be a tragedy for any Christian not to see here an exaggerated but legitimate plea for a more profound commitment to the spiritual realities of the Christian faith.

One of the most apparent differences between Christianity and these other religions is the manner in which they are frequently based on morality or some kind of absolute demand for self-realization as opposed to Christianity's offer of grace and supernatural strength. It may be tempting to believe that we are totally responsible for our own destiny and can therefore experience perfect realization or redemption in this life. If, however, we are honest with ourselves, we must realize the tyranny of these demands and the emotional suffering they bring. Paul writes continuously against the curse of the law and its unattainable goals. It is only after he finds his reconciliation and peace in Christ that he rejoices:

> For God has done what the law, weakened by the flesh, could not do: sending his own Son in the likeness of sinful flesh and for sin, he condemned sin in the flesh, in order that the just requirement of the law might be fulfilled in us, who walk not according to the flesh but according to the Spirit. (Rom. 8:3-4)

The Christian faith, to be sure, has its ethical responsibilities and absolute imperatives. Indeed, eschatological reward is described in the Christian faith as being based upon the works which have been accomplished by the believer. It is important, however, to realize that these works do not establish righteousness. Right relationship between the believer and God through faith creates the motivation and releases the divine energies which are needed to accomplish the good works.

The Claim for Uniqueness and Finality

There is a fundamental tension in all human experience and especially in religious experience between man's inescapable concern with the ultimate and the necessity of encountering this ultimateness through the particular. Since man is both a self-transcending and a tangible being, it will be necessary for his religious experience to satisfy both of these aspects of his nature. Paul Tillich sees here a basic clue for understanding the whole historical development of religion when he explains:

> The concreteness of man's ultimate concern drives him toward polytheistic structures; the reaction of the absolute element against these drives him toward monotheistic structures; and the need for a balance between the concrete and the absolute drives him toward trinitarian structures.[38]

While one need not postulate logically that the concrete or particular manifestation of religion be *trinitarian*, it does seem legitimate to ask what kind of particularity would best reflect the nature of ultimate reality. If an object of reverence is merely particular but has no capacity to communicate the transcendental dimension, then it can have no religious significance at all. If, however, that object possesses the quality of pointing beyond itself in a way which does not deny its own reality, the object may be viewed as at least potentially significant for religion. On the other hand, a religious value that is merely abstract can never really represent universality, because it is abstracted and thus separated from the particular which obviously exists in the universal. If one discovers, as Tillich reasons, a particular reality which is an embodiment and not a denial of the universal, and a universal which is not at the same time a denial of the particular, he may then have found that which fulfills his complete religious needs. It is here the Christian asserts that God, who is ultimately one and universal, has become particular in the person of Jesus Christ.[39] Christianity is therefore different from all the other world religions to the extent that Jesus Christ in his absoluteness and particularity is different from all other men.

However offensive the witness to the uniqueness and finality of Christ may be to some, there can be no doubt, as James Stewart declares, that these themes lie at the very heart of the New Testament proclamation.

> The facts of the Christian message were not just historic: they were *unique*, unrepeatable, absolute, final like the judgment

> trumpet, as indeed in a sense they *were* the judgment trumpet. That is why one of the great uncompromising notes of the New Testament is the Greek word, ἅπαξ, once and for all. This uniqueness of the particular event, the very conception with which mysticism and pantheism will have nothing to do, as being alien to their ideas of true spirituality—this very offence which to Greek speculative thought is "foolishness"—Christianity enthrones and makes its glory.[40]

Stewart then proceeds to marshall a host of scriptural passages where the "once for all" character of the gospel is made abundantly clear:

> The death he [Christ] died he died to sin, once for all. (Rom. 6:10)
>
> For Christ also died for sins once for all. (I Peter 3:18)
>
> I found it necessary to write appealing to you to contend for the faith which was once for all delivered to the saints. (Jude v. 3)
>
> [Christ] has no need, like those high priests, to offer sacrifices daily, first for his own sins and then for those of the people; he did this once for all when he offered up himself. (Heb. 7:27)
>
> So Christ, having been offered once to bear the sins of many, will appear a second time, not to deal with sin but to save those who are eagerly waiting for him. (Heb. 9:28)
>
> We have been sanctified through the offering of the body of Jesus Christ once for all. (Heb. 10:10)

He then concludes quite convincingly that the whole Bible is essentially an exposition of the "uniqueness of the events by which the human situation has been decisively transformed and a new relationship between God and man established for ever."[41]

The confidence which a Christian has in the finality of his faith is founded not just on a mere temporal condition, which he does not expect to recur, but also on the conviction that his Lord will never be qualitatively surpassed. There is in the believer's experience with Christ a finality which, according to H. H. Farmer, "here and now cuts right under, neutralizes, the radical infinalism of man's life, and shuts out once and for all any merely pessimistic devaluation of this present world."[42] One is conscious of being "rooted and grounded" in the personal love of God which in itself is final and complete (Eph. 3:17). The shepherd expressed this deep certainty long ago when he wrote, "The Lord is my shepherd, I shall not want" (Ps. 23:1). This consciousness of being loved absolutely and eternally in Christ is the foundation upon which the apostle Paul based his persuasion that neither "things present, nor things to come, . . . will be able to separate us from the love of God in Christ Jesus our Lord" (Rom. 8:39). Any claim like this regarding the future must by its very nature be based on a faith principle due to the fact that the future has not yet transpired. It can, however, be firmly established on the love of God experienced in Christ which is quite simply the most enduring reality known to man.

But how, it must be asked in conclusion, can one know he has experienced this love of God and received the necessary assurance regarding the finality of his Christian faith? Perhaps an illustration will serve the purpose well. In Lessing's classic drama, *Nathan the Wise*, a certain family had a magic ring which was handed down from generation to generation.[43] The ring was to be given to the best beloved and, according to the story, it had the power to make its wearer the most beloved of God and man. A father who had three sons could not decide which one he loved best, so he had two other rings made exactly like the ring of power and gave one to each of the three. After his death, they were inclined to quarrel as to which had the original ring, and they referred the matter to a very wise judge, each claiming that he had received his ring from his father's hand. The judge pointed out that the ring of power would itself decide the issue in the course of time, for its possessor would be the most loving and beloved. Lessing applies his parable to the three prophetic religions: Judaism, Christianity, and Islam. He is not supporting the belief that truth is a matter of indifference and that conduct is all important. He does want to maintain, however, that the final proof of theology is found in the quality of one's life.

The world can learn that Christianity has received the ultimate and final revelation only when Christians present the exclusiveness of this claim through the demonstration of their love.

CHAPTER IX

The Complementarity of Science and Religion

The popular world-view which currently permeates Western society and culture is unquestionably dominated by modern science. The universe, according to the general tenor of the scientific outlook, is believed to be self-contained with no transcendent or supernatural forces intervening or giving direction in any way. In this amalgamated residue of scientific and philosophical models the world simply exists naturally as matter and space extended to infinity. While various transformations of particles and energy transpire within this order, man himself is considered to be fundamentally the result of natural forces which have combined to produce him and provide his essential life support. Human values do emerge from these naturalistic sources and are to be freely chosen; however, there can be no assurance concerning either their universal relevance or lasting significance. Since science, with its near-miraculous advances in technology, is mainly responsible for this contemporary perspective, it is imperative that Christians understand as much as possible of their scientific heritage, its basic methodology, and especially those recent developments which relate most vitally to their faith.

It is ironical that in spite of the nearly total dominance of scientific naturalism in the present cultural milieu, the truly creative representatives in both science and religion are perhaps more willing than ever before to live peaceably with one another. After many centuries of antagonism, caused largely by a misunderstanding of their respective areas of responsibility, an era may be dawning where each discipline can appreciate the other's legitimate sphere and welcome its contribution.[1]

For one thing, there is today an increase of the sheer cumulative weight of information in both areas which inevitably demands intense specialization, making the overall implications of conflicting world-views more difficult to recognize and confrontation consequently less frequent. This increase in specialization no doubt also heightens the potential for internecine warfare within the disciplines themselves, thus releasing some pressures from the cross-area relationships.[2] And it should also not be overlooked that both science and religion are now encountering in Communism a form of political totalitarianism which not only threatens the integrity and dignity of the individual scientist and believer but also has assumed the awesome proportions of a deterministic metaphysic.[3] This common threat has to some degree drawn science and religion together on the side of freedom. There remain of course many areas of conflict, and these are no doubt destined to exist unless both science and religion come to a knowledge of the perfect truth. Wherever man rebels against the will of God there will be arrogance in science. And until faith and hope reside in that final love which enables us to understand fully even as we have been fully understood (I Cor. 13:12) there will be superstitious and obscurantist religion. If truth, however, is indeed *one*, the scientist must allow nothing to be true for him in religion which conflicts with his genuine scientific knowledge, and the Christian should accept none of the claims of science which contradict what he knows to be valid in his faith. Wolfhart Pannenberg summarizes this correlation well when he asks in his recent *Theology and the Philosophy of Science*, "*in what objects of experience* is God—as a problem—indirectly co-given, and what objects of experience can therefore be considered as possible traces of God?" He then responds, "The only possible answer is: *all objects*. . . . If 'God' is to be understood as the all-determining reality, everything must be shown to be determined by this reality and to be ultimately unintelligible without it."[4]

A Definition of Science

Science, from the Latin, scientia, knowledge, may be defined in the broadest sense as an abstract, highly selective yet free investigation which seeks to describe the behavior of a given realm with precision. It endeavors to allow the area under consideration to determine the most appropriate methodology for the inquiry and also to guide the interpreter toward the most adequate linguistic or symbolic responses. Natural science aspires to understand nature to the extent that it may discover certain patterns of continuity, uniformity, or at least high statistical probability, which will allow it to formulate general natural laws and theories and thus function on occasion predictively.[5] It may seem strange to speak of science as an abstract discipline because Western thought since Plato tends to think of a particular object which is being perceived as concrete whereas the larger conceptual context and the content of an idea are believed to be abstract. In reality, however, one really experiences and contemplates the whole world unless one seeks to isolate or abstract various segments of it for some specific purpose. When we therefore choose to investigate an object or a process we are in fact admitting the limitations of our perception and the necessity, for a while at least, to ignore the interrelationships which these surely have with reality as a whole.

For natural science even to begin, it must assume the existence of "nature," so this concept should be clarified before going further. According to Eric Rust, science understands nature to mean

> the general cosmic order, the aggregate of all observable or potentially observable entities, including man himself, insofar as man is a subject for scientific inquiry. It is thus the nexus of entities in the universe as they exist at the physical, vital, and

> psychological levels and as they are interrelated through their somatic and physical behavior.[6]

It is easy to see in this definition that the necessity to acknowledge one's basic point of departure and the principle of selectivity are present at a very early stage in the scientific enterprise. The assumption that there is a natural world *there* to be investigated is incidentally not very far removed from the kind of reasoning which assumes the existence of God in the ontological argument. In both cases, whether nature or God, the existence of an entity is *assumed* in order for one to be able to make rational sense of one's thinking. Be that as it may, science not only assumes the existence of the natural realm but its amenability to investigation and intelligible cohesion.

Although those employing the scientific method usually possess certain worthy personal qualities such as discipline in preparation, a spirit of free inquiry, community in research, and integrity in reporting results, the method itself deliberately intends to be metaphysically and axiologically neutral. While nature may encourage the scientist to believe that it is trustworthy, the method used to explore and demonstrate this orderliness is necessarily open. Arthur Pap in a very lucid essay entitled, "Does Science Have Metaphysical Presuppositions?" states this conviction forcefully:

> Nature happens to be so constituted that its course can be described by functional equations; and it is because scientists always found nature to be constituted that way that they came to develop the mathematical language of functionally connected variables. In any experimental inquiry now, to be sure, they betray their belief in uniformity by the very nature of their questions. . . . But only a minimum of psychology should be necessary to see that these scientific habits are the product of ever repeated experiences of uniformity.[7]

And most modern scientists would no doubt find themselves very much at home with Einstein's cryptic way of denying any metaphysical involvement: "For the scientist, there is only 'being,' but no wishing, no valuing, no good, no evil—in short, no goal."[8] This of course does not mean that the ultimate metaphysical context of one's scientific work can be ignored or his responsibility for an ontological commitment postponed indefinitely, but rather that as soon as science ceases to function descriptively within the natural realm and begins to interpret the whole of reality and its teleological goals it becomes philosophy; and once it claims to determine ultimate values it becomes religion.

For fear of predetermining the results of their inquiries, scientists are understandably reluctant to define the premises of their scientific method. In order to preserve the freedom to use many approaches to different phenomena, James Conant goes so far as to say that "there is no such thing as the scientific method."[9] The scientific method, if there is such, is therefore not so much a procedure which can be defined, as it is an approach to nature which is employed functionally, for according to Michael Polanyi, "no exhaustive statement of the premises of science can possibly exist. The common ground of science is, however, accessible to all scientists and is accepted by them as they become apprenticed to the traditional practice of science."[10] There are, nevertheless, certain recognizable patterns which emerge in the process of investigation which can characterize the scientific method as W. Wieland and R. Ebert perceive:

> Every experiment stands in an arranged context which is established by a *hypothesis;* it proceeds accordingly with a presupposition which must be itself free of contradiction and must have the adoption of a definite orderliness in the course of natural occurrences for its content; the presupposition becomes *theory*, if it is experimentally confirmed and is capable of *predicting* the results of the experiment . . . if several theories are capable of explaining a definite experimental situation, then in fact there is no further criterion of truth available for the natural scientist than the "beauty" and "simplicity" of a theory. The fact that experimentation is the most important method in natural science accounts for its close relationships to *technology*. Technology is "applied" natural science; on the other hand natural science itself can develop further through the continual refining of its methods of

> experimentation and observation only with the presupposition of modern technology.[11]

It is quite natural for science, by the very nature of its object and task, to prefer those aspects of its method which are capable of providing the greatest accuracy of interpretation and pragmatic demonstration. But no problems should arise between science and religion with the method thus described unless false religion attempts to determine what nature must be, or scientism masquerading as "the scientific method" tries to limit all knowledge to mechanical causes and that which is observable and quantitatively measurable. True dialogue can begin when religion has the faith to let nature be what it is, and science is willing to recognize that the truly real must also include that which is experientially and spiritually intelligible. In order to preserve this vital distinction, the German language provides the terms *Naturwissenschaften*, natural sciences, to refer to the physical sciences and *Geisteswissenschaften*, spiritual or human sciences, to describe the social sciences. In this latter sense Christian theology may be considered a science and yet not be confined to an experimental methodology which is more appropriate for investigating nature.

Historical Scientific Models

It should prove helpful to review, if even in an introductory manner, the major historical scientific world-views to which the Christian faith and its theological development have been related. The world which the Christian gospel first entered contained a conglomeration of animistic, naturalistic, dualistic, polytheistic, and mythological views where fate and purpose continually struggled for supremacy. Those who did not believe that the phenomenological world comprised the sum total of reality were left for the most part with the option of holding the world to be populated with sometimes benevolent but more frequently irrational powers, or accepting an irreconcilable dualism of eternal, immutable forms or patterns in the heavens which were only imperfectly embodied on earth. It was indeed *good news* when Christ came and the early evangelists went to a confused and frightened world and proclaimed that "in him all things were created, in heaven and on earth, visible and invisible, whether thrones or dominions or principalities or authorities—all things were created through him and for him. He is before all things, and in him all things hold together" (Col. 1:16-17). They preached moreover that God himself had come in the person of Christ to provide not only the redemption of man from sin but the rationale, the Logos, through which all men could perceive the purposes of God in his world and their own personal lives. Many in the early church were even willing to die as martyrs before they would sever their faith in Jesus Christ as personal savior from their belief in God as maker of heaven and earth, and their consciousness of the Holy Spirit's presence at work in the world. They deliberately decided that it was better to face the known evil of an executioner's sword than remain at the mercy of unknown cosmic powers in an unstable universe. It remained, however, for science in its various historical stages to appropriate and amplify these cosmological convictions into its own methods and models.

In the middle of the second century after Christ, the Ptolemaic astronomy, which was destined to dominate the scientific view of the world for the next 1400 years, gained ascendancy with its theory of the orbital movement of the moon, sun, and planets around the earth. The stars were but bright lights in a dark concave dome over all space. To be more exact, the planets, according to this interpretation, moved about the earth not only in a large orbit but also in small orbits upon the path of the larger orbit. These latter movements were called epicycles. According to Aristotle's philosophy which still largely conditioned this outlook, these orbits should be perfect because they are in the heavenly realm; however, since it was observed that these movements were not perfect (Ptolemy had discovered that the moon was irregular in its orbit), there developed a deep dualistic epistemological cleavage between the *intelligible* patterns of the celestial bodies and the *observable* phenomena of human experience and history. Unfortunately this dualism between the rational and sensible spheres entered Christian thought through Augustine's historical skepticism and his stress that God's revelation is known primarily through inner illumination. Later, when Aquinas sought deliberately to undergird his theology with the Aristotelian concept of causality, the dualistic division between the eternal immutable divine realm and the transitory unpredictable arena of human existence was further broadened and prolonged. Moreover, the Ptolemaic conviction that the earth was the cosmic center of the universe was destined to be used by the church to support its claims for authority in all spheres, including the scientific, consequently delaying the advent of modern science for centuries.

A major scientific revolution appeared on the horizon in the seventeenth century when Sir Isaac Newton developed his ingenious mathematical interpretations regarding the laws of mechanical causality. Copernicus prepared the way for the Newtonian cosmology when he established the heliocentric view of the universe. About this same time Kepler, through patient mathematical calculations and newly available data on the behavior of the planet Mars, was able to demonstrate more fully than ever before the elliptical orbit of the planets. Galileo's assumption that the universe consists of mass in motion governed by laws of mathematical dynamics[12] provided Newton with the clue that (contrary to Aristotle's law of motion, which believed that a moving body will come to a stop when it is no longer being propelled by a force) an object will not come immediately to a stop unless there is some force providing resistance. This new insight allowed Newton to formulate his famous law of inertia which teaches that every object will remain in a state of rest or continue in a straight line at the same speed unless some *force* causes it to *change*. Newton then proceeded to formulate his general law of gravitation in order to explain more adequately along quantitative lines what is involved in force and change: objects or mass particulars attract one another by a force which is directly proportional to the product of their respective masses, and inversely proportional to the squares of the distance between them. These laws which were believed to be valid throughout the universe inspired the confidence that the natural world could eventually be explained in terms of predictable mechanical causality. Many scientists hoped that, given time and the expected advances in scientific procedures and equipment, they would indeed be able to master the world.

It is obvious, however, that the old mechanical dualism of the Ptolemaic cosmology was not essentially changed but rather given greater sophistication and authority.[13] It was this Newtonian classical physics which also largely lay behind Immanuel Kant's metaphysical skepticism and his insistence that one could know only the phenomenal realm but could never really know "the world," "the soul," and "God," for these are concepts which "exist" only as categories in the mind, as it arranges phenomena through perception. It is moreover this dualistic heritage from Newton and Kant which makes it so difficult for modern man, who is conditioned by this scientific-philosophical model, to believe in providence, prayer, and miracles.

The model which currently dominates most scientific theory and procedure was ushered in by Albert Einstein with his truly revolutionary theory of relativity. The mechanical interpretations of Newtonian classical physics eventually broke down when they proved unable to explain the data being received from new experimentation, particularly in the areas of electricity, magnetism, and optics. James Maxwell, for example, discovered that electromagnetic phenomena did not conform to the Newtonian views of gravitation and thus began to interpret nature more in terms of fields of energy than of mass or substance. This in turn opened the way for Max Planck to develop his quantum theory which maintained somewhat paradoxically that matter does not so much "exist" but rather demonstrates certain restless "tendencies to exist" by individualizing its own identity in patterns of energy. These patterns are not so much seen as discerned through mathematical calculations and projections.

Albert Einstein took the discoveries from Maxwell and Planck yet a step further by teaching that space is not a three-dimensional realm nor is time a separate entity but rather that both are inseparably fused in a four-dimensional relationship which must be understood as the "space-time continuum." Although matter must still be *portrayed* with images of mass or particles, as atomic physicist Fritjof Capra explains, the theory of relativity means that

> the particles can no longer be pictured as static three-dimensional objects, like billiard balls or grains of sand, but must be conceived as four-dimensional entities in space-time. Their forms have to be understood dynamically, as forms in space and time. Subatomic particles are dynamic patterns, patterns of activity that have a space aspect and a time aspect. Their space aspect makes them appear as objects with a certain mass; their time aspect, as processes involving the equivalent energy. Relativity theory thus gives the constituents of matter an intrinsically dynamic aspect. The particles of the subatomic world are not only active by moving around very fast, they themselves are processes! The being of matter and its activity cannot be separated. They are but different aspects of the same space-time reality.[14]

Whatever else the new Einsteinian cosmology may involve—and the implications have by no means been finally assessed—it is nevertheless abundantly clear that the earlier Ptolemaic and Newtonian dualism is no longer tenable. There is here, as T. F. Torrance boldly declares, a "radical reorientation in knowledge in which structure and matter, form and being are inseparably fused together, spelling the end of the analytical era in science."[15] He goes on to add:

> For the first time, then, in the history of thought, Christian theology finds itself in the throes of a new scientific culture which is not antithetical to it, but which operates with a non-dualistic outlook upon the universe which is not inconsistent with the Christian faith, even at the crucial points of creation and incarnation.[16]

Not only has the old epistemological dualism been challenged, but categories such as time and process are receiving new attention in a way that may open the possibility for a fuller understanding of the Christian meaning of history and eschatology.

Religion and the Development of Science

It must now be asked, "What role, if any, has religion played in this historical development of science?" While there can be little doubt that ancient Greece, with men like Euclid, Aristarchus, and Archimedes, contributed significantly to the early beginnings of science, it is quite surprising and significant that science in the fullest sense did not arise there. The world will ever need to be grateful to the early Greek cosmologists for their capacity to sense the inherent unity of the universe and their struggle to conceptualize its natural patterns of behavior, but their efforts were still primarily speculative exercises which, when they remained concerned with nature, led eventually to the irrational futility of the Atomists. Not only was Plato's dualistic division of reality into eternal forms and their shadowy temporal manifestations an obstacle to science, but his view of creation by the "Demiurgos," who was forced to use recalcitrant matter, also discouraged investigation into nature. Aristotle, whose early interests in biology for the purposes of classification are surely to be commended, did not develop his scientific interests but gave greater attention to metaphysics, logic, and linguistics. His celebrated concept of First Cause left the Greeks with a very impersonal, abstract, unknowable force pulling nature to itself and was far more an impetus for speculation than scientific investigation. While one must admit that the origin and development of science is an extremely complex movement involving many personal, social, economic, political, and even geographical factors, it remains a historical fact, as Stanley L. Jaki observes, that

> science suffered a stillbirth not only in Greece but in all great ancient cultures, in India, in China, in pre-Columbian America, in Egypt, and in Babylon. A careful reading of their philosophical, religious, and scientific documents, many of which are available in modern language translations, indicates a common factor of those stillbirths. The factor was the belief in

> an eternal, cyclic recurrence of everything in a universe which was taken as the ultimate entity.[17]

When, however, the Greek passion for rationality in human thinking and the Judaic-Christian confidence in God's rational concern for creation and history were eventually fused into medieval Christian theology, the foundation was laid for modern science. The "inexpungeable belief that every detailed occurrence can be correlated with its antecedents in a perfectly definite manner, exemplifying general principles" is, according to A. N. Whitehead, the greatest contribution of medievalism to the formation of the scientific movement. He reasons furthermore in an oft quoted passage:

> When we compare this tone of thought in Europe with the attitude of other civilisations when left to themselves, there seems but one source for its origin. It must come from the medieval insistence on the rationality of God, conceived as with the personal energy of Jehovah and with the rationality of a Greek philosopher. . . .
>
> In Asia, the conceptions of God were of a being who was either too arbitrary or too impersonal for such ideas to have much effect on instinctive habits of mind. . . . My explanation is that the faith in the possibility of science, generated antecedently to the development of modern scientific theory, is an unconscious derivative from medieval theology.[18]

Religion has also contributed to science by teaching it, according to the great principle of the Reformation, that one learns from nature just as one learns from the Bible—by listening to it and being sensitive to its claims. Francis Bacon, who may be called the father of modern science, or at least the creative inspiration for the inductive method which lies at its base, sought very deliberately to employ John Calvin's method of interpreting "the books of God" to the task of understanding "the books of nature." He understood the scientist to be the priest of creation whose task it was to discern the secrets of nature and share them with his fellowmen to the glory of God. To accomplish this, one must be willing to respond to the object under investigation in a manner that is appropriate to its own peculiar quality. Just as one must be willing to obey the "Word of God," he must be willing to follow "the works of God" wherever they lead. This requires that an interpreter be humble and never seek to impose his own a priori thought patterns or preconceived concepts upon the object but rather allow it to manifest to him its true nature.[19]

Perhaps it is obvious from even this brief glimpse into the history of science that there is no real direct line of development in the sense of one discovery proceeding either logically or empirically to the next. Rather it seems that science progresses through a series of visions or breakthroughs very much akin to that which religion calls insight or even "revelation." Something of a creative leap often is taken after a certain functional plateau has been reached and existing hypothetical models are no longer able to account satisfactorily for the wealth of information being received. These advances, or in some cases revolutions, cannot be explained on the basis of the abundance of accumulative effort being extended upon inductive research and deductive reasoning. The point is illustrated beautifully by Max Planck who writes in his *Scientific Autobiography* that "when the pioneer in science sends forth the grasping feelers of his thoughts, he must have a vivid intuitive imagination, for new ideas are not generated by deduction, but by an artistically creative imagination."[20] In other words, the truly creative inspiration for science seems always to come from outside and a little beyond the current working model or system. There are many in the history of science like Galileo, Kepler, Boyle, Newton, Bacon, and Einstein who have even been willing to express their consciousness of a numinous feeling which often accompanied their endeavors. They spoke of thinking God's thoughts after him, reading the books of God's works and sitting down before the facts as a little child in order to learn the deeper mysteries of God. To cite only one example, Einstein wrote, when he was seventy-one years old to Maurice Solovine, a close friend and scientific colleague: "I have never found a better expression than the expression 'religious' for this trust in the rational nature of reality and of its peculiar accessibility to the human mind. Where this trust is lacking science degenerates into an uninspired procedure."[21] Such testimonies, when left standing alone, do not of course demonstrate the value of religious experience in general, much less the truth of the Christian faith. They may nevertheless invite both the scientist and the Christian to recognize the necessity for humble insight wherever truth is found.

Selected Contemporary Paradigms

Since it will obviously be impossible to survey the whole panorama of modern science, it must suffice to present some representative scientific theses or postures which can serve as paradigms for assessing the contemporary relationship between science and religion.

Cosmic Grandeur

Consider first the understanding which science has of the universe as a whole in its astronomical and cosmological framework. The planet earth with its core of molten metal is crusted over with a hard surface of siliceous rocks which are in turn overlaid with water, soil, and vegetation. The world contains over a hundred basic elements whose nuclear structures are stable enough to be observed and classified. Planet earth moves around its sun from which it receives energy through a nuclear reaction involving primarily hydrogen and helium. Now at this point allow A. R. Peacocke, an Oxford physicist, to stretch the human capacity for spatial-temporal comprehension to its limits when he explains that the sun

> has existed for about 5,000 million years and its hydrogen is likely to last for another 10,000 million years, but not for ever. The Earth, along with the other planets in the "solar system" moves round its star, the Sun, and this system is itself part of a single galaxy containing 10^{11} stars. The galaxy has the shape of a thin disc and it takes light 60,000 years to travel across it. We look along the thickest part of the disc when we look at the Milky Way. The solar system is near to the edge at a distance of 20–25,000 light years, that is about ⅔ of its radius, from the

> centre of the galaxy, about which it rotates once in every 200 million years. The extent of interstellar space relative to the planets is enormous, as strikingly depicted by Hoyle: if the scale is reduced by a factor of 10^{10}, the Sun becomes a ball 6 inches in diameter, Mercury is then 7 yards away, the Earth 18 yards away and the size of a speck of dust, Pluto 710 yards away, and the next nearest stars 2,000 miles. This immensity of interstellar space is not strictly empty but contains mainly hydrogen atoms (ca. 90 percent) in an extremely rarefied form as well as mineral "dust." But the cosmologist soon exhausts our available supply of superlatives, for our own galaxy is but one among 10^{9} galaxies each containing 10^{8} to 10^{11} stars, so that there are roughly 10^{17} to 10^{20} stars in the universe.[22]

Now that we possess such marvelous knowledge of the vast universe swirling about us it seems even more appropriate than in the days of the psalmist to ponder: "When I look at thy heavens, the work of thy fingers, the moon and the stars which thou hast established; what is man that thou art mindful of him, and the son of man that thou dost care for him?" (Ps. 8:3-4). Just as this psalm reflects paradoxically both our insignificance in the vastness and glory of the heavens and our worth in that God does care for us, so science reveals the boundless reaches of the universe yet waiting to be explored and at the same time the wonderful capacities of scientists who are able to comprehend such greatness and who have made such progress in channeling nature's vast resources toward our own purposes. It does seem, nevertheless, if one is willing to learn, that humility is a quality which science is uniquely qualified to teach. Nature must therefore be allowed through the unordained ministries of science to reveal to us both the wonders and limitations of our knowledge and our need of one who is greater than we ourselves and this world. Humility may even prepare us for the coming of God in the incarnate Christ who does *care for us indeed!*

Quite naturally, one's scientific explanation of the origin of the universe will have direct bearing upon the Christian conviction that God created the heavens and the earth. In the past science has proposed two major models to account for the origin of the natural world. The *evolutionary*, or *"big bang" theory*, reasons backward from the speed at which the galaxies are presently moving apart to postulate a time when all matter and energy were contained in a primeval mass. This mass eventually exploded to create the conditions whereby the stars and planets could be formed. The *steady state hypothesis*, based upon the belief that the distant galaxies have approximately the same density as those nearer to the earth, maintains that the universe exists now in approximately the same manner it always has. Yet a third *model of oscillation* has now appeared alongside the steady state theory to account for what scientists believe to be the expansion and contraction of the galaxies in the universe. While the consequences of entropy remain an eventual threat, this latter view sometimes reflects a sense of teleological balance within the cosmic process.[23] As long as the Christian is allowed to maintain his or her faith in God as the *ultimate* source of all that exists and the creator even of time itself, he or she need find no conflict in scientific descriptions of the *method* which God may use to accomplish his purposes with the natural universe. Scientific hypotheses to account for either the origin or behavior of the natural world are relevant for faith particularly as they may influence forms of expressing belief, but they should never be allowed to determine the limits of God's power or the content of one's personal encounter with God through Christ. Martin Luther captures the real heart of the issue here when he begins his Christian interpretation of God as creator of heaven and earth in his small catechism by declaring, "I believe that God has created *me*."[24] The whole thrust of biblical cosmology is that God in his power over nature is adequate to accomplish his *redemptive purposes*. If one therefore is experiencing God's redemption in Christ, this should be more than enough evidence that God can create and sustain the world through any method he may choose.

Atomic Wonder

Recent developments, especially in physics, have also increased man's sense of the microscopic grandeur of the universe when viewed in its atomic structure. Scientists have discovered that atoms, far from being the hard substances they were believed to be by the ancients, are now known to be essentially patterns of energy reflecting qualities much more akin to mind or spirit than to tangible physical objects. The layman needs to be reminded that atoms are so far removed from the ordinary world of sense experience that no one has ever in fact "seen" an atom; however, through experimentation and observation of the results when atomic theories are applied, atoms are nonetheless believed to be real. In order to get a more accurate impression of the infinitesimal dimensions involved in atomic formations it will be necessary once again to turn to the specialist. Fritjof Capra projects some of these dimensions graphically:

> The diameter of an atom is about one hundred millionth of an inch. To visualize this diminutive size, try the following: Imagine an orange blown up to the size of the earth. The atoms in the enlarged orange will then be as big as cherries.
>
> An atom, therefore, is extremely small compared to microscopic objects, but it is huge compared to the nucleus in its center. Even in a cherry-size atom, the nucleus would be invisible. If we blew up the atom to the size of a room, the nucleus would still be too small to be seen by the naked eye! To see the nucleus, we would have to blow up the atom to the size of a huge dome, say, the Houston Astrodome. In an atom of that size, the nucleus would be the size of a grain of salt! A grain of salt in the middle of the Astrodome and specks of dust whirling around in the vast space of the dome—this is how we can picture the nucleus and electrons of an atom.[25]

Solid things therefore "exist" as waves or patterns of probability that interconnect to form the observable objects men normally perceive through sense experience. According to Werner Heisenberg's principle of uncertainty or indeterminacy, science is at present unable to determine both the position of an electron and its momentum at the same time, thus making it impossible to construct a comprehensive causal determinism on the basis of modern atomic theory. While being very careful not to give the appearance of trying to establish religion on a foundation which could be easily swept away in the next scientific revolution, Arthur S. Eddington believes that the world of physics, which is largely derived from mental symbols, provides good evidence that ultimate reality is spiritual:

> Recognizing that the physical world is entirely abstract and without "actuality" apart from its linkage to consciousness, we restore consciousness to the fundamental position, instead of representing it as an inessential complication occasionally found in the midst of inorganic nature at a late state of evolutionary history.[26]

Eddington is even willing to go yet a step further and concludes that "the idea of a universal Mind or Logos would be a fairly plausible inference from the present state of scientific theory."[27] Although these atomic hypotheses do not pretend to prove that the universe is personalistic, they do mean the old mechanistic view of the world where mind was considered as an intruder is no longer valid. If there is therefore no convincing physical support for cosmological determinism, then the major scientific obstacle to allowing the witness of revelation to speak for itself has been, if not finally destroyed, at least rationally neutralized or contained.[28]

Organic Processes

Thus far the illustrations selected to represent the modern scientific concensus have come from the macroscopic realm of cosmological space and the microscopic sphere of atomic theory where the universe can be broken up into separate units or inorganic structures. Models constructed within these frames of reference are quite naturally going to be less dynamic than those drawn from the biological sciences where nature as organic life, and not matter and energy alone, provide the basic hermeneutical thrust. Consequently the more mechanical sciences such as physics and chemistry must always be interpreted alongside biology with its insistence on organic systems and life processes if a balanced understanding of science is to be maintained. Anyone, therefore, who wants to understand the relationship between science and religion today must be prepared to struggle with the dialectical tensions between the models which are built upon space-time-energy factors and those which are more life-system-process oriented. Since nature obviously includes both of these elements, any comprehensive scientific world-view cannot afford to allow either of the polarities to dominate or either of them to be neglected. This same counsel also seems appropriate for any comprehensive model of religion which seeks to relate the dialectical tensions between divine stability and the redemptive process to the world of contemporary science.

Ever since Charles Darwin published his monumental *Origin of Species* in 1859 the major stream of the biological sciences has developed along the lines of his major theses regarding the principle of natural selection: (1) All living creatures procreate more of their kind than can possibly survive within the limitations of food and space available to them. (2) These offspring possess an almost infinite variety among themselves. (3) There is a necessary struggle for existence among these beings due to the overpopulation. (4) The variety which exists among these living beings quite naturally means that some are better fit for longer life and greater reproductivity. (5) Those capacities which are better adapted for survival are naturally selected over successive generations. These various factors continually interact resulting in progressive adaptability and evolution of the species. At first Darwin believed that his evolutionary hypothesis was compatible with the concept of a purposeful creator for he concluded the *Origin of Species* with the following moving confession:

> There is a grandeur in this view of life, with its several powers, having been originally breathed by the Creator into a few forms or into one; and, that whilst this planet has gone cycling on according to the fixed law of gravity, from so simple a beginning endless forms most beautiful and most wonderful have been, and are being evolved.[29]

Later, however, in his autobiography Darwin indicated that he had come to the conviction through his discoveries that there was no need to postulate a divine being to account for the process. Regardless of what Darwin himself believed, there can be little doubt that the biological theses of evolution were pressed into the service of a metaphysical naturalism which tended increasingly to deny the possibility of any supernatural direction within or over the basic life-force.[30] However, biology is notoriously weak when it comes to questions of teleology because it does not possess within itself the philosophical means to determine what goals or values should be present within a given teleological set or context. Consequently, biologists have been, and are destined to remain, divided concerning the issue of whether there is design in the life processes.

The matter must eventually be determined, it seems, by one's overall system of values and sense of cosmic purpose. Perhaps a truce can now be established whereby biologists, teleologists, and Christians alike can appreciate the contribution evolution can make by describing the biological transformations that take place in the natural order of the species—while acknowledging its absolute impotence for explaining the ultimate origin and destiny of life. Paul Weiss, professor of biology at the Rockefeller Institute of New York willingly admits this limitation in his essay "Experience and Experiment in Biology" published in 1962:

> The center of gravity of the life sciences has steadily shifted on this scale from the descriptive and normative end of natural history toward the analytical and formulative end of the exact sciences. Of course, the assumption that biology could ever reach the physical end is a delusion, based either on lack of realistic acquaintance with living systems and their true nature or unawareness of the conceptual limitations of physical reductionism. This is not to question our success in reducing cellular phenomena to molecular terms. However, to pretend that the process can be reversed, that the molecular shambles can reassemble themselves into a functional living system without the cheating intervention of another living system is a conceptual perversion, whatever one may think of the primordial origin of life.[31]

In like manner, D. E. Green and R. F. Goldberger concede these same methodological boundaries in their book entitled *Molecular Insights into the Living Process* when they explain:

> There is one step [in evolution] that far outweighs the others in enormity: the step from macromolecules to cells. All the other steps can be accounted for on theoretical grounds—if not correctly, at least elegantly. However, the macromolecule to cell transition is a jump of fantastic dimensions, which lies beyond the range of testable hypothesis. In this area, all is conjecture. The available facts do not provide a basis for postulation that cells arose on this planet. This is not to say that some paraphysical forces were at work. We simply wish to point out that there is no scientific evidence.[32]

Although some might be willing to argue that there is a chance that the very indeterminacy or randomness of the molecule might at least hypothetically be able to account for the origin of protein molecules, there is simply not sufficient time for this to be even plausible. Edward McCrady postulates that:

> Even for the origin of one protein molecule by chance alone, Professor Charles-Eugene Guye has shown that 10^{243} billions of years would be required if the number of combinations were some 500 billion per second, and if the number of atoms from which its components came were equal to the number in the earth. But protein molecules are known to have arisen on this earth in a span of time less than 2 or 3 billion years. It would take an incredible act of faith to believe in so remote a probability as that this occurred by chance alone. Personally, I find it quite beyond my gullibility.[33]

Just as evolution alone proves inadequate to account for the origin of life, so is it incapable of explaining the capacity of man for self-consciousness and the pursual of transcendent goals. These dimensions can only be interpreted appropriately with values and categories derived from the life of the mind and spirit of the person rather than allowing the higher forms of thought, aspiration, and interpersonal relationships to be explained in terms of impulse, stimulation, and physical adaptability. Biology along with all the other sciences must base its hypotheses on the building blocks or smaller units of information discovered in its research. It should of course contain nothing in its hypotheses which is inconsistent with the lower units of information, but the larger mental patterns should always retain interpretative control. As long as the biological sciences are willing to remain within these legitimate scientific confines, realizing that they account neither for the origin of life nor its highest accomplishments, the Christian will be able to welcome their teleological descriptions.

The New Biology

There is a new revolution in biological science which is every bit as spectacular as the development in the new physics and perhaps even more awesome in its potential for constructive or destructive uses as far as man is concerned. This is the new biology inaugurated in 1953 when J. D. Watson and F. H. C. Crick discovered the molecular structure of DNA and its chemical counterpart RNA.[34] The functional relationship between DNA and RNA is not yet fully known, but it is believed that DNA serves as a blueprint or pattern that the cells are chemically programmed to follow and that RNA guides or implements the growth of these cells according to their DNA code. Rick Gore's popular presentation may help the nonexpert to grasp the plastic marvel of a human cell.

> Enormously long strands of DNA intertwine within the core of living cells. So narrow and tightly coiled is this DNA that all the genes in all the cells in a human body would fit into a box the size of an ice cube. Yet if all this DNA were unwound and joined together, the string could stretch from the earth to the sun and back more than 400 times.
>
> Moreover, biologists have found that virtually every cell contains the entire repertoire of genes for that plant or animal. One cell in my toe, say, has all the data in its DNA for making another man physically identical to me. That many instructions, if written out, would fill a thousand 600-page books. The unique experiences of our lives, of course, make us more than a product of our genes. Yet it is our DNA that sets the basic physical limits of what we can or cannot become.[35]

The psalmist was therefore certainly wiser than he knew when he praised his creator for the intricate formations of his body and its mysterious source:

> For thou didst form my inward parts,
> thou didst knit me together in my mother's womb.
> I praise thee, for thou art fearful and wonderful.
> Wonderful are thy works!
> Thou knowest me right well;
> my frame was not hidden from thee,
> when I was being made in secret,
> intricately wrought in the depths of the earth.
> Thy eyes beheld my unformed substance;
> in thy book were written, every one of them,
> the days that were formed for me,
> when as yet there was none of them. (Ps. 139:13-16)

However, modern biology is understandably not as interested in the creative origin of human life as it is in exercising control over its development. Crick's confident belief that the "decisive controls of life" can be reduced to a precise order of chemical determinance in the chain of DNA has led many biologists to assume that the basic life processes are ultimately explicable in terms of their biochemical interactions.[36] There are, however, those such as Michael Polanyi who maintain that DNA alone does not determine the biological structure of human life. For example, Polanyi argues that:

> The pattern of organic bases in DNA which functions as a genetic code is a boundary condition irreducible to physics and chemistry. Further controlling principles of life may be represented as a hierarchy of boundary conditions extending, in the case of man, to consciousness and responsibility.[37]

Naturally the pursual of this issue must be left to the scientists themselves. One result, however, is certain: molecular biologists can now alter the very rudiments of life by combining genes into completely new substances called "recombinant DNA." These powers now available through the new biology give man a control over his own destiny and that of his fellow creatures which he has never before possessed. The dangers inherent in faulty equipment, unperfected technique, and the ever-present possibility for selfish misuse literally frightened scientists into a self-imposed moratorium in their research until they could establish procedural guidelines to protect the community at large as well as the enterprise itself. The scientific establishment had never done anything like this before—not even when developing the atomic bomb! Experimentation is now proceeding in hopes that the greatest risks for danger have been recognized and can be avoided. The debate concerning the direction and extent of these frontiers is, however, destined to continue for some time to come. Dr. Shaw Livermore, professor of American history at the University of Michigan and member of a faculty committee to explore the possibilities for a DNA research center at that university, voices the concern of many when he wonders, quite simply, if man will have the intellectual and moral capacity to cope with such potential. He says, "I know of no more elemental capability, even including manipulation of nuclear forces. . . . It should not demean man to say that we may now be unable to manage successfully a capability for altering life itself."[38] Thus the new biology, like the other sciences, thrusts a challenge on modern man which is essentially spiritual. The promise from this field in such areas as agriculture, cancer prevention and cure, hereditary malformations, and biochemically related mental illness appear to be virtually unlimited. It is hoped that Christ's spirit will be allowed to direct these creative energies toward their highest potential.

Toward Rapprochement

Although the church must try to understand the world's contemporary scientific conditioning and communicate the gospel with a respectable awareness of those sensitive areas where it coexists with science, it should never become so identified with any scientific model that it compromises its prophetic responsibility to all strands of culture including science. If it is true as

Emile Cailliet says that "comprehensive philosophical views prove to be in part abandoned rationalizations of an obsolete science," then religion must be doubly on guard.[39] It has the perennial challenge to present its message in a relevant way to the popular mind, which has in all probability been shaped by a philosophy inspired in turn by a science that is no longer viable. A self-destructive tendency seems therefore to be built into any excessive concern of the church to be relevant. What often happens is that religion becomes so identified with a scientific perspective, such as the classical physics of Newtonianism, that believers can no longer distinguish between the content of their faith and the scientific world-view which is merely its cosmological stage-setting. Then when the old patterns of scientific thinking begin to change or are swept away by a scientific movement such as relativity, it appears as though the bases for religious faith have been destroyed and many begin to think that the gospel is no longer relevant. The challenge for the Christian is however, according to Paul, "Do not be conformed to this world but be transformed by the renewal of your mind," which means quite literally do not be schematized, συσχηματίζεσθε, by the thought patterns and fashion of the age, but rather let the will of God instruct you and the culture around you concerning "what is good and acceptable and perfect" (Rom. 12:2). If believers can therefore realize that every scientific explanation, when pursued to its quantitative limits, will eventually bring us to that ultimate threshold where the metaphysical questions remain open, we will then be better prepared to accept the descriptive contributions of science for what they are and will become more effective in our own vocation by confronting the scientist with ultimate questions.

The principle of complementarity formulated by Niels Bohr illustrates the willingness of modern science to admit that religion is not alone in its need for categories such as mystery and paradox. Bohr originally proposed this theory in 1927 in atomic physics to account for the evidence that the particle and wave hypotheses were exclusive of one another, and yet at the same time both indispensable to explain the transmission of light. According to one model, light travels from particle to particle or place to place while on the other hand it gives observers the impression of moving along waves of definite impulses. The implications of this principle have been explored in psychology by W. Pauli and P. Jordan, in logic by C. F. von Weizsacker, and in theology by H. Schrey and G. Howe; however, no one shows the significance of its scientific context for religion more clearly than Bohr himself. Notice, for example, how he extends the scientific principle of complementarity into religion when he seeks to reconcile the mutually exclusive though equally legitimate and indispensable claims of righteousness and love in religious experience:

> Although the narrowest possible unification of righteousness and love in all cultures presents a common goal, it must nevertheless be recognized that in every situation where the strict application of righteousness is demanded, there is no longer free room for the unfolding of love, and that on the other hand the highest demands which grow out of a feeling of love could be contrary to all concepts of righteousness. This situation, which is presented mythically in many religions through the conflict between various divine personifications of such basic qualities, is in fact one of the most appropriate analogies to the complementary relationship between physical phenomena which are described with varied elementary concepts.[40]

Surely the principle of complementarity is not intended as a final solution for the tensions between science and religion. But the fact that science itself recognizes the role of paradox would seem to enhance that category when it is applied to religious mysteries. If science accepts without fully explaining such necessary complements as the brain and the mind, physical causation and psychical freedom, the particle and wave theories of light, then such paradoxes as the deity and humanity of Christ, the sovereignty of God and the freedom of man along with the oneness and threefoldness of God, can perhaps become compatible with the way truly wise men respond to the mysterious realities of life.

Religion often responds to scientific theory in an ambiguous manner. Consider, for example, how the second law of thermodynamics is interpreted by some to support the belief in a creation and by others to herald the annihilation of the universe. The first law of thermodynamics deals with the conservation of energy, in distinction from the principle of the conservation of matter, and maintains that the amount of energy in the world though changing in form remains constant and available. Whereas the second law postulates that the tendency of all physical systems to seek their equilibrium means there will come a time when energy will no longer be available. This increase of entropy, as it is sometimes called, means not only that there appears to be an infinitesimal cooling down of energy-producing heat within the world's various physical systems, but implies that inevitably in the universe itself there is also an inherent tendency within natural systems toward disorder and randomness that is cosmically irreversible. So while some interpreters of nature profess to see a teleological pattern, or patterns, progressing to higher and more complex expressions of purpose, the physicist, according to this law, claims that the breakup of one physical pattern or system into another indicates a decrease in available energy and a gradual disintegration of cosmic order. Assuming this law to be scientifically valid, what is its significance for Christian faith? It is possible on one hand to disparage the power of the biblical creator, since the universe, according to this law, is now proving to be inadequately endowed. Yet it is equally valid to reason that since the world is progressing to a point in time where there will be no more energy, there must have been some earlier point in time, i.e., creation, when the world with all its energy *began*. The issue, however, may not be so much a temporal question in terms of an original creation or an end of time but rather in what sense is the believer *dependent upon the existence of the world?* The gradual demise of the universe may be a scientifically established law, and physicists will surely continue to function on the basis of this hypothesis unless they are convinced otherwise through sound scientific evidence. However, Christians have nothing to fear from this principle because they do not build their faith upon the existence of the *world* but upon their encounter with God through his Word, which also teaches them that this cosmos will pass away (I John 2:17). As long as we believe that we are kept in God's power, we can await with confidence his consummation of the world, whether or not it transpires within the framework of some recognized natural law, for we have been assured

> the day of the Lord will come like a thief, and then the heavens will pass away with a loud noise, and the elements will be dissolved with fire, and the earth and the works that are upon it will be burned up.
>
> Since all these things are thus to be dissolved, what sort of persons ought you to be in lives of holiness and godliness, waiting for and hastening the coming of the day of God, because of which the heavens will be kindled and dissolved, and the elements will melt with fire! But according to his promise we wait for new heavens and a new earth in which righteousness dwells. (II Peter 3:10-13)

Meanwhile the church will seek to act as wisely as possible in light of its scientific knowledge of available energy and continue to believe in the same universe of truth, but from yet another sphere, that Christ remains the Lord of creation, the Alpha and Omega (Rev. 22:13).

Another contribution which can come from the dialogue between modern science and religion is the realization that matter need no longer be considered antithetical to the human spirit, as it was in Platonic dualism, and to some degree in Newtonian physics, but can now be understood more fully as the tangible energizing counterpart of personality. In fact Teilhard de Chardin believes that within the very structure of matter itself there resides a spiritual impetus which is essential to human love and a sense of community.

> Considered in its full biological reality, love—that is to say, the affinity of being with being—is not peculiar to man. It is a general property of all life and as such it embraces, in its varieties and degrees, all the forms successively adopted by organized matter. . . . If there were no internal propensity to

> unite, even at a prodigiously rudimentary level—indeed in the molecule itself—it would be physically impossible for love to appear higher up, with us, in "hominised" form. By rights, to be certain of its presence in ourselves, we should assume its presence, at least in an inchoate form, in everything that is.[41]

However this may be from the scientific standpoint, the Christian doctrine of creation and incarnation coincide remarkably well with the new insights from science concerning the dynamic dimensions of matter. When the angel of the Lord says to a young Galilean girl, "the Holy Spirit will come upon you, and the power of the Most High will overshadow you," God is not only accomplishing something of profound redemptive significance but endorsing the spiritual value of matter as well (Luke 1:35). God is revealing that matter is not only made and sustained by him in creation but that moreover it possesses those qualities which are compatible with his self-revelation through a tangible incarnation. It is as though God in Christ takes up into himself the humble stuff of matter, the very elements which comprise the material form of all created things in order to underscore his involvement with nature and his commitment to fulfill his purposes in and through creation.

Modern science is furthermore capable of helping the Christian to understand more profoundly than ever before the significance of God's method of working through natural and historical *processes*. Science, not only through its abundant progress in the practical, technological spheres but also from its recent advances in astronomy, physics, chemistry, and biology, seems literally to cry out that the universe must be interpreted in dynamic terms. The whole cosmos and all its organic life, as this is crowned with the spiritual freedom of man, appears to be in a state of change and process. Now while Christians believe that "Christ is the same yesterday and today and for ever," we also know that God is involved with the whole of his creation at every moment of time (Heb. 13:8). Did not Christ declare on one occasion, "My Father is working still, and I am working" (John 5:17)? Without losing confidence in the steadfast nature of God and the faithfulness with which he accomplishes his purposes, contemporary Christians may welcome the process models in both science and philosophy as a challenge to their own participation in, and indeed contribution to, the work of God in the world.

Science and Miracles

If the preceding discussion can be deemed scientifically reliable, though obviously fragmentary and nontechnical, what can be said for the Christian claim that miracles have happened in biblical times, on occasion throughout history, and even remain a live possibility in today's world? One can, of course, treat the matter merely as a semantical question simply by understanding natural law as that which explains the natural course of events, thus ruling out the concept of the miraculous by definition. Another possibility is to expect that whatever might be considered miraculous, in a given age, will one day be explained by science. Yet a third alternative would be content to leave science and religion in separate compartments and force any claim for the miraculous into an isolated spiritual realm.[42] All of these proposals are bound to prove unacceptable to Christians who are convinced that their world and experience are united, that all truth resides ultimately in the one true God, and that their encounter with Christ through the biblical revelation is genuinely transcendent.

At the very outset one should be grateful for the understanding of nature which science has provided, since it is only within this larger context that the concept of miracle can have any meaning. Friedrich Schleiermacher was unquestionably right when he maintained: "It can never be necessary in the interest of religion so to interpret a fact that its dependence on God absolutely excludes its being conditioned by the system of Nature."[43] It is at just this point that modern science has provided an understanding of nature which allows the occurrence of miracle to be at least an intelligible claim for the past and an open possibility for the present. Albert Einstein is certainly not alone among modern scientists when he writes to Maurice Solovine concerning the miraculous quality of the world:

> You find it surprising that I think of the comprehensibility of the world (in so far as we are entitled to speak of such world) as a miracle or an eternal mystery. But surely, a priori, one should expect the world to be chaotic, not to be grasped by thought in any way. One might (indeed one *should*) expect that the world evidence itself as lawful only so far as we grasp it in an orderly fashion. This would be a sort of order like the alphabetical order of words of a language. On the other hand, the kind of order created, for example, by Newton's gravitational theory is a very different character. Even if the axioms of the theory are posited by man, the success of such a procedure supposes in the objective world a high degree of order which we are in no way entitled to expect *a priori*. Therein lies the "miracle" which becomes more and more evident as our knowledge develops. . . . And here is the weak point of positivists and of professional atheists, who feel happy because they think that they have not only pre-empted the world of the divine, but also of the miraculous. Curiously, we have to be resigned to recognizing the "miracle" without having any legitimate way of getting any further.[44]

Although Einstein to be sure is not giving a witness for miracle in a Christian sense, he is presenting an understanding of nature which is amenable to such a claim. Neither more nor less should be expected from science.

The common human experience wherein one exercises one's will and consequently sets an action or series of actions in motion and causes things to happen provides the basic analogical point of departure for the concept of miracle. For example a book lying on a desk is properly understood and interpreted within its given context of gravitation and inertia. When someone wills to pick it up and takes appropriate steps to accomplish that procedure, a different, if you please higher, frame of reference is necessary to comprehend the event. Moreover, if one should will the removal of the book, actually do so, and proceed to declare the intention of one's action, then yet a higher level of interpretation is available to explain the event. This is what the Christian believes takes place, on a much higher level of course, when a miracle occurs. Nature responds to a higher purposive will than mere mechanical motion, and the purpose of God is revealed through his accompanying word. Understood in this way miracle is not merely some extraordinary, inexplicable event but an intelligible manifestation of God himself as personal and loving in and through an unusual event.

A Christian definition of miracle, whether it be the claim that a miraculous event in the Bible has actually occurred or that some subsequent event corresponds strikingly with the biblical account of miracles, *will consequently involve these basic elements: (1) an interpretation of nature which allows at least the possibility of its being transcended by the creator, (2) reliable attestation and belief that the event cannot be explained on the basis of natural causes alone but occurs as the result of the will and power of Christ as this is (3) confirmed by his accompanying interpretative word which illuminates the meaning of the event and clarifies its redemptive purpose. In fact it is really the convergence of event and word which constitutes a Christian miracle*. For if God were to act solely through event there would be no real distinguishing factor between an episode which he might cause and any other occasion either ordinary or extraordinary. And if he only produced certain insights, even though these were capable of verbal formulations, there could be no valid distinction between his word and any other lofty insights or imaginations one might have. The integration of event and illumination through Jesus who is "mighty in deed and word" therefore provides the necessary hermeneutical balance for a proper understanding of miracle in the Christian faith (Luke 24:19).

According to the Gospel of John, Christ is willing to base his claim for divine sonship and authority confidently upon his miraculous deeds when he says, "If I had not done among them the works which no one else did, they would not have sin; but now they have seen and hated both me and my Father" (John 15:24). But remember now, Christ not only does the works, he interprets their meaning and relation to him. And according to the Gospel of Luke,

Christ realizes clearly that a miracle, even the raising of one from the dead, would be ineffectual unless one were willing to receive the divine word. In his parable of the rich man and Lazarus, he tells the rich man who wanted Lazarus to be raised from the dead and to warn his brothers of the danger of their fate: "If they do not hear Moses and the prophets, neither will they be convinced if some one should rise from the dead" (Luke 16:31). The New Testament, therefore, commends the faith of those who are open to possibilities of God's entering and acting within his world in extraordinary and wonderful ways, and who are willing to trust God and not presumptuously demand a sign (I Cor. 1:22). If indeed the Christian life is to be understood and experienced as personal faith and trust, the believer should not surrender his ultimate values or rationality to an impersonal system of natural laws, nor should he expect God to intervene every time man wishes, for either of these alternatives would make faith as trust impossible (see John 2:23-25; 4:46-53; 6:26; 11:39-44).

The Hymn of the Universe

It may now be concluded that science and religion are indeed complementary to one another in such basic areas as their insistence on the spiritual affinities and capabilities of matter, their mutual need for humility when confronting the infinite and mysterious, and the dependence which science has upon religion for values and religion upon science for an understanding of natural form and structure. The Christian can consequently look upon the whole natural universe as a sacramental altar upon which we may lay the fruits of our labors as an offering of thanksgiving to the Lord of all creation. *Everything*, except of course that which is deliberately contrary to the will of God, can according to the apostle Paul, bring honor to God and reflect the beauty and design of his creation: "Whether you eat or drink, or whatever you do, do all to the glory of God" (I Cor. 10:31). The challenge of correlating scientific labor and this Christian vision has probably never been more heroically embodied than in the work and life of

Teilhard de Chardin. Once while engaged in a paleontological expedition on the lonely plains of central China, Teilhard found himself without the prescribed sacred objects necessary for celebrating mass according to his Roman Catholic priestly order, whereupon he decided to employ the common elements all about him to consecrate the approaching day and all its work as a symbolic gift to the Lord:

> Since once again, Lord—though this time not in the forests of the Aisne but in the steppes of Asia—I have neither bread, nor wine, nor altar, I will raise myself beyond these symbols, up to the pure majesty of the real itself; I, your priest, will make the whole earth my altar and on it will offer you all the labours and sufferings of the world.
>
> Over there, on the horizon, the sun has just touched with light the outermost fringe of the eastern sky. Once again, beneath this moving sheet of fire, the living surface of the earth wakes and trembles, and once again begins its fearful travail. I will place on my paten, O God, the harvest to be won by this renewal of labour. Into my chalice I shall pour all the sap which is to be pressed out this day from the earth's fruits.
>
> My paten and my chalice are the depths of a soul laid widely open to all the forces which in a moment will rise up from every corner of the earth and converge upon the Spirit. Grant me the remembrance and the mystic presence of all those whom the light is now awakening to the new day.[45]

There is no better way to implement the full Christian significance of the belief that "the earth is the Lord's and the fullness thereof" than to explore the natural treasures of the universe and channel its energies for the service of our fellowman—and then offer these same labors and their results as an act of devotion to the Lord of creation (Ps. 24:1).

CHAPTER X

The Shadowside of Good

Once while struggling with the doctrine of the Trinity, Augustine became aware that his interpretation was not adequate to express the majesty of the triune God, and he confessed, "we say three persons, not in order to express it, but in order not to be silent."[1] Anyone daring to approach the awesome mystery of the good and its "shadowside," as reflected in the problem of evil and suffering, will surely experience this same feeling of inadequacy.[2] In fact, as Christians we may just have to be content to lessen the rational difficulties involved in our belief. There are, however, certain comforts and assurances that are available to heal the hurts and sustain us in our *faith*. Knowing these, we cannot keep silent. We will therefore endeavor to think reverently but realistically about this deepest of all human concerns, with the prayer that when the times of suffering come—and come they will—we may be confident that we have done everything within our power to be ready for the challenge and "having done all" we may be able "to stand" (Eph. 6:13).

The problem of evil and suffering is as old as human history and as new as the wordless awareness of this very moment that all is not well with oneself and the world. It is given classical philosophical expression by Epicurus, who, according to the Christian apologist Lactantius, taught that if both God and evil exist, there are four possible logical solutions: (1) God wants to remove evil but is unable; (2) he is able but unwilling; (3) he is neither willing nor able; (4) he is both willing and able.[3] Paradoxically this problem appears to become progressively more perplexing the higher one's belief concerning the power and goodness of God. Moreover, it is not just the existence of suffering that creates the difficulty, but the *inequity* of the distribution, the *enormity*, and *intensity* of the suffering which often constitute its greatest mystery. Thus at first appearance it seems that the power of God, or rather his lack of power to prevent suffering, is the crucial obstacle to belief. It may be, however, as Leonard Hodgson observes, that the primary issue concerns God's *character*. The essential question may be whether it is *morally* right for God to allow suffering: "It is alleged sinfulness of God in allowing the pain to exist which is the ground of disbelief. One might worship a God who suffers, but not a God who sins."[4] The real heart of the problem, therefore, seems rather to be the degree to which evil and suffering are *necessary* in the universe and human experience. The suffering which man brings upon himself and others, while certainly a formidable existential problem, can at least be accounted for theoretically. But the crucial issue concerns the "*possibility* of evil" or "*necessary* evil" which somehow must be allowed in order for reason, freedom, and goodness to exist in the world. When viewed from this perspective, it becomes clear that the problem of evil on its rational, theoretical side is fundamentally the negative counterpart to the ontological argument for the existence of God. *Must* I assume, this argument asks, the concept of a perfect being who exists in reality in order to be able to make rational sense of my thinking? Now the question is rather *must* I assume the concepts of imperfect, sinning, suffering beings who exist in reality in order to be able to make moral sense of my valuing? In other words, is it *necessary* for God to allow evil in order for him to be *God?*

Whereas *sin* is essentially personal, spiritual, moral rebellion against God himself, *evil* may be defined here provisionally as any threat to a cherished value or good, and *suffering* as that threat which in some manner, either tangibly or intangibly, brings personal distress. *Pain* in this context refers primarily to the physiological orientation of suffering. *There are therefore literally as many kinds of evil as there are values or goods to be threatened.* Some brief examples may serve to illustrate the infinite scope of the problem: If one values a certain pattern of order in nature, then any disruption of that order may rightfully be termed *natural evil;* where physical pleasure is deemed good, the presence of pain appears as *hedonistic evil;* when harmonious interpersonal relationships are believed to possess worth and then become estranged, one might speak of *relational evil;* if a certain esteemed moral standard is not properly maintained or fulfilled, *moral evil* is the appropriate designation; should the enduring quality of that which is ultimately good be in danger of destruction, this may be considered *ultimate* or *eschatological evil.*

We should be careful not to lose our sense of the mysterious quality of evil and suffering by focusing attention on the more objective mechanical aspects of the problem. There is always a danger that we will merely explore the problem from the outside by asking why the proper order of things has broken down or what caused a certain malfunction. These questions are surely valid preliminary practical considerations, but evil which is only observed ceases to be evil in that it is not *suffered.* Evil, according to Gabriel Marcel, can in reality only be grasped as evil to the extent that it *touches* someone personally as though one were involved in a lawsuit: "Being 'involved' is the fundamental fact; I cannot leave it out of account except by an unjustifiable fiction, for in doing so, I proceed as though I were God, and a God who is an onlooker at that."[5] There is, however, a danger in the other direction as well. For if suffering is considered primarily from the existential, subjective standpoint, the external structures may be overlooked. Consequently one may run the risk of considering oneself the God of one's own inner world. Both the subjective and objective dimensions of this mystery need to be carefully considered for they exist side by side in delicate dialectical tension.

Approaching Solution

There can understandably be as many views of the problem as there are interpreters and possible logical combinations within its essential elements.[6] The major streams of Western thought have nevertheless developed four major theological-philosophical "theodicies,"[7] or efforts "to justify the ways of God to man": the free-will defense, the soul-building model, existential transformationism, and the eschatological solution. As growing Christians we will no doubt want to incorporate aspects from each of these approaches into our Christian philosophy. It will be especially helpful, however, for us to realize that it is possible for only one motif to be in control, really in control, at any given moment of interpretation. Here they are in quick review.

The *free-will defense* has its orientation in Augustine and seeks to relieve God of responsibility for the problem by viewing evil as mere negation; it stresses the freedom of man and the historical fall of Adam and Eve as the cause for all evil and suffering in the race.[8] Evil in this context is largely construed in neoplatonic categories of "nonbeing." The evil which those first parents of the race chose, according to this defense, had no metaphysical existence but consisted essentially in their rejection of the good. Man's free choice of that which was not good is thus ultimately responsible for all natural evil, man's alienation from God, and the eternal separation of all those who remain estranged from their creator and redeemer.

The *soul-building* model, which finds early theological rootage in Irenaeus, does not shrink from ascribing responsibility for evil and suffering to God because he must ontologically be the cause of all that exists in his universe.[9] Since freedom to choose good necessarily involves the structural *possibility* for evil choices, God must have assumed the responsibility for evil when he created man as a free personal being. It is not the historical event of the fall of man that provides the point of departure for this view, but rather those recurring temptations and challenges throughout our lives which enable us to become disciplined and liberated children of God. The classical view of hell as eternal separation from God is often denied or minimized by this pedagogical model.

Those who, like H. Wheeler Robinson, R. Bultmann, and Victor Frankl, stress *existential transformation* are not concerned as much with the origin of evil or with soul-building as a process, but seek above all to confront suffering with a strong, courageous will in order to experience meaning in the present moment. Christians who hold this view surely do not make suffering itself a value but understand quite realistically that life is full of suffering and want to develop their vision and capacity to welcome the challenges of life. If there is to be any realization of a broad historical or communal purpose, according to this perspective, it must begin with individuals who transform their particular encounter or threat into a personal victory and a symbol of courage for others.

The *eschatological solution*, represented by John Hick in philosophy and Jürgen Moltmann and Wolfhart Pannenberg in theology, interprets evil and suffering within a linear chronological perspective and maintains that in this life there will always remain an indefinable surd, or intractable, element in the problem which can only be resolved in the future.[10] If there is no future hope that certain ills will be overcome and understood, then there is no solution possible for much human suffering and loss. The goal, however, toward which our life has been moving may eventually prove itself worth all the suffering which has gone before. The eschatological approach does not claim, of course, to be able to demonstrate a final solution here and now because the future has not arrived. It does, however, in the meantime extend the *logical framework* of the problem toward those temporal dimensions which may yet provide a final solution.

The Problem of the Good

There will be elements from each of the above four models present in the following reflections upon the problem; however, the primary concern in the ensuing discussion will not be historical observations or critical evaluations regarding these views but an effort to set forth some basic principles which will enable us to formulate our own systematic approach. From the very beginning it will be helpful to encourage the interpreter of this great mystery to *stay on the offensive* and probe the primary metaphysical question, "Where does one originally get the *good* or the value which is being threatened?" In other words, it will be unreasonable to expect anyone to give up his or her Christian faith in the face of evil and suffering until those who deny the faith can account satisfactorily for the *presence* of value—any value—in the universe! If the basic ontological question is as we mentioned earlier, "Why is there something rather than nothing?" then the crucial question for any theodicy must be, "Why do I expect good of that something?" Surely no one wants a mere verbal victory in such a vital area, but there is far more than a formal logical or linguistic dialectic involved here. The ontological depth of this issue may be illustrated by asking why men continue to live even though they realize full well there is in this life no escape from suffering, pain, and eventual death. All human life involves faith as Franz Kafka ventures:

> That there is with us a lack of faith, one cannot say. All by itself the simple fact of our life and its value for faith cannot be exhausted. . . . "Man can indeed not live not." Even in this "can indeed not" resides the frantic power of faith; in this contradiction the power receives form.[11]

This unconscious love of life in spite of the inevitable logic that suffering is an integral part of the equation is portrayed dramatically by Ivan in Dostoyevsky's *The Brothers Karamazov*. Ivan, the materialistic skeptic who boldly threatens to take the whole world between his two fists, is appalled by the lack of justice in the world. Nevertheless he confides to his sensitive brother, Alyosha:

> Do you know I've been sitting here thinking to myself: that if I didn't believe in life, if I lost faith in the woman I love, lost faith

> in the order of things, were convinced in fact that everything is a disorderly, damnable, and perhaps devil-ridden chaos, if I were struck by every horror of man's disillusionment—still I should want to live and, having once tasted of the cup, I would not turn away from it till I had drained it! . . . The centripetal force on our planet is still fearfully strong, Alyosha. I have a longing for life, and I go on living in spite of logic.[12]

Notice that Ivan does *not* commit suicide but continues to live in spite of life's rational contradictions. Obviously one does not solve the problem of evil merely by posing the question of original value. The issue, however, remains clear: unless one can first account for the origin and existence of the good, one has no right to disparage life and faith because of the problem of evil. The shadows could not be present were it not for the light.

One must moreover be cautious that one does not consider evil as mere privation which is brought about by the misuse of the human will. While granting this may appear to give some temporary relief by removing God from the responsibility of creating evil, it can never account for the ontological destructiveness of evil. Karl Jaspers is right when he argues that evil "is not just a limit; it is a destructive negation. What can destroy must be something. Nothingness, which is not, cannot destroy; as it destroys, it exists. Evil is no absence of being. It has being."[13] Those analogies which portray evil as privation are especially suited to depict the impersonal quantitative aspects of the problem. They appear at first to be profoundly personalistic yet they are in fact little more than abstractions. This imagery furthermore can never do justice to the biblical teaching of Satan as a personal being who aggressively pursues man with cunning strategies for the purpose of destroying him. Nor does it deal satisfactorily with that existential dread which we experience when we believe ourselves to be really tempted and threatened. The absence of any good which one may have grown accustomed to or begun to feel one deserves, will of course bring suffering. If, however, evil is merely an absence of some good occasioned by the failure of the will, then one should be able to redirect one's will and compensate for that which one feels is lacking and causing one's suffering. The biblical stress concerning the enslaving power of Satan which actually debilitates our power to remedy our own situation seems more adequate to explain the human condition of sin and the suffering which it brings. No, evil *is* something, or perhaps more accurately stated, the expression of *someone* quite destructive—and thus far more than mere negation.

The problem of evil may be somewhat mitigated by accepting the necessity of the stability of the natural environment for there to be any possibility of a personalistic world and moral growth. Consider for a moment what kind of potential for personal development there would be in a world where gravity never pulled against one's own desires, the inevitable collision of objects was always averted at the last moment, and historical continuity in choices played no role in proscribing responsibility. Some kind of reliable natural order is absolutely mandatory in a personal world for as H. H. Farmer says, "a world where every castle was of sand, to be washed away within a few hours by the tide, would be no fit place for personality to grow in."[14] The seeming rigidities and sharp edges of the structures of reality will continue to be the occasion of much pain and bewilderment. We must, however, be prepared to design, produce, and sustain a better universe in every single created unit and all conceivable combinations before we have the right to condemn this world as it now exists. The man of faith, it is hoped, would rather stand alongside Job and bow before the Creator who asks: "Where were you when I laid the foundation of the earth? Tell me, if you have understanding. Who determined its measurements—surely you know! Or who stretched the line upon it?" (Job 38:4-5). There is therefore a sense in which Leibniz's confident assertion of this as the best of all possible worlds is biblically valid, not in the shallow optimistic, rationalistic way in which he used it, but as a declaration of faith in the power, wisdom, and love of Him who is the best of all possible gods!

Although quantitative and structural dimensions are surely involved in every encounter with evil and suffering,

Christians must always come in the last analysis to interpret their solution within the framework of personalistic analogies. This is true simply because it is one's personal *values* which are threatened by the presence of evil and suffering. David Hume is typical of many who taunt the theist with arguments inspired by impersonal imagery when he likens the maker of the universe to an architect who is capable of building a perfect house. Why, he asks, would he deliberately allow imperfections in the structure which would inevitably lead to confusion and all kinds of discomforts? And yet again he scoffs, if a builder were constructing a cage for his pet would he not do everything within his power to provide for the comfort of the creature?[15] Dostoyevsky provides an even clearer illustration of the limitations of impersonal imagery in handling this problem when in *The Brothers Karamazov* he has Ivan ask Alyosha:

> Tell me yourself, I challenge you—answer. Imagine that you are creating a fabric of human destiny with the object of making men happy in the end, giving them peace and rest at last, but that it was essential and inevitable to torture to death only one tiny creature—that baby beating its breast with its fist, for instance—and to found that edifice on its unavenged tears, would you consent to be the architect on those conditions? Tell me, and tell me the truth.[16]

These analogies do have logical and pictorial force, provided their impersonal contexts are clearly recognized for what they are worth: an adequate building is to be preferred over a faulty one; a comfortable cage is better for a pet than one which is uncomfortable; and no one should sacrifice a child to construct a happy "society." Their relevance for the problem of evil and human suffering, however, changes drastically when the primary value to be conserved is free and responsible selfhood. Imagine for a moment two happily married young people who are longing intensely to share their affection with a child of their very own. Realizing full well that certain pain, sorrows, disappointments, and even eventual death must surely come along with the joys of parenthood, should they honestly choose to be content with a plastic doll which would never know suffering? This analogy of the parent-child relationship has its limitations to be sure, just as the former impersonal ones; nevertheless, if one's highest values are indeed personal in nature, then one should strive to defend and describe these values in language which is predominantly personalistic.

While one must continually avoid becoming indebted to evil for the existence of good, there may be some merit in admitting that human values are largely determined by the fact that man experiences them within certain limitations. For example, the anticipation of heaven as a realm and communion of ultimate spiritual perfection and blessedness takes on profound meaning for us in view of the transitional quality of our human life here and now. If one were, however, to consider the hypothetical possibility of endless life on this earth, one would have to confess that many human values such as love, courage, and faithfulness would be so drastically altered in quality as to become virtually nonexistent. At least it seems reasonable to suppose that some of the basic qualities of these values are derived in part from the fact that in the present age they are all involved with certain spatial-temporal and existential limitations.[17] This sobering and poignant thesis is portrayed parabolically in the ancient legend of Jubal. The story imagines those early years of the human race:

> In the old, soft, sweet days before men knew death, when all that was known of it was the single black spot in the memory of Cain, his descendants lived in gladsome idlesse; they played, they sang, they loved, they danced, in a life that had no gravity and no greatness; but when the second death came, and men saw that there had come to one of their own race a sleep from which there was no awaking, a new meaning stole into life. The horizon which limited it defined it, and made it great. Time took a new value; affection, by growing more serious, became nobler; men thought of themselves more worthily and of their deeds more truly when they saw that a night came when no man could work. Friends and families lived in a tenderer light when the sun was known to shine but for a season; earth became lovelier when they thought the place which knew them now would soon know them no more. The limit set to time drove

> their thoughts out towards eternity. The idea of the death, which was to claim them, bade them live in earnest, made them feel that there was something greater than play; for the death had breathed into life the spirit out of which all tragic and all heroic things come.[18]

Such mystical optimism should not be allowed to blur the biblical focus on death as God's punishment for man's sin; however, we might in some small measure soften the agony of death if we could believe that God has actually intensified the value of human life itself by prescribing its essential limitations.

The Priority of Freedom

Whatever final form one's theodicy may take there should be abundant recognition of the significance of human freedom. Aldous Huxley, writing from his humanistic perspective, may help to unveil something of the psychical and structural dimensions of human freedom when the Savage in his *Brave New World* declares his rebellion against the comfortable impersonal utopia which his pursuers are attempting to force upon him. The Savage shouts:

> "But I like the inconveniences."
> "We don't," said the Controller. "We prefer to do things comfortably."
> "But I don't want comfort. I want God, I want poetry, I want real danger, I want freedom, I want goodness. I want sin."
> "In fact, . . . you're claiming the right to be unhappy."
> "All right then," said the Savage defiantly, "I'm claiming the right to be unhappy."
> "Not to mention the right to grow old and ugly and impotent; the right to have syphilis and cancer; the right to live in constant apprehension of what may happen tomorrow; the right to catch typhoid; the right to be tortured by unspeakable pains of every kind." There was a long silence.
> "I claim them all," said the Savage at last.[19]

These are chilling words to any sensitive human being, especially to the Christian who wants to abhor sin, share the pain of the world, and be an agent in its redemption.

Nevertheless, in some ultimate sense, *God himself* must have decided that it was better to allow these possibilities, yes, even in their tragic form, than make a shadowless world without freedom. In other words, God so values freedom that he is even willing to allow it to be used against him. This divine gift of freedom to a race that becomes rebellious against God is characterized by Karl Jaspers in the dramatic phrase: "God versus God—this is the situation."[20]

Insofar as evil and its consequent suffering and death result from an indefensible free choice against the good, so must the origin and nature of evil also remain a mystery. Any attempt to explain one's choice of evil denies the very essence of freedom and removes the problem of evil from the realm of religion into rational morality. When this happens, according to Wolfgang Trillhaas, one fails to realize that evil

> transcends the borders of morality in that it denotes that conscious opposition against the recognized good. It is a mystery viewed morally that anyone acts against his insight and avowed conviction. In morality, however, there is no mystery. In morality everything is capable of explanation.[21]

Perhaps no one has felt the mysterious depth of freedom and its relation to evil more profoundly than Augustine when he prayed:

> Behold my heart, O God, behold my heart, which Thou hast put upon in the bottom of the abyss. Now, behold, let my heart tell Thee, what it sought there, that I should be gratuitously wicked, having no temptation to that evil deed itself. It was foul, and I loved it, I loved to perish, I loved my own fault, not that for the sake of which I committed the fault, but my fault itself I loved. Foul soul, falling from the firmament to expulsion from Thy presence; not seeking aught through the shame, but the shame itself![22]

If human rebellion of such enigmatic proportions lies as the root cause of all the suffering we must endure, then the honest interpreter must acknowledge that there is little here that might be called an *explanation* of our plight. For sin by its very nature is unreasonable. If, however, one is willing to concede that God in his righteousness must punish sin, both at its original appearance in the race and at its recurrence throughout history, by sending suffering and death, then it seems reasonable to conclude that the *ultimate* cause of evil in the universe is the freedom God allows his creatures. Whereas the *proximate*, or *secondary*, cause must be the exercise of human freedom which *irrationally* chooses sin.

Evil, Satan, and Sin

While this is surely not the place to enter into an elaborate exposition of the biblical teaching concerning Satan, no treatment of the problem of evil will be complete without addressing this issue. There is in Christian tradition and literature a recurring and at times dominating mythological interpretation of the origin of Satan as a fallen angel which claims to be based on Isaiah 14:12-15:

> "How you are fallen from heaven,
> O Day Star, son of Dawn!
> How you are cut down to the ground,
> you who laid the nations low!
> You said in your heart,
> 'I will ascend to heaven;
> above the stars of God
> I will set my throne on high;
> I will sit on the mount of assembly
> in the far north;
> I will ascend above the heights of the clouds,
> I will make myself like the Most High.'
> But you are brought down to Sheol,
> to the depths of the Pit."

The rise of this view is largely due to the translation of "Day Star" in the Hebrew text into the word "Lucifer," which means light bearer, in the Latin Vulgate. This word Lucifer was subsequently personified in Christian tradition and popularized in dramatic imagery by John Milton in

Paradise Lost. However, little biblical substantiation can be found for considering this passage in Isaiah as an account of Satan's origin. R. B. Y. Scott's treatment in *The Interpreter's Bible* is a much more accurate interpretation. The text before us, he explains, recalls an ancient Canaanite cosmic drama which tells

> of the attempt of the morning star to scale the heights of heaven surpassing all other stars only to be cast down to earth by the victorious sun. . . . This became in turn the story of the aspiring of a minor deity to reach the highest heaven where the supreme god dwelt in remote and lonely splendor, and finally the symbol of the ambition and downfall of an earthly monarch. He who has climbed so high will be cast down to the depths, better, "the uttermost depths" of the Pit of Sheol.[23]

Although Milton appears to have a weak biblical foundation for his view of Satan as a fallen angel, he nevertheless pierces to the heart of the satanic nature, and perhaps to the essence of human sin as well when in *Paradise Lost* he has Satan cry defiantly, "It is better to reign in hell than to serve in heaven."[24] For in spite of the fact that Satan is portrayed in varied roles in scripture, for example he even appears to be an instrument of God's testing on occasion, the dominant impression remains from his relationship to Christ that Satan is the very essence of rebellion against God.

Looking at the history of Israel's thought, we see a growing understanding of the concept of Satan as a personal being. The reason for this may be more epistemological than ontological in that the revelation of God is received more and more along personal lines as the coming of Christ draws near; consequently, the power or powers which oppose God are correspondingly conceived in more personal terms. At any rate, the Old Testament reveals a growing conflict between God and evil as though there is a cosmic antagonism between them which will inevitably erupt sometime in the future. Kurt Lüthi in his book on God and evil concludes his presentation of the Old Testament concept of evil by describing this immanent cosmological conflict: "The motif of the battle begins to sound uniquely in the strikingly important reminder of the primordial battle of Jaweh against the chaos and—as a prelude to the New Testament witness—in the Isaiah Lucifer passage: 'How you are fallen from heaven, you brilliant star!' "[25] Throughout the Old Testament, however, there remains little question that God is sovereign over every form of evil, whether it be chaos, a serpent, a satanic being, demons, or the sinful choices of man.

In the New Testament, Christ struggles against Satan and demons in realistic confrontation, yet there, as in the Old Testament, God is unquestionably in control. Not only is Satan conceived along more personal lines than in the Old Testament, but he is credited with being the ruler of a kingdom with innumerable potent servants. Moreover he "is represented as entering into men and as the responsible author (not merely the personification) of their evil deeds and passions."[26] According to the Synoptic Gospels, the power which Christ demonstrates in casting out demons is one of the earliest and clearest signs that the kingdom of God has come: "But if it is by the Spirit of God that I cast out demons, then the kingdom of God has come upon you" (Matt. 12:28). And on one occasion Christ declares that he has seen Satan fall as lightning from heaven (Luke 10:18). This is unquestionably a reference to the Lucifer image in Isaiah, but it is important to realize that Christ is not referring to the origin of Satan but rather to the limitation of his power because of Christ's superiority over demons during his earthly ministry. While Paul does not hesitate to proclaim that the principalities and powers of the world have been ultimately defeated through the victory of Christ's cross and resurrection (Col. 2:8-23), he insists that man must repent and believe in order to receive the power to overcome sin. In a word, through his life, death, and resurrection, Christ has come to deliver all who believe on him from the bondage of sin, death, and fear. Thus the writer of Hebrews declares:

> Since therefore the children share in flesh and blood, he himself likewise partook of the same nature, that through death he might destroy him who has the power of death, that is, the

> devil, and deliver all those who through fear of death were subject to lifelong bondage. (2:14-15)

If one might now be allowed to use the symbolism of the Lucifer passage without its traditional metaphysical connotations, God has in Christ been victorious over the darkness of the night of sin and death. It is therefore with rapturous delight that one reads in the book of Revelation God's promise to the believer who remains faithful: "I will give him the morning star!" (Rev. 2:28).

While all suffering is not the result of one's own personal sin either in the past or the immediate situation, the Bible does teach that there is a direct relationship between Adam's sin, or original sin, and the appearance of suffering and death in the human race. It says very plainly that "as sin came into the world through one man and death through sin, . . . so death spread to all men because all men sinned" (Rom. 5:12). According to C. Anderson Scott, the Bible speaks as though "Death employed Sin to stab for itself an opening into human nature."[27] Devout Christians may sincerely be divided over their interpretations of *how* the original sin of man is related to the facts of suffering and death. There need however be little debate that moral evil, or to use Kant's more philosophical term, "radical evil," permeates every strata of human life intensifying our anguish on every encounter with suffering and death. Paul writes, "The sting of death is sin, and the power of sin is the law" (I Cor. 15:56). Now H. H. Farmer clearly applies the meaning of this scripture to the problem of evil when he perceives

> that sin is the chief source of the bitterness and perplexity of suffering; it throws a shadow across vision, making it appear other than it is. If suffering has an insupportable sting in it, crushing and embittering the soul, it is not because it is, so to say, suffering *per se*, but because it meets and enters into an alliance with the lovelessness of man without, and with a profound disquietude and dissatisfaction with ourselves within, a disorganized and corrupted inner life estranged and alienated from God . . . sin is the only disaster which at the end of the day really matters. . . . In the discernment of that truth the victory over suffering is won.[28]

The removal of the separation between man and God, and between man and his fellowmen—which characterizes sin—is therefore the central concern of biblical redemption. If the message of reconciliation and forgiveness can be truly received, the horror and meaninglessness of suffering and death can to an amazing extent be overcome.

God with Us

One of the most comforting themes in the Christian message is that God is in the midst of human suffering sharing every hurt and sorrow. Long ago Isaiah dared to believe that suffering could be redemptive. Even then he dreamed of the Christ who would come and bear our sin and share our burdens:

> Surely he has borne our griefs
> and carried our sorrows;
> yet we esteemed him stricken,
> smitten by God, and afflicted.
> But he was wounded for our transgressions,
> he was bruised for our iniquities;
> upon him was the chastisement that made us whole,
> and with his stripes we are healed.
> All we like sheep have gone astray;
> we have turned every one to his own way;
> and the LORD has laid on him
> the iniquity of us all.
>
> He was oppressed, and he was afflicted,
> yet he opened not his mouth;
> like a lamb that is led to the slaughter,
> and like a sheep that before its shearers is dumb,
> so he opened not his mouth. (Isa. 53:4-7)[29]

Jesus of Nazareth certainly fulfills the biblical expectation that the messiah would be a "man of sorrows, and acquainted with grief" (Isa. 53:3). He is rejected by most of his own people, misunderstood by his family, weeps over the death of a friend, agonizes in prayer, laments the destruction of his cherished land, and experiences indescribable pain and loneliness until he cries out at his death: "My God, my God, why hast thou forsaken me?"

(Mark 15:34). Christ's identification with, and involvement in, our human suffering is proclaimed sensitively by Helmut Thielicke when he imagines Christ telling his followers:

> Every wound I lay my healing hand upon has ached a thousand times in me; every demon I cast out has leered at me; I died the death that I myself defeated; I let my own body be torn and buried in the earth. Who among you suffers that I do not suffer with you? Who among you dies and I do not die with you? I am your comrade and brother in every pain, whatever your lot may be. Do you understand that? Then understand this too: He who sees me sees the Father, and he who sees me suffering with you sees the Father suffering. God suffers pain for you and with you; do you understand this?[30]

This comforting refrain is illustrated in eloquent prose by George Eliot in the novel *Adam Bede*. In the following moving passage a young woman preacher of the early Methodists named Dinah writes to Seth, her suitor, concerning her faith in God's involvement with the suffering of the world:

> For then, the very hardship, and the sorrow, and the blindness, and the sin I have beheld and been ready to weep over—yea, all the anguish of the children of man, which sometimes wraps me round like sudden darkness—I can bear with a willing pain, as if I was sharing the Redeemer's cross. For I feel it, I feel it—infinite love is suffering too—yes, in the fullness of knowledge it suffers, it yearns, it mourns; and that is a blind self-seeking which wants to be freed from the sorrow wherewith the whole creation groaneth and travaileth.[31]

Is it not this conviction that God is deliberately and inextricably involved with human suffering that enabled the early Christians not only to endure hardships and persecution but to *rejoice* in them? Perhaps this is the reason why Paul believed that he might in a relative sense "complete what is lacking in Christ's affliction for the sake of his body, that is, the church" (Col. 1:24).

Although it is a delicate matter to interpret, and must be held with love, it is nonetheless a valid biblical insight that God often uses suffering to bring one to a consciousness of spiritual reality that could come in no other way. C. S. Lewis is one of the few contemporary writers who has the courage to develop this theme. Notice carefully that he speaks primarily of God's address to the evil man:

> Until the evil man finds evil unmistakably present in his existence, in the form of pain, he is enclosed in illusion. Once pain has roused him, he knows that he is in some way or other "up against" the real universe: he either rebels (with the possibility of a clearer issue and deeper repentance at some later stage) or else makes some attempt at an adjustment, which, if pursued, will lead him to religion. . . . No doubt Pain as God's megaphone is a terrible instrument; it may lead to final and unrepented rebellion. But it gives the only opportunity the bad man can have for amendment. It removes the veil; it plants the flag of truth within the fortress of a rebel soul.[32]

Lest we feel that we are immune from such a divine confrontation it would be well for us to consider how God, according to his loving purposes, occasionally sends punishment in order to discipline his children. This is a painful though unmistakable biblical teaching which the early church found difficult to understand, as do Christians today. The writer to the Hebrews, however, presents the matter quite soberly but without apology: "My son, do not regard lightly the discipline of the Lord, nor lose courage when you are punished by him. For the Lord disciplines him whom he loves, and chastises every son whom he receives" (Heb. 12:5-6). A considerable amount of spiritual maturity must be attained before one can even entertain the possibility that one's suffering is sent by God for discipline. And it would be a wise rule never to draw the conclusion that another person's suffering is a result of God's decree. Above all, however, we can know that God loves his children better even than they can love themselves. Should God's disciplining hand fall heavily upon any of his children, they may rest assured that God wishes nothing more than the wholeness of their salvation. As difficult as it may seem at the time, there is in the experience of punishment rightly received God's presence which, as Spurgeon used to preach, can enable one to "kiss the hand that wields the rod." The returned prodigal may still suffer some of the consequences of his sin and sometimes chafe at his disciplined lot, but it is enough for him to know that he is back at home *in the Father's house!*

The New Testament also makes it perfectly clear that the Christian can *expect* suffering to arise from the fact that the world is perennially hostile to Christ and his followers. Christ warns of the time that shall come when his enemies "will lay their hands on you and persecute you, delivering you up to the synagogues and prisons, and you will be brought before kings and governors for my name's sake" (Luke 21:12). Christ, according to John, explained: "If you were of the world, the world would love its own; but because you are not of the world, but I chose you out of the world, therefore the world hates you" (John 15:19). Even Paul's thorn in the flesh, whatever it may have been, is associated with his fidelity to Christ and is in some sense occasioned by the persecutions which he received from the enemies of the church:

> Three times I besought the Lord about this, that it should leave me; but he said to me, "My grace is sufficient for you, for my power is made perfect in weakness." I will all the more gladly boast of my weaknesses, that the power of Christ may rest upon me. For the sake of Christ, then, I am content with weaknesses, insults, hardships, persecutions, and calamities; for when I am weak, then I am strong. (II Cor. 12:8-10)

It is precisely at this point that Paul's handling of suffering differs most clearly from the classical Old Testament treatment in the book of Job. Christof Gestrich delineates the distinction as follows:

> Job suffers, *although* this actually should not be, because according to the Law he is a righteous man. And Job suffers in the depths of his being to be sure also *in* this righteousness of the Law which is confirmed by him. On the contrary Paul reckons his own pharisaical righteousness in the Law, which was once his greatest prize, for refuse; and his goal is now that he might gain Christ and participation in his suffering (Phil. 3:7, 10)! This desired suffering is even allotted to him, because he receives the new righteousness.[33]

While the Christian should never seek suffering for its own sake or for the sake of being rewarded, it is quite possible for him to rejoice that he is found worthy to suffer for his Lord. At least some in the early church possessed enough faith to believe that their suffering for the sake of the gospel could bring glory to Christ. They exhort one another therefore to rejoice in suffering: "In this you rejoice, though now for a little while you may have to suffer various trials, so that the genuineness of your faith, more precious than gold which though perishable is tested by fire, may redound to praise and glory and honor at the revelation of Jesus Christ" (I Peter 1:6-7). We might well ponder for a moment which is the greater miracle: the resurrection of Jesus which produces such faith, or the gift of faith which realizes such victory through suffering—and then be thankful we need not choose between the two for both are ours in Christ.

The raw strength of determination to endure insurmountable difficulties and never admit defeat is commendable provided, of course, our goals are worthy. The heroic defiance of uncontrollable circumstances in Albert Camus' *The Myth of Sisyphus* is an appropriate literary expression of that kind of humanistic effort which seeks to transform a situation by sheer force of will. Sisyphus, according to the myth, has been condemned by the gods to push a tremendous stone to the top of a mountain only to see it totter for a moment and roll down to the base where again the striving toward the summit must begin. In spite of this recurring futility and frustration, Sisyphus, in Camus' existentialist interpretation, teaches us

> the higher fidelity that negates the gods and raises rocks. He too concludes that all is well. This universe henceforth without a master seems to him neither sterile nor futile. Each atom of that stone, each mineral flake of that night-filled mountain, in itself forms a world. The struggle itself toward the heights is enough to fill a man's heart. One must imagine Sisyphus happy.[34]

Although one may receive inspiration from this mythological symbol of courage, the imagery still needs to be more firmly rooted in experience. Perhaps Victor Frankl's testimonies of personal triumph from the Nazi extermination camps in World War II can provide just this needed dimension. He writes that while most of his fellow prisoners were asking the question

> "Will we survive the camp? For if not all this suffering has no sense." The question for me was, "Has all this suffering, this dying around us, a meaning? For if not, then ultimately there is no sense to surviving."
>
> For a life whose meaning stands or falls on whether one escapes with it or not—a life, that is, whose meaning depends on happenstance—would not really be worth living at all.[35]

Frankl's personal example and noble convictions regarding the inherent meaning of life, even when experienced at its worst, are surely existentially valid. They are even *phenomenologically* very close to the confidence of Paul that "in all these things we are more than conquerors." There is, however, a crucial ontological difference in that Paul adds "through him who loved us" (Rom. 8:37).

Notice how masterfully John Claypool presents this ontological difference within a Christian context when he interprets Paul's assurance that no temptation, trial, or tribulation will ever be too great for man because God will make a way to endure it (I Cor. 10:13). His sermon based on this text bears the candid title, "When You Are Up Against It." After explaining carefully that one of the biblical ways of handling trouble is to be miraculously rescued by God, and still another alternative is for the individual himself to exert his own will and perhaps change the circumstances that are causing the problem, he then proceeds to the major thrust of this message when he admits that there are times in life when the only possibility remaining is to change one's attitude toward the unalterable situation. In a passage which is wrenched from his very heart and unsurpassed in pathos and courage, he recalls:

> Four and a half years ago, I found myself really "up against it" when my little girl was diagnosed with leukemia, and I responded like anyone would do—I prayed for a miracle of healing, and I did everything in my power to alter the circumstances medically. But then one snowy January night

> the battle for life was lost, and I found myself face to face with a situation that neither God nor I could alter. The event of death happened, a stark immutable reality. It would have been very easy in those moments to have embarked on a pilgrimage of bitterness that could have lasted for the rest of my days. I could have refused to accept this fact and gone into insanity or curdled resentment. But Paul's example was instructive to me here, for I came to realize that my "thorn in the flesh" was not removeable. My alternative was not to change my circumstances but rather to change my attitude toward it and thus in creative openness to let it make of me what it would. And though it was very difficult, this is what I tried to do, and I am here to testify that Paul's promise came true. It did make me a more sympathetic traveler down the "road of life." The very gift of life itself has become more intensely valuable to me than it was before, and I have found again and again in these last four years that I was able to move close and share meaningfully with other people because of this "thorn in the flesh." Therefore I would have to say good has come out of this experience. This is no explanation for the tragedy of a little girl's dying, and it certainly does not make the experience of loss easy or light, but it does confirm the promise that in every circumstance there is a possibility for good. No tragedy need be total tragedy. No difficulty needs to be utterly devastating. Even when we get to the place that there is nothing we can do except submit and accept the unchangeable, even this has the potential of good about it.[36]

While the emphasis here falls unquestionably upon the need for surrender to God's will and the exercise of courage in the present existential moment, the wider perspectives concerning the indwelling, strengthening presence of Christ and his Spirit, and the assurance of eschatological victory should never be neglected.

Our Eschatological Hope

William Sanday once said that in the New Testament the center of gravity lies beyond the grave. Whether one expresses it like this or not, there is the need to recognize that there are many mysterious and insoluble elements within the problem of evil and suffering which must await an eschatological solution. If we were forced to say the final word today, we would have to confess we have no real answer to these problems. Fortunately, however, we are surrounded by those like C. S. Lewis who have already begun to anticipate the future which God promises in his Word. Lewis intimates, and all the while hopefully:

> At present we are on the outside of the world, the wrong side of the door. We discern the freshness and purity of the morning, but they do not make us fresh and pure. We cannot mingle with the splendours we see. But all the leaves of the New Testament are rustling with the rumour that it will not always be so.[37]

The pages of the New Testament abound with the hope that while "we are God's children now; it does not yet appear what we shall be, but we know that when he appears we shall be like him, for we shall see him as he is" (I John 3:2). Yet no single passage of scripture expresses more convincingly or succinctly the significance which the eschatological dimension possesses for the problem of evil and suffering than Romans 8:18 where Paul concluded: "I consider that the sufferings of this present time are not worth comparing with the glory that is to be revealed to us."

Tarry therefore a little longer on this eschatological theme, not so much to conclude the argument, for what I can say has surely been said by now. Confirm this hope, however, in the only way that faith can be validated—by beginning to *experience* the joy of heaven and the healing which it brings by living here and now within the presence of Christ. Let me introduce you to one who not only has the right to speak on evil, suffering, and death, but who has perhaps proclaimed the message of Christian hope more forcefully and eloquently than anyone else in the English language. He is Arthur John Gossip, who preaches from Jeremiah's fearful warning: "If thou hast run with the footmen, and they have wearied thee, then how canst thou contend with horses? and if in the land of peace, wherein thou trustedst, they wearied thee, then how wilt thou do in the swelling of the Jordan?" (Jer. 12:5 KJ). His famous sermon, "But When Life Tumbles In, What Then?" was his first message after his wife's dramatically sudden death.

His conclusion of this homiletical masterpiece must be shared at length because its very cadence vibrates with joy and every word, defying deletion, reflects some delicate hue of that glory which is to come:

> But there is one thing I should like to say which I have never dared to say before, not feeling that I had the right. We Christian people in the mass are entirely unchristian in our thoughts of death. We have our eyes wrongly focused. We are selfish, and self-centered, and self-absorbed. We keep thinking aggrievedly of what it means to us. And that is wrong, all wrong. In the New Testament you hear very little of the families with that aching gap, huddled together in their desolate little home in some back street; but a great deal about the saints in glory, and the sunshine, and the singing, and the splendour yonder. And, surely, that is where our thoughts should dwell. I for one want no melancholious tunes, no grey and sobbing words, but brave hymns telling of their victory. . . . Think out your brooding. What exactly does it mean? Would you pluck the diadem from their brows again? Would you snatch the palms of victory out of their hands? Dare you compare the clumsy nothings our poor blundering love can give them here with what they must have yonder where Christ Himself has met them, and has heaped on them who can think out what happiness and glory? I love to picture it. How, shyly, amazed, half protesting, she who never thought of self was led into the splendour of her glory. . . . To us it will be long and lonesome: but they won't even have looked round them before we burst in. In any case, are we to let our dearest be wrenched out of our hands by force? Or, seeing that it has to be, will we not give them willingly and proudly, looking God in the eyes, and telling Him that we prefer our loneliness rather than that they should miss one tittle of their rights.
>
> . . . When we are young, heaven is a vague and nebulous and shadowy place. But as our friends gather there, more and more it gains body and vividness and homeliness. And when our dearest have passed yonder, how real and evident it grows, how near it is, how often we steal yonder. For, as the Master put it: Where our treasure is, there will our heart be also. Never again will I give out that stupid lie, "There is a happy land, far, far away." It is not far. They are quite near. And the communion of the saints is a tremendous and most blessed fact. . . .
>
> Nowadays, for example, to pray is to turn home. For then they run to meet us, draw us with their dear familiar hands into the Presence, stand quite close to us the whole time we are there—quite close while we are there.
>
> . . . And so back to life again, like a healthyminded laddie at some boarding-school, who, after the first hour of home-sickness,

> resolves, if he is wise, he will not mope, but throw himself into the life about him, and do his part and play the game, and enjoy every minute of it—aye, and does it too—though always, his eyes look ahead for the term's end, and always his heart thrills and quickens at thought of that wonderful day when he will have not memories and letters only, but the whole of his dear ones really there, when he will be with them again and they with him. Well, that will come in time. . . .
>
> I don't think you need be afraid of life. Our hearts are very frail; and there are places where the road is very steep and very lonely. But we have a wonderful God. And as Paul puts it, what can separate us from His love? Not death, he says immediately, pushing that aside at once as the most obvious of all impossibilities.[38]

Now until we are there with those who are dear to us, and above all with the Lord who has gone before, we may rest in the faith, even in the depths of despair, that whatever of our suffering God may have allowed, he has more than atoned for with his gift of Christ and the place he has gone to prepare. We should therefore not despise our freedom but do what we can to endure, relieving as much suffering as we can and encouraging one another—and this "all the more as you see the Day drawing near" (Heb. 10:25).

CONCLUSION

A Meditation on *Personal* Faith

If Christ is indeed the creative center of all reality and ultimate value, as maintained throughout the preceding discussions, then there are several corollaries which should be amplified in order to comprehend the full *personalistic* dimensions of a Christian philosophy. Because we believe that God has revealed himself in Christ, in the Bible, and by the continuous presence of his Spirit through the church, as Christians we can incorporate the following affirmations into our personal philosophy:

1. *God as Father, Son, and Holy Spirit is essentially absolute personal being.* God not only reveals himself in a threefold pattern or economy as Father, Son, and Holy Spirit but exists in his very being as these three persons. Far from being a merely speculative projection, the doctrine of the trinity is deeply rooted in Christian experience. We know *God* because he has come into history in *Christ* and the believer encounters God himself in the presence of his *Holy Spirit*. Unless all three persons are indeed divine, we could never really be certain that we know God. Instead, we might just be encountering some numinous manifestations.[1]

God as Father, Son, and Holy Spirit is *absolute*. Biblical words such as creator, Lord, omnipotent, and everlasting strive to express the quantitative grandeur of God's nondependence on anything else for his being and power.

Although he is person, he is never limited to mere human personhood. His very deity extends to the limits of man's conceptions of energy, time, and space—and beyond. Genuine encounter with God will inevitably lead one to the contemplation of the divine mystery and the realization that God is the creative source of all that is worthwhile and lasting in this world and the next.

At the same time, this infinite, divine source of life is profoundly *personal*. Pannenberg expresses this conviction well when he explains:

> The origin of everything real is essentially infinite. So our questioning after that upon which we know ourselves to be dependent is also infinite, insofar as this questioning again moves beyond every answer and nowhere comes to rest. We seek the unity of everything real in order to become certain of the unity of our existence. The origin in which we seek this unity can be grasped only in trust, since it is infinite. Since in its essence this origin is not controllable, we can only think of it as a person—as a personal God.[2]

This same transcendent-personal polarity is reflected in the early biblical portrayal of God as the supreme creator who walks with man in the garden in the cool of the evening. It will be remembered that when God called Moses to deliver his people

> then Moses said to God, "If I come to the people of Israel and say to them, 'The God of your fathers has sent me to you,' and they ask me, 'What is his name?' what shall I say to them?" God said to Moses, "I AM WHO I AM." And he said, "Say this to the people of Israel, 'I AM has sent me to you.' " (Exod. 3:13-14).

God is the one who exists; he goes out before us, and we will not know him until we meet him out there at his appointed place; but above all, he is the *personal* Lord, the one who says "I"! God is not a part of nature, a river, a tree, the sun, or a force. He is neither a sacred object nor a concept, but the living personal one who continually crashes into our experience to declare "I say unto you."

The psalmist acknowledges with gratitude the immanent personal presence of God when he asks:

Whither shall I go from thy Spirit?
Or whither shall I flee from thy presence?
If I ascend to heaven, thou art there!
If I make my bed in Sheol, thou art there!
If I take the wings of morning
and dwell in the uttermost parts of the sea,
even there thy hand shall lead me,
and thy right hand shall hold me. (Ps. 139:7-10)

It is this eternal "thou-art-thereness" which constitutes the essence of God according to the Christian faith.

Nowhere, however, has this depth of personal being been more clearly revealed than in the coming of God's Son in Christ Jesus. John declares: "No one has ever seen God; the only Son, who is in the bosom of the Father, he has made him known" (John 1:18). And Paul prays, "*that I may know him* and the power of his resurrection" (Phil. 3:10, italics added). With lucid brevity H. H. Farmer of Cambridge dares to summarize the central affirmation of the Christian faith as being the conviction that "God himself came, and comes, into human history in the person of Jesus Christ. Jesus Christ is God himself in action within history 'for us men for our salvation,' in a way that is unique, final, adequate, and indispensable."[3] Man is continually in danger of trying to make God into an object and, as Emile Cailliet has often said, we are always "colonizing reality with abstractions"—but the absolute, infinite one is above all person.

2. *God is personal and salvation is essentially surrender to and encounter with the personal being of God himself.* Christian salvation is not the result of an impersonal, mechanical force, submission to fate, nor one's assent to this concept even though it is a Christian doctrine. Rather, salvation is quite simply trust in Christ. Contrary to the will of God who reveals his "I say unto you," we seek to silence the divine voice and defiantly assert that we will have our own way. Along with those described early in Genesis, we have in many varied and subtle ways tried to place ourselves in charge of the world and claimed to be as God. Our false persona runs counter to the "I AM" of God, so we live estranged and anxious in a home where the Father is away.

However, we would never have known how deep our wound or how dark our path is had not Christ come to live next door. He tells Nicodemus not that he is following the wrong method or that he merely needs more strength but says in profound simplicity, "Truly, truly, I say to you, unless one is born anew, he cannot see the kingdom of God" (John 3:3). The transformation called for could not be more drastic! One must become a *new person*. We need a new self which will surrender to the harmonies of God's "I say unto you." When this happens salvation as encounter transpires and one anticipates something of that divine symmetry between the redeemed self and all things which Dante envisioned in his *Paradise*: "desire and will were rolled— even as a wheel that moveth equally— by the Love that moves the sun and the other stars."[4] In our dying to Christ we may therefore confess with Paul: "I have been crucified with Christ; it is no longer I who live, but Christ who lives in me; and the life I now live in the flesh I live by faith in the Son of God, who loved me and gave himself for me" (Gal. 2:20).

When, however, the whole of Christian faith and theology is interpreted according to this personalistic model, the high priority of human freedom necessitates the possibility that one can ultimately reject God's personal love. The New Testament makes it perfectly clear that God does not wish "that any should perish, but that all should reach repentance" (II Peter 3:9). But it also teaches with equal force that "God is not mocked" (Gal. 6:7). When God therefore, as Brunner says, takes "Himself, His love, infinitely seriously," this means that he must also take man and his freedom "infinitely seriously." Wherever man in his sin rejects divine love, the wrath of God is inevitable and morally justified. "Because it is true that Jesus Christ alone is the Light and the Life, it cannot be otherwise than that outside of Christ there is darkness, death, destruction."[5] John Bunyan is therefore biblically quite sound when he describes the King of the Celestial City refusing to admit one who comes not by the way of the Cross but in his own strength. He writes with both compassion and conviction, "Then I saw that there was a way to Hell even from the gates of Heaven."[6]

3. *If God is, indeed, personal being and redeems through personal relationship with his Son by the presence of his personal Spirit, then there is abundant encouragement to believe he has a personal will for each life.* The most basic religious question anyone can ask is, "Does God know my name?" The answer is yes, for Christ teaches, "Pray, then, like this: Our Father. . . ." He encourages us to use the intimate phrase of a little child talking to his loving earthly father. And don't forget, even though two sparrows may be sold for a penny, "Not one of them will fall to the ground without your Father's will. [For] even the hairs of your head are all numbered" (Matt. 10:29-30).

Every individual is, therefore, unique and relatively irreplaceable. It might challenge us to be more distinctly like ourselves to realize with Cailliet that "according to the new science of genetics which proceeds on the calculus of probabilities, once my father had known my mother and conception had taken place, there was about one chance in three hundred thousand billion that the individual I now am would be born."[7] We can see now more clearly how foolish it is to try to be somebody else. Quite simply, it can't be done. By trying to do so, we will also miss our own mark and, what is more important, we will defeat God's purpose in making us. Perhaps if we can increasingly discover and express our own individuality, we can even grow in the understanding and charity which is so essential in allowing others to be themselves.

God does have a very special will for every life. However, be careful not to fall into a mechanical impersonalism and start looking for his will as though it were a blueprint, an irresistible force, or an abstract concept. The wisest counsel in this regard is at the same time the most simple: anytime you want to know God's will, you may ask him.

4. *True selfhood is found only through personal participation in the community of Christ's church.*

> What life have you if you have not life together?
> There is no life that is not in community
> And no community not lived in the praise of God.

And now you live dispersed on ribbon roads,
And no man knows or cares who is his neighbor
Unless his neighbor makes too much disturbance,
But all dash to and fro in motorcars,
Familiar with the roads and settled nowhere.

And the wind shall say: "Here were decent godless people
Their only monument the asphalt road
And a thousand lost golf balls."[8]

With this haunting refrain T. S. Eliot captures many hollow echoes of our lonely age. Augustine spoke for all men when he wrote those memorable lines of man's longing for God: "Thou hast formed us for Thyself, and our hearts are restless till they find rest in Thee."[9] The beloved theme remains incomplete, however, until one adds, "Thou has formed us for Thyself—*and one another*."

There is no question that Augustine knows the value of a vital communal Christian life when he recounts so movingly the conversion of Victorinus. For years the old pagan teacher of rhetoric had taunted his Christian friends by declaring himself a Christian, but they would reply, "We will not believe you are a Christian until we see you in the Church," whereupon he would answer derisively, "Is it then walls that make Christians?" But one day Victorinus was willing to acknowledge his need for the witness of the church and its community and declared: "Let us go to the church; I wish to be made a Christian." He was given instruction and eventually the time came for his public confession and baptism. Augustine tells about the occasion with a tenderness and love that is truly Christian, catholic, and contemporary:

> So, then, when he ascended to make his profession, all, as they recognized him, whispered his name one to the other, with a voice of congratulation. And who was there amongst them that did not know him? And there ran a low murmur through the mouths of all the rejoicing multitude, "Victorinus! Victorinus!" Sudden was the burst of exaltation at the sight of him; and suddenly were they hushed, that they might hear him. He pronounced the true faith with an excellent boldness, and all desired to take him to their very heart—yea, by their love and joy they took him thither; such were the hands with which they took him.[10]

A love which begins in the Christian community and spreads to the world around is therefore not an option, or merely some external appendage to the Christian life, but an organic expression of the personalistic quality of Christian experience.

5. *There is only one channel through which to share faith in a personal God—and that is by personal witnessing.* It may be wise strategically to stress different kinds of evangelistic approaches such as mass media, benevolence, crisis ministry, journalism, and institutional evangelism in order to reach different kinds of people, but in the strictest theological sense there is no such thing as *impersonal* evangelism. Somehow the art object, television production, book, bread, or bricks must become incarnate, tangible expressions of one's *personal* faith confronting another *person* with the *person* of Christ.

While there is only one "name under heaven given among men by which we must be saved," there are as many ways of sharing this gospel as there are individual persons (Acts 4:12). One who might not feel gifted with the grace to witness to strangers for brief moments is not thereby excused from the responsibility of sharing his or her faith. For evangelism, if it is radically personal, throws the door wide open to us according to the strengths of our own individuality. How much richer the Christian life becomes when we learn the simple lesson that "the body does not consist of one member but of many. . . . God arranged the organs in the body, each one of them, as he chose. If all were a single organ, where would the body be? As it is, there are many parts, yet one body" (I Cor. 12:14-20). Let us, therefore, in the richness of our own unique individuality share our personal faith.

6. *Since God is personal and the whole Christian life is constituted along personal lines, it follows that God will sustain his personal relationship with the believer unto everlasting life.* Very simply and biblically expressed, the Christian will never really die, for Jesus says: "I am the resurrection and the life; he who believes in me, though he die, yet shall he live, and whosoever lives and believes in me shall never die" (John 11:25-26). If we should pass from

this life before Christ returns, we may expect to know the agonizing wrench of separation from those we love, regrets over unfinished tasks, and most probably excruciating accompanying physical pain. However, it can be for any one of us who trusts in Christ as it was for Christian and Hopeful in John Bunyan's *Pilgrim's Progress*. As they approach the river of death, which has no way around nor bridge across, they ask about the depth of the water and are told, "You shall find it deeper or shallower, as you believe in the King of the place." Upon entering the water Christian begins to sink and cries to his companion that the billows and waves are going over his head. To this Hopeful responds, "Be of good cheer, my Brother, I feel the bottom and it is good." Christian soon finds solid ground to stand on and "the rest of the River was but shallow."[11]

NOTES

CHAPTER I—*KNOWING THAT YOU KNOW GOD*

1. Epistemology—from ἐπιστήμη, knowledge—according to W. Wieland, "is that philosophical discipline which seeks to understand the essence, origin, elements, causes and conditions of the human process of knowing. Above all, however, it explores the possibility of a criterion for the correctness of the content of knowledge. That means it examines the agreement between the object of knowledge and its concept or the relationship of thought to the circumstance toward which it is directed. The search for the essence of the knowing process is as old as philosophy itself; as a special discipline it has arisen only in recent times. The term *Erkenntnistheorie* (theory of knowledge or epistemology) was first coined in connection with the philosophy of Kant. . . . Narrow relationships exist, however, not only to metaphysics, but also to psychology and to logic. Psychology can also occupy itself with the knowing function, and its particular results can be very significant for epistemology. It can, however, never answer the question of the criterion of truth for the knowing process. In like manner there is also a distinction from logic. Formal logic also reveals conditions which must be fulfilled if knowing should be true. It must, nevertheless, always presuppose the concept of truth itself." *Die Religion in Geschichte und Gegenwart*, Dritte Auflage, Zweiter Band, "Erkenntnistheorie," by W. Wieland. (All translations from the German, unless otherwise noted, are the author's own.)

2. A. A. Milne, *The Christopher Robin Story Book* (New York: Dutton, 1955), pp. 40-42; 48-49.

3. Paul Tillich, "Reason and the Quest for Revelation," *Systematic Theology*, vol. 1 (University of Chicago Press, 1951), p. 71.

4. John Wisdom, "Gods," *Essays on Logic and Language*, ed. Antony Flew (Oxford: Basil Blackwell & Mott, 1951), pp. 192-93.

5. Immanuel Kant, *Critique of Pure Reason*, trans. Norman K. Smith (London: Macmillan, 1950), p. 93.

6. Aristotle, *Metaphysics*, trans. Richard Hope (New York: Columbia University Press, 1952), 4.4, p. 68.

7. Blaise Pascal, *Pensées*, trans. W. F. Trotter (New York: Dutton, 1947), 277, p. 78.

8. Michael Polanyi, *Personal Knowledge* (University of Chicago Press, 1958), p. 64.

9. Eunice Tietjens, "The Most-Sacred Mountain," in *Modern Religious Poems* (New York: Harper, 1964), lines 14-21, pp. 202-03.

10. John Dewey, *Reconstruction in Philosophy* (Boston: Beacon Press, 1948), pp. 156-57.

11. The historical orientation for the role of reason in Western thought can be found in Aristotle's famous principles of identity, contradiction, and the excluded middle. (1) The principle of identity means that a thing is itself and must remain that while under consideration in a rational discourse (*Anal. Pri.* 2.22). Example: A is A. (2) The principle of contradiction maintains that a thing cannot be and not be at the same time or that a proposition cannot be both true and false in a given line of inquiry (*De. Cat.*, c. 10; *Met.* 4.3 ff). Example: A is B, and A is not B cannot both be true. (3) The principle of excluded middle insists that there can be no alternative between affirmation and denial within a given logical context (*Anal. Post.* 1.11). Example: A is B or A is not B. For clarification of these terms, see Dagobert D. Runes, ed., *The Dictionary of Philosophy* (New York: Philosophical Library, 1965), pp. 67, 102, 140. These principles have a long and complicated history; however, their value remains in that they set forth at least some preliminary guidelines which help us avoid contradictions and inconsistencies when we attempt to think rationally.

12. John B. Cobb, Jr., "The Intrapsychic Structure of Christian Existence," *Journal of the American Academy of Religion*, 36:4 (December, 1968), 330.

13. John Oman, *Vision and Authority*, rev. (London: Hodder & Stoughton, 1928), pp. 107, 112-13.

14. H. H. Farmer, *Toward Belief in God* (London: SCM Press, 1942), p. 54.

15. Paul Tillich, *Systematic Theology*, vol. 1, p. 76.

16. Daniel P. Fuller, *Easter Faith and History* (Grand Rapids: Eerdmans, 1965), p. 259.

17. Saint Justin Martyr, *The First Apology*, in *The Fathers of the Church*, trans. Thomas B. Falls (New York: Christian Heritage), 1.14, p. 47.

18. T. F. Torrance, *Theology in Reconstruction* (London: SCM Press, 1965), p. 141.

19. Carl Jung, *Memories, Dreams, and Reflections*, ed. Aniela Jaffe, trans. Richard and Clara Winston (New York: Random House, 1963), p. 355.

CHAPTER II—COME LET US REASON

1. The word "argument" is used in this discussion as a logical term to mean as Wesley Salmon exlains: "a conclusion standing in relation to its supporting evidence. More precisely, *an argument is a group of statements standing in relation to each other*. An argument consists of one statement which is the conclusion and one or more statements of supporting evidence." Wesley C. Salmon, *Logic* (Englewood Cliffs, N.J.: Prentice-Hall, 1963), p. 3. A proof, then, in this context will be a claim that an argument is valid within its acknowledged logical set or framework.

Additional general readings on the arguments can be found in John Hick, "Grounds for Belief in God," *Philosophy of Religion*, 2d ed. (Englewood Cliffs, N.J.: Prentice-Hall, 1973), pp. 15-30 and in his *Arguments for the Existence of God* (London: Macmillan, 1970); Malcolm Diamond, *Contemporary Philosophy and Religious Thought* (New York: McGraw-Hill, 1974); Frederick Ferré, *Basic Modern Philosophy of Religion* (New York: Scribner's, 1967); *Encyclopedia of Religion and Ethics* (New York: Scribner's, 1922), *s.v.* "Theism," by A. E. Taylor; *Die Religion in Geschichte und Gegenwart*, Dritte Auflage, Zweiter Band, *s.v.* "Gottesbeweise," by J. Klein; and each of the classical arguments is discussed by title in *The Encyclopedia of Philosophy* (New York: Macmillan, 1967).

2. Walt Whitman, "Song of the Universal," *The Collected Writings of Walt Whitman*, ed. H. Blodgett and S. Bradley (New York University Press, 1965), p. 226.

3. Saint Anselm, *Proslogium*, trans. S. N. Deane (La Salle, Ill.: Open Court, 1958), pp. 6-7.

4. Anselm, S. *Anselm's Cantuariensis Archiepiscopi Opera omnia ad fidem codicum recensuit Franciscus Salesius Schmitt*, I 103, 14 ff quoted in Karl Barth, *Anselm: Fides Quaerens Intellectum*, trans. Ian W. Robertson (Atlanta: John Knox Press, 1960), p. 161.

5. Anselm, S. *Anselm's Cantauriensis* quoted in Karl Barth, *Anselm*, p. 161.

6. Alan Gragg, *Charles Hartshorne* (Waco, Texas: Word, 1973), p. 99. Cf. Charles Hartshorne, *Anselm's Discovery: A Reexamination of the Ontological Proof for God's Existence* (La Salle, Ill.: Open Court, 1965), pp. 30, 34, 99, 134.

7. An understanding of the ontological argument is essential for any legitimate assessment of the role of the proofs in Christian thought for it lies, often unrecognized, at the foundation of all the others. Immanuel Kant was perhaps the first to conclude that "the physico-theological (teleological) is based upon the cosmological, and this upon the ontological proof of the existence of a Supreme Being; and as besides these three there is no other path open to speculative reason, the ontological proof, on the ground of pure conceptions of reason, is the only possible one, if any proof of a proposition so far transcending the empirical exercise of the understanding is possible at all." Immanuel Kant, *Critique of Pure Reason*, trans. J. M. D. Meiklejohn (New York: Willey, 1943), p. 353. This thesis appears throughout Kant's treatment of the arguments in his *Critique of Pure Reason*, pp. 327-58. For further discussion of the ontological argument see Charles Hartshorne, *The Logic of Perfection* (La Salle, Ill.: Open Court, 1965); *The Many Faced Argument*, ed. J. H. Hick and A. C. McGill (New York: Macmillan, 1967); *The Ontological Argument*, ed. Alvin Plantinga (Garden City, N.Y.: Doubleday, 1965).

8. Thomas Aquinas, *Summa Theologica* I. 2. 1. reply to objection 2.

9. There are, as might be expected, many ways to interpret causality: (1) Aristotle thought of movement from potency to actuality (2) Hume spoke of the association of sequences (3) Kant interpreted it more along the line of a priori structures of the mind (4) modern science often views it in terms of statistical probabilities (5) whereas most of us today still function within a commonsense Newtonianism that believes if A hits B with enough force A will cause B to move. See John Hick, *Philosophy of Religion*, 2d ed. (Englewood Cliffs, N.J.: Prentice-Hall, 1973), p. 21.

10. Thomas Aquinas, *Summa Theologica* I. 2. 3. Aquinas' Five Ways,

according to J. Klein, "are one way which is founded on the unproven presupposition of the identity of essence and existence in God." Klein, "Gottesbeweise," p. 1750.

11. *Ibid.* The cosmological argument, along with the whole body of Aquinas' theology, was officially endorsed by the Roman Catholic church at the First Vatican Council in 1870 as declared by its third session and recorded in *The Dogmatic Constitution of the Catholic Faith*.

12. Germain Grisez, "A Child Learns to Talk about God," *Beyond the New Theism—A Philosophy of Religion* (University of Notre Dame, 1975), pp. 14-15.

13. Grisez, *Beyond the New Theism*, pp. 16-17.

14. *Ibid.*, p. 18.

15. *Ibid.*

16. *Ibid.*, p. 52.

17. *Ibid.*, p. 53.

18. Frederick Ferré, *Basic Modern Philosophy of Religion* (New York: Scribner's, 1967), p. 144.

19. Relevant material on the cosmological argument can be found in Anthony Kenny, *The Five Ways* (New York: Schocken Books, 1969); E. L. Mascall, *He Who Is* (London: Longmans, Green, 1943); Austin Farrer, *Finite and Infinite*, 2d ed. (London: Dacre Press, 1960); Samuel M. Thompson, *A Modern Philosophy of Religion* (Chicago: Regnery, 1955); and Germain Grisez, *The New Theism* (University of Notre Dame Press, 1975).

20. William Paley, *Natural Theology* (London: Printed for J. Faulder, 1810), pp. 1-8.

21. Gerald Manley Hopkins, "God's Grandeur," *Ancients and Moderns: An Anthology of Poetry* (New York: Harper, 1971), p. 200.

22. The teleological argument is also treated in the following works: F. R. Tennant, *Philosophical Theology*, vol. II (Cambridge University Press, 1930); Lecomte Du Nouy, *Human Destiny* (New York: David McKay, 1947); A. E. Taylor, *Does God Exist?* (New York: Macmillan, 1947); Peter Bertocci, *Introduction to the Philosophy of Religion* (Englewood Cliffs, N.J.: Prentice-Hall, 1951); Teilhard de Chardin, *The Phenomenon of Man* (New York: Harper, 1959); Richard Taylor, *Metaphysics* (Englewood Cliffs, N.J.: Prentice-Hall, 1963), p. 94 ff; Thomas McPherson, *The Argument from Design* (London: Macmillan, 1972); and R. G. Swinburne, "The Argument from Design—a Defense," *Religious Studies*, 8 (1972), 193-205. For an examination of this argument in relation to evolution see Ian Barbour, *Issues in Science and Religion* (Englewood Cliffs, N.J.: Prentice-Hall, 1966), part 12.

The problem of evil and suffering, of course, vitally concerns the relevance of the teleological argument and will be considered carefully in a later discussion.

23. Kant, *Critique of Pure Reason*, p. 331.

24. *Ibid.*, p. 359.

25. Immanuel Kant, *Critique of Pure Reason*, 2d ed., trans. Norman K. Smith (London: Macmillan, 1929), p. xxx.

26. Immanuel Kant, *Critique of Practical Reason*, trans. Lewis White Beck (University of Chicago Press, 1949), p. 226.

27. *Ibid.*, pp. 227, 228.

28. Although Kant's version of the moral postulate is unique, the general line of reasoning which he follows is present in Hastings Rashdall, *The Theory of Good and Evil*, vol. II (Oxford: Clarendon Press and Oxford

University Press, 1907), book III, chapter 1, sections IV and V, pp. 206-213, 219-20. This selection is reproduced in J. Hick, ed. *The Existence of God* (New York: Macmillan, 1964), pp. 144-52; J. H. Cardinal Newman, *A Grammar of Assent*, ed. C. F. Harrold (New York: David McKay, 1977); George I. Mavrodes, *Belief in God* (New York: Random House, 1970); and C. S. Lewis, *Mere Christianity* (New York: Macmillan, 1976), pp. 15-66.

29. Etienne Gilson, *God and Philosophy* (New Haven: Yale University Press, 1959), p. 89.

30. Paul Tillich, "The Religious Situation in Germany Today," *Religion in Life*, 3:2 (1934), 167.

31. Frederick Ferré, *Basic Modern Philosophy of Religion* (New York: Scribner's, 1967), p. 143.

32. R. L. Sturch, "God and Probability," *Religious Studies*, 8:4 (December, 1972), 354.

33. Gaunilon's objection and Anselm's reply can be found in *The Many Faced Argument*, ed. J. H. Hick and A. C. McGill (New York: Macmillan, 1967), pp. 9-32.

34. David Hume, *Dialogues Concerning Natural Religion* (New York: Hafner, 1948), p. 40.

35. *Ibid*., p. 39.

36. See William of Occam, *Sum of All Logic*, quoted in E. A. Moody, *The Logic of William of Occam* (London: Sheed & Ward, 1935), I. 12. 6R., pp. 49-50.

37. H. H. Farmer, *Revelation and Religion* (London: Nisbet & Company, 1954), p. 53.

38. Wolfgang Trillhaas notes in this connection that the classical proofs "have two presuppositions in common which both bring to expression an untroubled optimistic world view. One presupposition is that reality is unquestionably meaningful and purposefully ordered. And the other presupposition concerns the capacity of our understanding—namely, that it can recognize this reality in its order and purposefulness." *Religionsphilosophie* (Berlin: Walter de Gruyter, 1972), p. 46.

39. Robin Attfield, "The God of Religion and the God of Philosophy," *Religious Studies*, 9:1 (March, 1973), 7.

40. John Hick, *Arguments for the Existence of God* (New York: Herder & Herder, 1971), p. xiii.

41. Anselm, S. *Anselm's Cantauriensis*, quoted in Barth, *Anselm*, p. 170.

42. Barth, *Anselm*, p. 171.

43. George Adam Smith, "Isaiah," *An Exposition of the Bible* (Hartford, Conn.: The S. S. Scranton Company, 1904), p. 619, col. 2.

CHAPTER III—THE MOVING IMAGE OF ETERNITY

1. William H. Dray, *Philosophy of History* (Englewood Cliffs, N. J.: Prentice-Hall, 1964), p. 4.

2. Erich Kahler, *The Meaning of History* (New York: Braziller, 1964), p. 17.

3. *Ibid*., pp. 17-18.

4. R. S. Collingwood, *The Idea of History* (Oxford: Clarendon Press, 1946), p. 213.

5. Alan Richardson, *Christian Apologetics* (London: SCM Press, 1950), p. 107.

6. *Die Religion in Geschichte und Gegenwart*, Dritte Auflage, Zweiter Band, "Geschichte und Geschichtsauffassung: Geschichts-philosophie," by Hans-Georg Gadamer. In German just as in English the context of a word must largely determine its meaning; however, *Historie* usually means that which has actually happened in a way that could be established by the historical-critical method, whereas *Geschichte* refers to that which has occurred in the past with varying degrees of tangibility but which possesses potential existential significance for today. The writer will seek to make his meaning of *Historie* clear by such expressions as "actually happened," "happened in fact," or "tangible event."

7. Rudolf Bultmann, *Jesus and the Word* (New York: Scribner's, 1958), p. 8.

8. Rudolf Bultmann, "New Testament and Mythology," in Hans Werner Bartsch, ed. *Kerygma and Myth*, vol. I, trans. R. H. Fuller (London: Billing and Sons, 1953), p. 16.

9. Bultmann, "New Testament and Mythology," p. 41.

10. *Ibid.*, p. 42. There is a striking difference between Bultmann as a demythologizer of the Christian message for today and this same scholar as a historical, exegetical interpreter of the New Testament in its first-century setting. Observe, for example, how he admits that an acceptance of the miracle of the resurrection is an integral part of the early kerygma: "In Romans x.9 . . . Paul indicates the content of the Christian faith in one sentence in which he is consciously expressing, not a conception peculiar to himself, but that which is taken for granted by every Christian preacher: *if you confess* (ὁμολογεῖν) with your lips that Jesus is Lord and believe (πιστεύειν) in your heart that God raised him from the dead, you will be saved. Since in the synonymous parallelism (ὁμολογεῖν) and (πιστεῶειν) have the same meaning, it is clear that the Christian faith consists in recognizing Jesus as Lord and at the same time accepting ('believing to be true') the miracle of the resurrection." Rudolf Bultmann and Artur Weiser, "Faith: Associated Concepts in the New Testament," from *Bible Key Words*, vol. III from Gerhard Kittel's *Theologisches Wörterbuch zum Neuen Testament*, trans. and ed. by Dorothea M. Barton, P. R. Ackroyd, and A. E. Harvey (New York: Harper, 1960), p. 70.

11. Gerhard Ebeling, *Theology and Proclamation*, trans. John Riches (Philadelphia: Fortress Press, 1962), p. 57.

12. *Ibid.*, p. 64 ff.

13. *Ibid.*, p. 77.

14. For an excellent summary of the non-Christian literature and its importance see Maurice Goguel, "Non-Christian Sources of the Gospel Story," chap. II, *The Life of Jesus*, trans. Olive Wyon (New York: Macmillan, 1944), pp. 70-104.

15. Flavius Josephus, *Antiquities of the Jews*, found in *The Works of Josephus*, trans. William Whiston (Philadelphia: John C. Winston, 1957), book XX, chap. IX, 1., p. 598.

16. *Ibid.*, book XVIII, chap. III, 3., p. 535.

17. See his detailed discussion of this passage in *The Life of Jesus*, pp. 77-82.

18. Tacitus, *Ann.* as quoted in Günther Bornkamm, *Jesus of Nazareth*,

trans. Irene and Fraser McLuskey with James M. Robinson (London: Hodder & Stoughton, 1960), 15.4., p. 27.

19. Bornkamm, *Jesus*, p. 28.

20. Albert Schweitzer, *The Quest of the Historical Jesus*, trans. W. Montgomery (New York: Macmillan, 1922), p. 396.

21. Bornkamm, *Jesus*, p. 24.

22. C. F. D. Moule, *The Birth of the New Testament*, 2d ed. (London: A. & C. Black, 1966), p. 9.

23. Jürgen Moltmann, *Theology of Hope*, trans. James W. Leitch (London: SCM Press, 1967), pp. 172-73.

24. The word for proof, τεκμήριον, according to H. B. Hackett, "does not occur elsewhere in the New Testament, and is a very expressive term. Plato uses it to denote the strongest possible logical proof, as opposed to that which is weaker, and Aristotle employs it to signify demonstrative evidence." Acts and Romans, Vol. IV. *An American Commentary on the New Testament*, ed. Alva Hovey (Philadelphia: The American Baptist Publication Society, 1882), p. 31.

25. T. Müller, *Das Heilsgeschehen im Johannesevangelium, eine exegetische Studie, zugleich der Versuch einer Antwort an Rudolf Bultmann* (Zürich: Gotthelf Verlag, 1961), p. 136.

26. See Helmut Thielicke, "The Resurrection Kerygma," *The Easter Message Today*, by Leonhart Goppelt, Helmut Thielicke, and Hans Rudolf Müller-Schwefe, trans. Salvator Attanasio and Darrell Guder (Nashville: Thomas Nelson, 1964), p. 79.

27. David Hume, *Enquiry Concerning Human Understanding* (La Salle, Ill.: Open Court, 1927), pp. 122 ff. See especially opening sections of part II.

28. *Ibid*., p. 121, final paragraph of part I.

29. Malcolm L. Diamond, *Contemporary Philosophy and Religious Thought* (New York: McGraw-Hill, 1974), p. 68.

30. This line of defense is put forward rather early in the church's history when around 240 A.D. Origen in *Contra Celcus* pleads: "But I think that the clear and certain proof (of the resurrection) is the argument from the behaviour of the disciples, who devoted themselves to a teaching which involved risking their lives. If they had invented the story that Jesus had risen from the dead, they would not have taught with such spirit, in addition to the fact that in accordance with this they not only prepared others to despise death but above all despised it themselves." *Ante-Nicene Fathers*, taken from Roland H. Bainton, *Early Christianity* (New York: Van Nostrand, 1960), II. 57., pp. 116-17.

31. Reinhart Staats' investigations into the historical, theological background of the concept of "fact" leads him to formulate the following definition: "Facts are only perceivable through experience. In theology, facts are generally convincing indications whereby common natural experiences can be brought together with historical events from the biblical tradition into a uniform experience. Their certainty remains limited at best to a high degree of probability." Reinhart Staats, "Der theologiegeschichtliche Hintergrund des Begriffes Tatsache," in *Zeitschrift für Theologie und Kirche*, 70:3 (1973), 325-26.

32. C. S. Lewis, *Miracles* (New York: Macmillan, 1947), p. 114.

33. Hans W. Frei, *The Identity of Jesus Christ* (Philadelphia: Fortress Press, 1967), p. 139.

34. Frei, *Identity of Jesus Christ*, p. 148. This interpretation of Frei also

illustrates the relevance of the kind of reasoning employed in the ontological argument. Here one acknowledges the *necessity* of believing Jesus is alive in order to make *rational* sense of his understanding of Jesus as the resurrection and the life.

35. Form-Criticism which seeks to analyze the literary structure of its sources in order to understand more fully the original intention of the authors has also rather conclusively proven the impossibility of interpreting the Christ of the New Testament along merely historical lines. F. F. Bruce, for example, concludes that "perhaps the most important result to which Form-Criticism points is that, no matter how we classify the gospel material, we never arrive at a non-supernatural Jesus. . . . All parts of the gospel record are shown by these various groupings to be pervaded by a consistent picture of Jesus as the Messiah, the Son of God; all agree in emphasizing the messianic significance of all that He said and did, and we can find no alternative picture, no matter how thoroughly we scrutinize and analyze successive strata of the Gospels. Thus Form-Criticism has added its contribution to the overthrow of the hope once fondly held, that by getting back to the most primitive stage of gospel tradition we might recover a purely human Jesus, who simply taught the Fatherhood of God and the brotherhood of man." F. F. Bruce, *The New Testament Documents, Are They Reliable?* (Grand Rapids: Eerdmans, 1960), p. 33.

36. *Die Religion in Geschichte* und *Gegenwart*, Dritte Auflage, *s.v.* "Auferstehung Christi: Im NT," by H. Conzelmann.

37. Gerhard Delling, in *The Significance of the Message of the Resurrection for Faith in Jesus Christ*, trans. R. A. Wilson (Naperville, Ill.: Alec R. Allenson, 1968), p. 90.

38. E. Troelsch, "Ueber historische und dogmatische Methode," *Gesamelte Schriften*, II (1898), pp. 729 ff. (esp. p. 731) quoted in Moltmann, *Theology of Hope*, pp. 175-76.

39. Daniel L. Migliore, "How Historical Is the Resurrection?" *Theology Today*, 33 (April, 1976), 14.

40. Erich Dinkler, *Die Religion in Geschichte* und *Gegenwart*, Dritte Auflage, Zweiter Band, Geschichte und Geschichtsauffasung: Neutestamentlich, p. 1481.

CHAPTER IV—CHRIST—THE CLUE TO REALITY

1. Ontology, or its synonym, metaphysics, is traditionally defined as "the science of being as such." According to Runes' *Dictionary of Philosophy*, ontology is to "be distinguished from the study of being under some particular aspect." It is seeking to understand first causes and "the 'causes' which are the objects of metaphysical cognition are said to be 'first' in the natural order (first principles), as being founded in no higher or more complete generalizations available to the human intellect by means of its own natural powers." Dagobert D. Runes, ed., *The Dictionary of Philosophy* (New York: Philosophical Library, 1965), p. 196. The major task of ontology, according to John Herman Randall, Jr.'s more technical definition, is to analyze "the generic traits manifested by existences of any kind, the characters sure to turn up in any universe of discourse—those traits exhibited in any '*ousia*' or subject-matter whatever, the fundamental and pervasive distinctions in terms of which any subject-matter may be

understood." John Herman Randall, Jr., "Metaphysics: Its Function, Consequence and Criteria," *The Journal of Philosophy*, 43:15 (July 18, 1946), 403-4.

2. Malcolm L. Diamond, *Contemporary Philosophy and Religious Thought* (New York: McGraw-Hill, 1974), pp. 370-74.

3. Margery Williams, *The Velveteen Rabbit or How Toys Become Real* (Garden City, N.Y.: Doubleday, 1976), pp. 16-20.

4. Alfred North Whitehead, *Religion in the Making* (New York: Macmillan, 1927), p. 50.

5. The reader will find an informative historical treatment of the relationship between ontology and theology as interpreted particularly from the contemporary continental theological perspective in Hermann Diem, "Dogmatik zwischen Personalismus und Ontologie," *Evangelische Theologie*, 15 (1955), 408-15.

6. Gerhard Ebeling, "Theology and Reality," Inaugural Lecture at the University of Zürich, November 10, 1956, in his *Word and Faith* (London: SCM Press, 1960), p. 199.

7. Karl Barth, *The Word of God and the Word of Man*, trans. Douglas Horton (New York: Harper, 1957), p. 196.

8. Karl Barth, *Church Dogmatics*, vol. 1, part 1, trans. G. T. Thompson (Edinburgh: T. & T. Clark, 1949), pp. 103-4.

9. T. F. Torrance, "Newton, Einstein and Scientific Theology," *Religious Studies*, 8 (September, 1972), 248.

10. Scripture often teaches or implies that men have an awareness of God which does not come from the historical Christ or scriptures: Ps. 19:1-4; John 1:9; Acts 14:17; 17:22-31; Rom. 1:19-21, 32; 2:12-16.

11. Torrance, "Newton, Einstein and Scientific Theology," 248-49. For a positive estimate of the place of natural theology as seen particularly in its post-Barthian continental development see Christof Gestrich, "Die unbewältigte natürliche Theologie," *Zeitschrift für Theologie und Kirche*, 68:1 (1971), 82-120. In a superb article on this problem, John Bennett, while acknowledging the danger of unaided theistic reasoning and admitting that theistic faith needs both the "fulfillment and correction from the Christian revelation," confides that theism "does have a basis that is in part independent of that revelation and can give some support to it. It does provide pointers to the truth of Christian faith which can be seen, dimly perhaps, apart from Christian faith. Such pointers may be of no interest to the person who sees God in Christ with unchanging assurance. I only ask such a person to withhold his theological scorn from those of us, of whom I am one, whose assurance is less unchanging and who are grateful for every glimpse of truth which is available outside the Christian circle." John C. Bennett, "Are There Tests of Revelation?" *Theology Today*, 12 (April, 1955), 83-84. See also John B. Cobb, Jr., *A Christian Natural Theology* (Philadelphia: Westminster Press, 1965).

12. Willard V. Quine, "On What There Is," *Review of Metaphysics* (September, 1948), 29.

13. Paul Tillich, *Systematic Theology*, vol. I, p. 71.

14. Gabriel Marcel, "On the Ontological Mystery," in *The Philosophy of Existence*, trans. Manya Harai (New York: Books for Libraries Press, 1969), pp. 6-7.

15. Marcel, *Philosophy of Existence*, p. 13.

16. Tillich, *Systematic Theology*, vol. 1, p. 101.

17. T. F. Torrance, *Space, Time and Incarnation* (London: Oxford University Press, 1969), pp. 53-54.

18. An illustration of this principle on the scientific level is provided by Max Black when, in dealing with the relationship between scientific models and their subjects, he confesses, "we pin our hopes upon the existence of a common structure in both fields." Max Black, *Models and Metaphors* (Ithaca: Cornell University Press, 1962), p. 238.

19. Karl Barth, preface to the second edition of *The Epistle to the Romans*, as it appears in Jürgen Moltmann, *Theology of Hope* (London: SCM Press, 1967), p. 380.

20. Hugh Montifiore, "Towards a Christology for Today," in A. R. Vidler, ed., *Soundings: Essays Concerning Christian Understanding* (Cambridge University Press, 1966), p. 167.

21. For example, Matt. 11:27, 24:42; Mark 13:24-27; John 1:1-18, 10:30; I Cor. 1:30, 8:6; II Cor. 4:6, 8:9; Eph. 1:3, 19-23; Phil. 2:5-11; Col. 1:15-20; Heb. 1:1-4, 13:8.

22. Emil Brunner, *The Mediator*, trans. Olive Wyon (Philadelphia: Westminster Press, 1947), p. 310.

23. Gerhard von Stammler, "Ontologie in der Theologie?" *Kerygma und Dogma*, 4:3 (Juli, 1958), 159.

24. Heinrich Ott, "Objectification and Existentialism," in Hans-Werner Bartsch, ed., *Kerygma and Myth*, vol. II (London: S.P.C.K., 1962), pp. 317-18.

25. R. H. Fuller, *The Foundations of New Testament Christology* (New York: Scribner's, 1965), p. 248.

26. Karl Barth, *Church Dogmatics*, vol. 1, part 1, pp. 487, 490.

27. Wolfhart Pannenberg, *Jesus—God and Man* (Philadelphia: Westminster Press, 1968), p. 136. Cf. Gerhard Ebeling's interpretation of the Hebrew meaning of truth where he offers this definition: "Real is what has a future" (*Faith*, p. 208), and notice further his approval of the following description from H. von Soden: "Truth is not something that lies somehow at the bottom of things or behind them and would be discovered by penetrating their depths or their inner meaning; but truth is what will transpire in the future. The opposite of truth would so to speak not really be illusion, but essentially disillusion (in the commonly accepted sense of disappointment). What is lasting and durable and has a future is true, and that holds supremely of the eternal as being imperishable, everlasting, final, ultimate." "Was ist Wahrheit?" *Urchristentum und Geschichte*, Ges. Aufsätze und Vorträge, ed. H. von Campenhausen, vol. I (1950), 10 f., quoted by Ebeling, *Faith*, p. 209.

28. Oscar Cullmann, *The Christology of the New Testament*, trans. Shirley C. Guthrie and Charles A. M. Hall (Philadelphia: Westminster Press, 1959), p. 9.

29. James Barr, *Old and New in Interpretation* (London: SCM Press, 1964), p. 86.

30. Torrance, *Incarnation*, pp. 67-68.

31. Paul Holmer, "Philosophical Criticism and Christology," *The Journal of Religion*, 34 (April, 1954), 99.

32. Paul Lehman, "Logos in a World Come of Age," *Theology Today*, 3 (October, 1964), 275-76.

33. Ebeling, "Theology and Reality," p. 200.

CHAPTER V—WHERE YOUR TREASURE IS

1. Axiology (from the Greek αξιοσ, worthy or of like value) is that area of philosophy which investigates the nature, criteria, and metaphysical status of *value*. According to H. Hülsmann, "axiology is the interpretation of value as a strict theory of value, analogous to logic and in distinction from a pure practice or theory of practice as a teaching concerning action." "Axiologie," *Historisches Wörterbuch der Philosophie*, Band 1, Herausgegeben von Joachim Ritter (Darmstadt: Wissenshaftliche Buchgesellschaft, 1971), p. 737. In a similar vein, William K. Frankena explains, "In its widest use 'value' is the generic noun for all kinds of critical or pro and con predicates, as opposed to descriptive ones, and is contrasted with existence or fact." *The Encyclopedia of Philosophy* (New York: Macmillan, 1967), *s.v.* "Value and Valuation," by William K. Frankena.

2. Jean Paul Sartre, "Existentialism Is a Humanism," *Existentialism from Dostoevsky to Sartre*, ed. Walter Kaufmann, trans. P. Mairet (Cleveland and New York: World, 1969), pp. 295-97.

3. Bertrand Russell, *Why I Am Not a Christian* (New York: Simon & Schuster, 1957), p. 12.

4. James S. Stewart, *The Wind of the Spirit* (London: Hodder & Stoughton, 1968), pp. 12-14.

5. Stewart, *Wind of the Spirit*, pp. 115, 116.

6. Wolfhart Pannenberg, *Jesus—God and Man*, trans. Lewis L. Wilkins and Duane A. Priebe (Philadelphia: Westminster Press, 1968), p. 73.

7. Gabriel Marcel, "On the Ontological Mystery," *The Philosophy of Existence*, trans. Manya Harai (New York: Books for Libraries Press, 1969), p. 14.

8. Austin Farrer offers a provisional definition for the philosophical concept of goodness as being that which one cannot help approving. Austin Farrer, *Love Almighty and Ills Unlimited* (Garden City, N.Y.: Doubleday, 1961), p. 23.

9. Marcel, *Philosophy of Existence*, p. 16.

10. *Ibid.*

11. St. Augustine, *The Confessions*, trans. F. J. Sheed (New York: Sheed & Ward, 1947), 1.1., p. 3.

12. Johann Wolfgang von Goethe, *Wilhelm Meister's Apprenticeship and Travels*, trans. Thomas Carlyle (New York: John O. Williams, 1882), 2.8.5., p. 51.

13. Blaise Pascal, *Pensées*, trans. H. F. Stewart (New York: Pantheon Books, 1950), #312, #313, p. 173.

14. Jürgen Moltmann, *Theology of Hope*, trans. James W. Leitch (London: SCM Press, 1967), pp. 137-38.

15. Quoted in Bertrand Russell, *A History of Western Philosophy* (New York: Simon & Schuster, 1945), p. 264.

16. Mark 5:34; Luke 5:31 / John 10:10 / Luke 19:9; Rom. 1:16; Phil. 2:12 / John 14:27.

17. S. Kierkegaard, *Leben und Walten der Liebe*, trans. Schrempf, p. 19 f., quoted in Günther Bornkamm, *Jesus of Nazareth*, trans. Irene and Fraser McLuskey with James M. Robinson (London: Hodder & Stoughton, 1960), p. 113.

18. Martin Buber, "Urdistanz und Beziehung" *Werke I Schriften zur Philosophie* (München: Kösel-Verlag KG, 1962), p. 423.

19. Wolfgang Weidlich, "Befragung der philosophischen Theologie

der radikalen Fraglichkeit," *Zeitschrift für Theologie und Kirche*, 70:2 (1973), 237.

20. H. R. Niebuhr, *The Meaning of Revelation* (New York: Macmillan, 1941), p. 93.

21. E. Evans, *The Clarendon Bible*, Corinthians (Oxford: Clarendon Press, 1930), p. 73.

22. Gerhard Ebeling, "Lebensangst und Glaubensanfechtung," *Zeitschrift für Theologie und Kirche*, 70:1 (1973), 80-81.

23. Moltmann, *Theology of Hope*, p. 91.

24. John H. Hick, *Philosophy of Religion* (Englewood Cliffs, N.J.: Prentice-Hall, 1973), p. 91.

25. John Bunyan, *The Pilgrim's Progress* (London: Dent, Everyman's Library, 1964), p. 181.

CHAPTER VI—THE FUTURITY OF BEAUTY

1. The word *aesthetics* arises from the Greek, αἰσθάνομαι, "to perceive by the senses," and was first used in the philosophy of art by Alexander Gottlieb Baumgarten around 1750 in his *Aesthetica* to distinguish sensuous perception as a means of experiencing beauty from analytical logic which leads to a knowledge of truth. The somewhat indeterminate nature of contemporary aesthetics as a discipline within philosophy is characterized by Edouard Morot-Sir when he explains rather enigmatically that aesthetics "is like a savage child who wanders gaily through the corridors of the House of Man's Knowledge, without ever managing to settle down in a home of his own. On some occasions he refuses to let a willing person adopt him; on others, he is thrown out after a while because of his strange and independent nature. . . . Perhaps the savage child which is now wandering through the House of Man's Sciences will eventually play the role of the Prodigal Son." Eugene F. Kaelin, *An Existentialist Aesthetic: The Theories of Sartre and Merleau-Ponty* (Madison: University of Wisconsin Press, 1962), foreword, vii, xi. Excellent current discussions on the history of and introduction to aesthetics can be found in *Historisches Wörterbuch der Philosophie*, 1971 ed., *s.v.* "Ästhetik," by Joachim Ritter; *The Encyclopedia of Philosophy* (New York: Macmillan, 1967), *s.v.* "History of Aesthetics," by M. C. Beardsley, pp. 18-35, and *s.v.* "Problems of Aesthetics," by J. Hospers, pp. 35-56.

2. The close linguistic affinity which the ancient Greeks allowed between their word for beauty, καλόσ, and their verb to call, καλέω, is observed by Thomas Aquinas when he speaks of God as the cause of beauty and harmony because it is he who calls all things to himself for his purpose. *Exposition of Dionysius on the Divine Names*, chapter 4.

3. C. E. M. Joad, *Matter, Life and Value* (London: Oxford University Press, 1929), p. 398.

4. Alfred North Whitehead, *Adventures of Ideas* (New York: Macmillan, 1933), p. 350.

5. Immanuel Kant, *Werke*, Band V: *Kritik der Urtheilskraft* (Berlin: zweite Auflage bei F. T. Lagarde, 1793, herausgegeben von Otto Buek, verlegt bei Bruno Cassirer, 1922), I.I.1.49., p. 430. Essentially the same realistic accent falls in one of Kant's major theses in his definition of beauty where he understands, "The beautiful is that which without any

concept (i.e., no rational category can exhaust its depth) is recognized as the object of a necessary satisfaction." Kant, *Werke*, I.I.1.22., p. 311.

6. Martin Heidegger, "Der Ursprung des Kunstwerkes," *Holzwege* (Frankfurt-am-Main: Vittorio Klostermann, 1950), p. 33. (The essay as it now stands consists of several parts which appeared in lecture and written form during 1935, 1936.)

7. The writer is indebted to Johannes Pfeiffer for encouraging the attempt to distinguish the peculiar feature of selected arts, and while the emphases shown here are not identical nor even the arts chosen always the same ones, gratitude must be acknowledged for the suggestion. Johannes Pfeiffer, "On Karl Jaspers' Interpretation of Art," *The Philosophy of Karl Jaspers*, ed. Paul Arthur Schilpp (New York: Tudor, 1957), p. 711.

8. In his definitive article on the historical development of aesthetics, Joachim Ritter interprets Immanuel Kant as presupposing that beauty is essentially the "appropriateness of the object without utility 'as though a judgment of the divine would contain the basis of the unity of the manifold.' " Joachim Ritter, "Ästhetik," p. 565. The quotation from Kant can be found in Kant, *Werke*, Einleitung, IV., p. 249.

9. Pierre Teilhard de Chardin, *The Phenomenon of Man* (London: Collins, Fontana Books, 1960), pp. 292-93.

10. Jean Paul Sartre, *Literature and Existentialism*, trans. Bernard Trechtman (New York: Citadel Press, 1949), p. 57.

11. Robert Leet Patterson, *A Philosophy of Religion* (Durham, N.C.: Duke University Press, 1970), p. 279.

12. Although a recognition of the personalistic nature of reality is usually wanting in Plotinus' larger system, he nevertheless voices a similar dissatisfaction with a mere rational understanding of beauty and even provides a vivid example of the way beauty is dependent on a moral foundation and the manner in which it often points forward toward a higher goal: "Beauty is dead until it takes the light of The Good, and the soul lies supine, cold to all, unquickened even to Intellectual-Principle there before it. But when there enters into it a glow from the divine, it gathers strength, awakens, spreads true wings, and however urged by its nearer environing, speeds its bouyant way elsewhere, to something greater to its memory: so long as there exists anything loftier than the near, its very nature bears it upwards, lifted by the giver of that love." Plotinus, *The Enneads*, trans. Stephen MacKenna, 2d ed. rev., B. S. Page (London: Faber & Faber, 1956), VI.7.22., p. 579.

13. Jacques Maritain, "Poetry and the Perfection of Human Life," *The Responsibility of the Artist* (New York: Scribner's, 1960), p. 114.

14. Karl Barth, *Church Dogmatics*, vol. 3, part 3, ed. G. W. Bromiley and T. F. Torrance (Edinburgh: T. & T. Clark, 1961), p. 298.

15. Paul Tillich also indicates an awareness of this ontological principle when he tells how once he contemplated a work of modern art and felt compelled to ask the question: "What does this picture express in terms of an ultimate interpretation of human existence?" And his answer was, "It too expresses power of being in terms of an unrestricted vitality in which the self-affirmation of life becomes almost ecstatic." Paul Tillich, "Existential Aspects of Modern Art," in *Christianity and the Existentialists*, ed. Carl Michalson (New York: Scribner's, 1956), p. 135.

16. Paul Tillich, *Protestantismus und Expressionismus* (Hamburg: Friedrich-Wittig-Verlags-Almanach, 1959), p. 87. Essentially this same

emphasis is made by Hans Eckehard Bahr with a refreshing Christological boldness when he concludes in his splendid treatment of the subject: "The disclosure of the ways in which all life unhesitatingly runs its course is the maximum to be expected of artistic possibilities of work. If this disclosure takes place in a work, then one is able to raise questions from it which, moreover, only God can answer. Then is this work unintentionally a preparer of the way for a higher truth, a disciplinarian which points to Christ (Gal. 3:24)." Hans Eckehard Bahr, *Theologische Untersuchung der Kunst, Poiesis* (München: Siebenstern, 1965), p. 169.

17. Karl Jaspers, *Philosophie* (Berlin: Springer Verlag, 1948), p. 292.

18. *The Confessions of St. Augustine*, trans. J. C. Pilkington (Cleveland: Fine Editions Press, n.d.), IV.XVI.30., p. 62.

19. Rudolf Otto, *The Idea of the Holy*, trans. John W. Harvey, 2d ed. (London: Oxford University Press, 1957), p. 178.

20. Jacques Maritain, *Creative Intuition in Art and Poetry* (London: Harvill Press, 1953), pp. 166-67.

21. Roger Hazelton, "Theology as Conversation: With the Arts," *New Accents in Contemporary Theology* (New York: Harper, 1960), p. 25.

22. Thomas of Celano, *The Lives of St. Francis of Assisi*, trans. A. G. Ferrers Howell (London: Methuen & Company, 1908), p. 79.

23. Karl Heim, *Jesus, The World's Perfector*, trans. D. H. van Daalen (London: Oliver & Boyd, 1959), pp. 195-96.

CHAPTER VII—THE SOUND OF MEANING

1. Hans-Georg Gadamer, "Man and Language," *Philosophical Hermeneutics*, trans. and ed. David E. Linge (Berkeley: University of California Press, 1976), p. 62.

2. The significance of silence in a linguistic context is treated briefly and ably by Wolfgang Trillhaas in "Das Schweigen," *Religionsphilosophie* (Berlin: Walter de Gruyter, 1972), pp. 260-69.

3. Ronald W. Langacker, *Language and Its Structure* (New York: Harcourt, Brace Jovanovich, 1967), p. 238; see also pp. 14, 16-21. Cf. Charles F. Hockett, "Man's Place in Nature," *A Course in Modern Linguistics* (New York: Macmillan, 1958), pp. 568-85 and Noam Chomsky, "A Review of Verbal Behavior by B. F. Skinner," *Language*, 35 (1959), 26-58.

4. Helen Keller, *The Story of My Life* (Garden City, N.Y.: Doubleday, 1954), pp. 256-57.

5. Maurice Merleau-Ponty, *Phénoménologie de la Perception* first published in Paris 1945, German translation R. Boehm, 1966, quoted in "Das Sprachverständnis von Maurice Merleau-Ponty" by Winfried Rorarius, in *Zeitschrift für Theologie und Kirche* 72:1 (1975), 90.

6. Charles Hartshorne, *The Logic of Perfection and Other Essays in Neoclassical Metaphysics* (La Salle, Ill.: Open Court, 1962), pp. 152-53.

7. T. F. Torrance, *Theology in Reconstruction* (London: SCM Press, 1965), pp. 19-20.

8. Thomas Aquinas, *Summa Theologica*, I.Q. 13.

9. *The Oxford Dictionary of the Christian Church*, 2d ed. (London: Oxford University Press, 1974), *s.v.* "Analogy."

10. Erich Przywara, *Religionsphilosophie katholischer Theologie* (München: Oldenbourg, 1926), p. 31, quoted in Niels C. Nielson, Jr.,

"Analogy as a Principle of Theological Method Historically Considered," *The Heritage of Christian Thought*, ed. Robert E. Cushman and Egil Grislis (New York: Harper, 1965), p. 201. Gerhard Ebeling, in like manner, declares that language reveals "the presence of the hidden" by making present what would not be immediately obvious. "The function of language, therefore, is seen in a particularly impressive way in its power of transcending the present moment. It is able to make present what no longer exists and what does not yet exist. Without language we would have no relationship with the past and the future; we would be imprisoned in the present moment and banished to our very immediate environment. The same is true of the transcendence that leads to the whole complex of circumstances in which what is immediately present to us is located, and from there to what it signifies, what is proclaimed in it and the thoughts it provokes." Gerhard Ebeling, *Introduction to a Theological Theory of Language*, trans. R. A. Wilson (Philadelphia: Fortress Press, 1973), pp. 54-55.

11. A. M. Hunter, *Interpreting the Parables* (London: SCM Press, 1960), p. 63.

12. A. M. Farrer, *Finite and Infinite* (London: Dacre Press, 1943), p. 23.

13. Heinrich Ott, *Theology and Preaching* (London: Lutterworth Press, 1961), pp. 72-73.

14. Sigmund Freud, *Vorlesungen zur Einführung in die Psychoanalyse* (1917). In: *Ges. Werke* XI, 1969, 422. Quoted in Gerhard Ebeling, "Lebensangst und Glaubensanfechtung," *Zeitschrift für Theologie und Kirche*, 70:1, 94.

CHAPTER VIII—CHRISTIANITY AND CONVERGING FAITHS

1. Jürgen Moltmann warns that any effort on the part of the Christian to dialogue with those following the non-Christian religions must begin with the realization that "theology" in a formal sense is a specialized Christian discipline which has really only come into its own since the Middle Ages and has no exact counterpart in the other faiths. The Christian must therefore be willing to pursue his discussion on the level of devotional procedure, traditional practices, and moral values, and not expect too much from an intellectual or theological comparison. Jürgen Moltmann, *The Church and the Power of the Spirit* (New York: Harper, 1975), p. 160.

2. Emile Cailliet, *Journey Into Light* (Grand Rapids: Zondervan, 1968), pp. 26-27.

3. A. N. Whitehead, *Religion in the Making* (New York: Macmillan, 1927), p. 16.

4. H. H. Farmer, *Revelation and Religion* (London: Nisbet & Company, 1954), pp. 78-79.

5. *Die Religion in Geschichte und Gegenwart*, Dritte Auflage, s.v. "Religion," by G. Mensching, p. 961.

6. Frederick Ferré, *Basic Modern Philosophy of Religion* (New York: Scribner's, 1967), p. 69.

7. G. Dawes Hicks, *Philosophical Bases of Theism*, pp. 32 ff., cited in Robert Leet Patterson, *A Philosophy of Religion* (Durham, N.C.: Duke University Press, 1970), p. 5.

8. John Oman, *Natural and Supernatural* (Cambridge University Press, 1950), p. 57.

9. Heinz von Zahrnt, "Religiöse Aspekte gegenwärtiger Welt- und Lebenserfahrung," *Zeitschrift für Theologie und Kirche*, 1 (März, 1974), 99-100.

10. Peter Berger in his book, *A Rumor of Angels: Modern Society and the Rediscovery of the Supernatural* (Garden City, N.Y.: Doubleday, 1969) is even willing to claim that there is a certain transcendental character accompanying the following everyday phenomena: the necessity for order, the fact of play, hope, the conviction of an invisible righteousness, and the presence of humor. Wolfgang Trillhaas commends the phenomenological approach of Berger and quotes from his discussion on play as an appropriate example of the way transcendence interpenetrates our everyday experience: "It belongs quite concretely to the usual everyday world. In this experienced reality it is nevertheless a signal, a sign of transcendence. Because its actual intention points beyond itself and beyond the 'nature' of man toward 'supernatural' justification." Wolfgang Trillhaas, *Religionsphilosophie* (Berlin: Walter de Gruyter, 1972), p. 71.

11. R. Puligandla, "Could There Be an Essential Unity of Religions?" *International Journal for Philosophy of Religion* (Spring, 1971), p. 15.

12. *Chāndogya Upaniṣad* 3:14, in *The Principal Upaniṣads*, trans. S. Radhakrishnan (London: George Allen & Unwin, 1953), pp. 391-92.

13. *Vedânta-Sûtras*, trans. George Thibaut, in *Sacred Books of the East*, vol. 34 (Oxford: Clarendon Press, 1890), II.I. 22., p. 345.

14. See Rig-Veda 6:47:18; Rig-Veda 3:27:7; Katha Up. 2:2:9.

15. Sankara, *Brahmasutrabhasya*, in *Sacred Books of the East*, Vol. 34, I.I.5., p. 51.

16. Eknath Easwaran, *The Bhagavad Gita for Daily Living* (Berkeley: Blue Mountain Center of Meditation, 1975), p. 349.

17. *Katha Upanishad*, vol. I, part I, 3:7-8, trans. Swami Nikhilananda (New York: Harper, 1949), p. 150.

18. *Young Buddhist Handbook* (Bureau of Buddhist Education, Buddhist Churches of America, 1966), pp. 53-54.

19. *The Questions of King Milinda*, trans. T. W. Rhys Davids in *The Sacred Books of the East*, vol. 35, *ibid*., book II, chap. I, pp. 43-44.

20. The *Dhammacakkappavattana-sutta*, in *Samyutta-nikaya*, vi.II., trans. W. Rahula, quoted in John Bowker, *Problems of Suffering in Religions of the World* (Cambridge University Press, 1970), pp. 239-40.

21. Sri Aurobindo, *The Life Divine, A Source Book in Indian Philosophy*, ed. S. Radhakrishnan and C. A. Moore (Princeton University Press, 1957), pp. 586-88.

22. Hermann Hesse, *Siddhartha*, trans. Hilda Rosner (Toronto: McClelland & Stewart, 1951), pp. 120-22.

23. *Theragatha*, canto X ("Kisa-gotami") trans. P. Vajiranana and Francis Story, *The Buddhist Doctrine of Nibbana* (Kandy: Buddhist Publication Society, 1971), p. 18.

24. *Udana*, 80, in *The Minor Anthologies of the Pali Canon*, part II, trans. F. L. Woodward (London: Oxford University Press, 1948), pp. 97-98.

25. *A Shorter Encyclopedia of Islam* (Leiden: E. J. Brill, 1953), *s.v.* "Allah," by D. B. MacDonald.

26. In his article on religion in *Die Religion in Geschichte und Gegenwart*, G. Mensching makes a major distinction between a religion of revelation and a religion of a book explaining: "By book-religion one

understands not only religions with holy scriptures, but religions in which the holy book as such has central significance and in many ways even enjoys cultic reverence. Islam is for example both a revelation and also a book-religion. . . . Christianity in Jesus' time was a revelation-religion, however, no book-religion." Mensching, "Religion," p. 965.

27. M. M. Pickthall, *The Meaning of the Glorious Koran* (New York: Mentor Books, 1953), p. 445.

28. *Ibid.*

29. *Ibid.*, from the foreword.

30. According to Geoffrey Parrinder's indispensable study of *Jesus in the Qur'ān, Jesus is far more than a prophet in Islamic scripture; nevertheless, his divine significance is never fully grasped: "In Islam there is clearly a mystery about Jesus. It was accepted generally that his birth was unusual*, comparable only with that of Adam. On the common interpretation of sūra 4, 156/157 Jesus would be the only man in history who had not died. But if it felt after the mystery, this interpretation did not grasp it. The stark tragedy of the crucifixion reveals depths of the human and divine natures that remain unapprehended. Yet the challenge remains, to search for the truth of the revelation of love and the relationship of God to man which appeared in the person of Christ. 'What think ye of Christ?' is still a question to be answered." Geoffrey Parrinder, *Jesus in the Qur'an* (New York: Oxford University Press, 1977), p. 173.

31. Tor Andrea, "Muhammed: The Man and His Faith," in Robert A. Ellwood, Jr., *Words of the World's Religions* (Englewood Cliffs, N.J.: Prentice-Hall, 1977), pp. 390-91.

32. Koran 7:5-8; 21:48; 23:103-5; 101:6-8.

33. *Sacred Books of the East*, 56:12-23; 9:263, quoted in Robert E. Hume, *The World's Living Religions* (New York: Scribner's, 1947), p. 227.

34. Arnold Toynbee, *An Historian's Approach to Religion* (New York: Oxford University Press, 1956), pp. 274-78. Elsewhere Toynbee even suggests what he believes would satisfy the essential needs for corporate liturgical worship in the new universal religion:

Christe, audi nos.

Christ Tammuz, Christ Adonis, Christ Osiris, Christ Balder, hear us, by whatsoever name we bless Thee for suffering death for our salvation.

Christe Jesu, exaudi nos.

Buddha Gautama, show us the path that will lead us out of our afflictions.

Sancta Dei Genetrix, intercede pro nobis.

Mother Mary, Mother Isis, Mother Cybele, Mother Ishtar, Mother Kwanyin, have compassion on us, by whatsoever name we bless thee for bringing Our Savior into the World.

Sancte Michael, intercede pro nobis.

Mithras, fight at our side in our battle of Light against Darkness.

Omnes Sancti Angeli et Archangeli, intercedite pro nobis.

All ye devoted bodhisattvas, who for us your fellow living beings and for our release have forborne, aeon after aeon, to enter into your rest, tarry with us, we beseech you, yet a little while longer. . . .

Arnold Toynbee, *A Study of History*, vol. 10 (New York: Oxford University Press, 1934–43), pp. 143, 275-77.

35. R. C. Zaehner's criticism therefore seems valid when he asserts: "Professor Toynbee's 'essential truths' unfortunately do not coincide with the facts; he is making the great religions say what he personally

thinks they ought to say." R. C. Zaehner, ed., *The Concise Encyclopedia of Living Faiths* (New York: Hawthorn Books, 1959), p. 414. The serious student in this area will not want to miss this scholarly volume, especially its conclusion, pp. 413-17.

36. Hans Küng, *On Being a Christian*, trans. Edward Quinn (Garden City, N.Y.: Doubleday, 1976), p. 103.

37. Harvey Cox, "Why Young Americans Are Buying Oriental Religions," *Psychology Today* (July, 1977), 39.

38. Paul Tillich, *Systematic Theology*, vol. 1, p. 221.

39. Tillich, *Systematic Theology*, vol. 1, pp. 16-17.

40. James S. Stewart, *A Faith to Proclaim* (New York: Scribner's, 1953), p. 21.

41. *Ibid.*

42. Farmer, *Revelation and Religion*, p. 204.

43. Gotthold Ephraim Lessing, *Nathan der Weise* (New York: Hinds, Noble and Eldredge, 1898), Act III, Scene 7. An English translation of the drama may be found in Gotthold Ephraim Lessing, *Laocoon, Nathan the Wise and Minna von Barnhelm* (New York: Dutton, 1930), pp. 113-220.

CHAPTER IX—THE COMPLEMENTARITY OF SCIENCE AND RELIGION

1. The classical treatment of this age-long conflict is Andrew Dixon White's work, *A History of the Warfare of Science with Theology* (New York: Appleton-Century-Crofts, 1896).

2. See Martin E. Marty, "Science versus Religion: An Old Squabble Simmers Down," *Saturday Review* (December 10, 1977), 29-35.

3. Howard B. Jefferson, "The Christian Tradition and Physical Science," in *The Vitality of the Christian Tradition*, ed. George F. Thomas (New York: Harper, 1945), p. 267.

4. Wolfhart Pannenberg, *Theology and the Philosophy of Science*, trans. Francis McDonagh (Philadelphia: Westminster Press, 1976), p. 302.

5. Arthur C. Danto provides a helpful distinction between law and theory as scientific terms: "Let us characterize a law all of whose nonlogical terms are observational as an empirical law. A theory may be regarded as a system of laws, some of which are empirical. Not every empirical law is part of a theory—nor are all the laws of a theory empirical, for some of a theory's laws employ theoretical terms, which are nonobservationable. Theoretical terms, if they denote at all, refer to unobservable entities or processes, and it is with respect to changes at this covert level that one explains the observed regularities as covered by empirical laws." Arthur C. Danto, "Problems of Philosophy of Science" in *The Encyclopedia of Philosophy*, vol. 6 (New York: Macmillan and Free Press, 1967), p. 299.

6. Eric C. Rust, *Science and Faith: Towards a Theological Understanding of Nature* (New York: Oxford University Press, 1967), p. 3.

7. Arthur Pap, "Does Science Have Metaphysical Presuppositions?" *Readings in the Philosophy of Science*, ed. Herbert Feigl and May Brodbeck (New York: Appleton-Century-Crofts, 1953), p. 33.

8. Albert Einstein, "The Laws of Science and the Laws of Ethics," *Readings in the Philosophy of Science*, p. 779.

9. James B. Conant, *Science and Common Sense* (New Haven: Yale University Press, 1951), p. 45.

10. Michael Polanyi, *Science, Faith and Society* (London: Oxford University Press, 1946), p. 75.

11. *Die Religion in Geschichte und Gegenwart*, Dritte Auflage, s.v. "Naturwissenschaft: Systematisch," by W. Wieland and R. Ebert.

12. Polanyi, *Science, Faith and Society*, p. 71.

13. Newton himself never intended his mechanical physics to be employed against belief in the supernatural, for in his second edition of the *Principia* he defended himself against the charge of atheism declaring: "it is not to be conceived that mere mechanical causes could give birth to so many regular motions. . . . This most beautiful system could only proceed from the counsel and dominion of an intelligent and powerful Being." Cited in Mary B. Hesse, *Science and the Human Imagination* (London: SCM Press, 1954), p. 54.

14. Fritjof Capra, "The Tao of Physics: Reflections on the Cosmic Dance," *Saturday Review* (December 10, 1977), 28.

15. T. F. Torrance, "The Church in the New Era of Scientific and Cosmological Change," *Theology in Reconstruction* (Grand Rapids: Eerdmans, 1975), p. 270.

16. *Ibid.*

17. Stanley L. Jaki, "God and Creation: A Biblical-Scientific Reflection," *Theology Today*, 30 (July, 1973), 114. See also Mary B. Hesse, *Science and the Human Imagination* (London: SCM Press, 1954), pp. 43-46; Herbert Butterfield, *The Origins of Modern Science* (New York: Macmillan, 1951); and R. S. Cohen, "Alternative Interpretations of the History of Science," *The Scientific Monthly*, 80 (1955).

18. A. N. Whitehead, *Science and the Modern World* (New York: Macmillan, 1941), pp. 18-19. Stanley L. Jaki provides another illustration for this thesis when he explains why science did not arise in the Muslim world: "The disciples of Muhammed fell heir to both the Bible and the Greek scientific corpus, but they read both through the unsteady glasses provided by the Koran which often attributes utter willfulness to Allah, the Creator. Because in Allah the balance between reason and will is heavily tilted toward the latter, the Arabic Scholars opted for a mental dichotomy which destroyed their chances for turning the Greek scientific heritage into a self-sustaining enterprise. On the one hand, they became overzealous admirers of Aristotle and his world-view and argued, on the other hand, against the possibility of strictly valid physical laws, because such laws would put a constraint on Allah's sovereign freedom of action. Thus the main service of the Arabs to science was limited to channeling Greek science to medieval Christian Europe." Jaki, "God and Creation," 116.

19. T. F. Torrance, "Newton, Einstein and Scientific Theology," *Religious Studies*, 8 (September, 1972), 233.

20. Max Planck, *A Scientific Autobiography* (London: Williams & Norgate, 1950), p. 109.

21. Albert Einstein, Lettres à Maurice Solovine, reproduits en facsimilé et traduites en français (Paris: 1956), pp. 102-3, cited by Stanley L. Jaki, "Theological Aspects of Creative Science," *Creation, Christ and Culture—Studies in Honour of T. F. Torrance*, ed. Richard W. A. McKinney (Edinburgh: T. & T. Clark, 1976), pp. 162-63.

22. A. R. Peacocke, *Science and the Christian Experiment* (London: Oxford University Press, 1971), pp. 47-48. Peacocke's estimate concerning the duration of the solar system is based on his confidence in the second law of thermodynamics which will be discussed later.

23. *Ibid.*, pp. 50-51, 120-39.

24. This passage is quoted and discussed in a christological context in Karl Barth, *Dogmatics in Outline*, trans. G. T. Thompson (London: SCM Press, 1949), p. 60 ff.

25. Capra, "The Tao of Physics," p. 22.

26. A. S. Eddington, *The Nature of the Physical World* (Cambridge University Press, 1928), p. 32 as quoted in John Macquarrie, "Some Physicists' Views on Philosophy and Religion," *Twentieth Century Religious Thought* (London: SCM Press, 1963), p. 247, see pp. 243-48.

27. *Ibid.*, p. 338.

28. One must be very careful, as Ian G. Barbour warns, not to be guilty of an idealistic reductionism which is essentially no different methodologically from the older mechanical reductionism which is now being replaced: "We rejected arguments for idealism based on the role of the observer, the prominence of mathematics, and the new view of matter. Probability-waves may be less 'substantial' than billiard-ball atoms, but the new atom is no more 'mental' or 'spiritual' than the old. If science is indeed selective and its concepts limited, it would be as dubious to attempt to build a metaphysics of idealism on modern physics as it was to build a metaphysics of materialism on classical physics. We also maintained that the attempt to found a concept of human freedom on atomic indeterminacy is as guilty of reductionism as was the earlier denial of freedom on the basis of classical physics." Ian G. Barbour, *Issues in Science and Religion* (Englewood Cliffs, N.J.: Prentice-Hall, 1966), p. 315.

29. Charles Darwin, *The Origin of Species*, vol. 2 (New York: Appleton-Century-Crofts, 1896), pp. 306-06.

30. Although the history of the conflict between naturalistic evolution and literalistic biblicism cannot be developed here, it must be recognized that the vast majority in the Christian church considered evolution, particularly when it soon became extrapolated by Herbert Spencer into a cosmic determinism, as a threat to the biblical doctrine of creation. Evolution came into the Christian camp, as Andrew Dixon White describes vividly, "like a plough into an anthill. Everywhere those thus rudely awakened from their old comfort and repose had swarmed forth angry and confused." Andrew Dixon White, *A History of the Warfare of Science with Theology in Christendom*, vol. 1 (New York: Appleton-Century-Crofts, 1936), p. 70. The foremost opponent of evolution for the Christian forces was Bishop William Samuel Wilberforce who debated Thomas Huxley at Oxford in 1860. At the 1860 meeting of the British Association for the Advancement of Science, Wilberforce, referring to the ideas of Darwin, who was absent because of illness, congratulated himself in a speech that he was not descended from a monkey. To this boast Huxley gave his famous reply: "If I had to choose, I would prefer to be a descendent of an humble monkey rather than of a man who employs his knowledge and eloquence in misrepresenting those who are wearing out their lives in the search for truth." *Ibid.*, p. 70.

31. Paul Weiss, "Experience and Experiment," *Science* (May 11, 1962), 468.

32. D. E. Green and R. F. Goldberger, *Molecular Insights Into the Living Process* (New York: Academic Press, 1967), pp. 406-07.

33. Edward McCrady, "Religious Perspectives in Biology," *Theology Today*, 9:3 (October, 1952), 322.

34. Watson and Crick inferred from a diffraction pattern a model of a

deoxyribonucleic acid molecule as a twisted, double helix. See Alister Hardy's explanation of this technical issue in *The Living Stream* (New York: Harper, 1965), pp. 108-14.

35. Rick Gore, "The Awesome Worlds Within a Cell," *National Geographic*, 150 (September, 1976), 356-57.

36. Hardy, *Living Stream*, p. 114.

37. Michael Polanyi, *Knowing and Being*, ed. Marjorie Green (University of Chicago Press, 1969), pp. 238-39, see especially pp. 225-39. Compare also Barry Commoner, *Science and Survival* (New York: Viking Press, 1966), pp. 37-44 and G. G. Simpson, *This View of Life* (New York: Harcourt Brace Jovanovich, 1964), pp. 68-69.

38. William Bennet and Joel Gurin, "Science That Frightens Scientists: The Great Debate Over DNA," *The Atlantic Monthly* (February, 1977), 59.

39. Emile Cailliet, *The Christian Approach to Culture* (New York: Abingdon-Cokesbury Press, 1953), p. 174.

40. This excerpt is from an unpublished essay presented at a "Unity of Knowledge Congress" celebrating the bicentennial of Columbia University in New York on October 28, 1954, as cited in Günter Howe, "Zu den Aüsserungen von Niels Bohr über religiöse Fragen" *Kerygma und Dogma*, 4:1, 35.

41. Chardin, *Phenomenon of Man*, p. 290.

42. See Douglas K. Erlandson, "A New Look at Miracles," *Religious Studies*, 13 (December 1977), 417-28, for an excellent discussion of these alternatives and their contemporary representatives.

43. Friedrich Schleiermacher, *The Christian Faith*, trans. from 2d German ed., ed. H. R. Mackintosh and J. S. Stewart (Edinburgh: T. & T. Clark, 1948), p. 178.

44. Einstein, as cited by Jaki, *Creation, Christ and Culture*, p. 164.

45. Pierre Teilhard de Chardin, "Mass on the World," in *Hymn of the Universe* (New York: Harper, 1965), p. 19.

CHAPTER 10—THE SHADOWSIDE OF GOOD

1. Augustine, *De Trinitate* 5.9.10.

2. The negation of the good, according to W. Trillhaas, has no philosophical solution: "The formulation of the question which is contained in the problem of evil endeavors to make the imperceivable world visible and transform a religious need, that means one which can be overcome only in the subjectivity of faith, into a question which is formulated as a metaphysically soluble one. Because all questions of faith possess the tendency to objectify themselves metaphysically, the problem of evil must be recognized as an irrepressible question, however, it is by its very nature at the same time an insoluble [metaphysical] question." *Die Religion in Geschichte und Gegenwart*, Dritte Auflage, *s.v.* "Theodizee," by W. Trillhaas, p. 746.

3. Lactantius, *A Treatise on the Anger of God*, chap. 13. Cf. chaps. 12, 15, 16, 17, and 21.

4. Leonard Hodgson, *Towards a Christian Philosophy* (London: Nisbet & Company, 1943), p. 184.

5. Gabriel Marcel, "On the Ontological Mystery," in *Philosophy and Religion: Some Contemporary Perspectives*, ed. Jerry A. Gill (Minnesota: Burgess, 1968), p. 41.

6. For example, reality may be considered as wholly good and therefore evil as nonexistent; reality on the other hand may be seen as all evil with good as entirely absent; reality could be neutral toward good and evil; goodness might be real and evil an illusion or vice versa; good and evil may both exist in the same universe with equal status or varying degrees of prominence. Furthermore, any of these alternatives may be interpreted within a static substance-metaphysical model or as a part of reality in the process of development. See Hodgson, *Towards a Christian Philosophy*, pp. 182-83.

7. "Theodicy" is formed from θεός, God, and δίκη, justice, and refers to any attempt to free God from the charges of impotence or immorality. The term is attributed to G. W. Leibniz in 1710.

8. See Augustine, *Enchiridion* 4, trans. E. Evans; (London: S.P.C.K., 1953), pp. 8, 10, 23. John Hick gives an extended treatment of the Augustinian type of theology in his *Evil and the God of Love* (New York: Harper, 1966), pp. 43-96.

9. Consider also John Hick's exposition and recommendation of the Irenaean form of theodicy in *Evil and the God of Love*, pp. 217-21, 279-98.

10. The reader must strive to be certain that his understanding of this solution, as well as any theories concerning the origin of Satan or the fall of Adam and Eve, goes deeper than a mere *chronological* solution. Just because one feels one knows the first time evil appeared in the cosmos is no clear indication that one understands the true nature of evil or why God may have allowed evil to appear at all. The same warning is valid should one profess to know that at some point in the future the problem of evil will be resolved.

11. Franz Kafka, *Hochzeitsvorbereitungen auf dem Lande und andere Prosa aus dem Nachlass* (1966), p. 54, as quoted in Heinz Zahrnt, "Religiöse Aspekte gegenwärtiger Welt-und Lebenserfahrung," *Zeitschrift für Theologie und Kirche*, 1 (März, 1974), 107.

12. Fyodor Dostoyevsky, *The Brothers Karamazov* (New York: Modern Library, 1950), pp. 273-74.

13. Karl Jaspers, *Philosophical Faith and Revelation*, trans. E. B. Ashton (New York: Harper, 1967), p. 246.

14. H. H. Farmer, *The World and God* (London: Nisbet & Company, 1935), pp. 298-99.

15. David Hume, *Dialogues*, part XI (Oxford: Clarendon Press, 1935), p. 251.

16. Dostoyevsky, *Brothers Karamazov*, p. 291.

17. John Hick has an excellent discussion of this hypothesis in a section called "Critique of the Idea of the Immortal Ego" in *Death and Eternal Life* (New York: Harper, 1976), pp. 407-14.

18. Andrew Martin Fairbairn, *The Philosophy of the Christian Religion* (New York: Macmillan, 1902), p. 143.

19. Aldous Huxley, *Brave New World* (New York: Bantam Books, 1946), p. 283.

20. Jaspers, *Philosophical Faith*, p. 224. See also Steven P. Davis, "A Defense of the Free-Will Defense," *Religious Studies*, 8:4 (1972), 335.

21. Wolfgang Trillhaas, *Religionsphilosophie* (Berlin: Walter de Gruyter, 1972), pp. 190-91.

22. Augustine, *Confessions* 2.4.

23. *The Interpreter's Bible*, vol. 5 (Nashville: Abingdon Press, 1956), p. 262.

24. *Paradise Lost* 1.263.

25. Kurt Lüthi, *Gott und das Böse* (Zürich: Zwingli Verlag, 1961), p. 159. This is perhaps the best book available on the biblical background of the problem of evil.

26. *The Interpreter's Dictionary of the Bible*, vol. 4 (Nashville: Abingdon, 1962), *s.v.* "Satan," by T. H. Gaster, p. 227.

27. C. Anderson Scott, *Christianity According to St. Paul* (Cambridge University Press, 1932), p. 51.

28. Farmer, *The World and God*, p. 247.

29. Reflecting on this passage, John Bowker concludes: "Here is perhaps the supreme contribution of Israel to the human response to suffering, that suffering can be made redemptive, that it can become the foundation of better things, collectively, if not individually. Such a view cannot be or rather ought not to be, imposed on others in their grief, but it can be accepted for oneself." John Bowker, *Problems of Suffering in Religions of the World* (Cambridge University Press, 1970), p. 21.

30. Helmut Thielicke, *Our Heavenly Father*, trans. John W. Doberstein (New York: Harper, 1960), p. 23.

31. George Eliot, *Adam Bede* (New York: Dodd, Mead, 1947), p. 309.

32. C. S. Lewis, *The Joyful Christian* (New York: Macmillan, 1977), pp. 209-10.

33. Christof Gestrich, "Homo peccator und homo patiens. Das Verhältnis von Sünde und Leiden als Problem der theologischen Anthropologie und der Gotteslehre," *Zeitschrift für Theologie und Kirche*, 72:2 (1975), 265.

34. Albert Camus, *The Myth of Sisyphus and Other Essays*, trans. Justin O'Brien (New York: Knopf, 1958), p. 123.

35. Viktor Emil Frankl, "On Logotherapy and Existential Analysis," *American Journal of Psychoanalysis*, 18:1 (1958), 36.

36. John R. Claypool, "When You're Up Against It," from his printed sermons, 12:26 (January 28, 1973), p. 6.

37. C. S. Lewis, "The Weight of Glory," *The Weight of Glory and Other Addresses* (New York: Macmillan, 1949). p. 13.

38. Arthur John Gossip, "But When Life Tumbles In, What Then?" published in *The Hero in Thy Soul*, Scribner's, 1928 and in Andrew W. Blackwood, *The Protestant Pulpit* (Nashville: Abingdon-Cokesbury, 1957), pp. 202-4.

CONCLUSION

1. Dogmatic theologians such as Karl Barth, Emil Brunner, and Paul Tillich have presented elaborate expositions of this theme; however, the reader will find excellent brief treatments in: R. C. Crawford, "Is the Doctrine of the Trinity Scriptural?" *Scottish Journal of Theology*, 20:3 (September, 1967), 282-94; G. A. F. Knight, *A Biblical Approach to the Doctrine of the Trinity* (Edinburgh: Oliver and Boyd, *Scottish Journal of Theology*, Occasional Papers, No. 1, 2d ed., 1957); H. Richard Niebuhr, "The Doctrine of the Trinity and the Unity of the Church," *Theology Today*, 3 (October, 1946), 371-84. Emile Cailliet has a very helpful statement on the history and significance of the word "person" in *Christian Approach to Culture*, p. 43.

2. Wolfhart Pannenberg, *What Is Man?* trans. Duane A. Priebe

(Philadelphia: Fortress Press, 1970), p. 33. For further discussion of the methodological principle that one's understanding of "person" must be derived from that which is itself personal see Thomas Aquinas, *Summa Theologica*, I.90.2. Cf. also I.118.2, and further, Augustine Shutte, "Indwelling, Intersubjectivity and God," *Scottish Journal of Theology*, 32:3 (1979), 201-16.

3. *The Interpreter's Bible*, vol. 1 (New York: Abingdon Press, 1952), p. 5.

4. Philo M. Buck, Jr., and Hazel Stewart Alberson, *An Anthology of World Literature* (New York: Macmillan, 1940), p. 491.

5. Emil Brunner, *Dogmatics: The Christian Doctrine of God*, vol. 1, trans. Olive Wyon (Philadelphia: Westminster Press, 1940), p. 170.

6. John Bunyan, *Pilgrim's Progress*, p. 162.

7. Emile Cailliet, *The Dawn of Personality* (New York: Bobbs-Merrill, 1955), p. 180.

8. T. S. Eliot, "Choruses from 'The Rock,' " in *Collected Poems 1909–1935* (London: Faber & Faber, 1937), pp. 101-2, 103.

9. Augustine, *Confessions* 1.1.

10. *Ibid.*, 8.2.

11. John Bunyan, *Pilgrim's Progress*, pp. 156, 157.

INDEX OF NAMES

INDEX OF SUBJECTS

INDEX OF BIBLICAL REFERENCES